THE IDEA OF THE MUSLIM WORLD
A Global Intellectual History

By Cemil Aydin
Publication Date: April 2017
$29.95 | 293 pp.
ISBN: 978-0-674-05037-2
History / Religion
Harvard University Press

For more information please contact:
Emilie Ferguson
Senior Publicist
eferguson@harvardup.co.uk
020 3463 2352

European price: £23.95
European pub date: 27th April 2017

Visit our Web site
www.hup.harvard.edu

THE IDEA OF THE MUSLIM WORLD

The Idea of
the Muslim World

A Global Intellectual History

CEMIL AYDIN

Harvard University Press

Cambridge, Massachusetts & London, England

2017

First printing

Library of Congress Cataloging-in-Publication Data
Names: Aydin, Cemil, author.
Title: The idea of the Muslim world :
a global intellectual history / Cemil Aydin.
Description: Cambridge, Massachusetts : Harvard University Press, 2017. |
Includes bibliographical references and index.
Identifiers: LCCN 2016046007 | ISBN 9780674050372
(hardcover : alk. paper)
Subjects: LCSH: Muslims—Public opinion—History. | Group identity—
Islamic countries—History. | Islamic countries—Civilization. |
Islamic countries—Civilization—Western influences.
Classification: LCC BP52 .A94 2017 | DDC 909/.09767—dc23
LC record available at https://lccn.loc.gov/2016046007

For Juliane, Leyla, and Mehtap

Contents

THE IDEA OF THE MUSLIM WORLD

Introduction

What Is the Muslim World?

Roughly a fifth of people now living are Muslims. Their societies, located in every corner of the globe, vary in language, ethnicity, political ideology, nationality, culture, and wealth. Yet throughout modern history, Muslims and non-Muslims have appealed to an imagined global Muslim unity. One need only look at the headlines to see that this unity does not exist: today, the very people who claim to speak on behalf of all Muslims target other Muslims as their enemies; Muslim societies are more divided than ever, riven by civil wars and protracted conflicts across borders. Even so, the illusion of Muslim unity persists.

This illusion is captured most succinctly in the universally popular notion of a "Muslim world," with its own collective history and future, often contrasted with a putative "West." But we rarely question the historical roots and conceptual shortcuts inherent in such terms. Since when do political leaders, intellectuals, and everyday people talk about a Muslim world? How has it encompassed a civilization, religious tradition, and geopolitical unit? Why are the same people who take for granted the existence of a Muslim world reluctant to talk about a Christian world, an African world, or a Buddhist world in the same way? Why has the idea of the Muslim world become so entrenched, despite the obvious naïveté of categorizing one and a half billion people, in all their diversity, as an imagined unity?

When President Barack Obama made his 2009 address "to the Muslim world" in Cairo, he was confirming the modern assumption that there is a global Muslim community to be engaged.[1] Obama was trying to undo the damage President George W. Bush's war on terror had done to America's image among Muslims. To that end, Obama praised the historical contributions of Muslims in areas such as algebra, medicine, navigation, and printing. He also criticized Americans' negative stereotypes about Muslim faith traditions. He mentioned the positive moral values of these traditions and lauded American Muslims. This was a kind of sweetener before he put forward his government's views about the political tensions between the United States and diverse Muslim societies. It was an odd gesture. Would it be acceptable, or even sensible, to appeal to the contributions of East Asian civilization, Buddhism, and Confucianism before addressing America's political disputes with China?

Alongside Obama and so many others in the so-called West, Muslim leaders and intellectuals rely on the notion of the Muslim world to describe, simultaneously, the geopolitics, civilization, and religious tradition of diverse millions. About two decades before President Obama's speech, in January 1988, Iran's Ayatollah Ruhollah Khomeini wrote a letter to Mikhail Gorbachev on behalf of the Muslim world, urging the Soviet leader not to be misled by the capitalist West and to study the spiritual and political values of Islam. Khomeini ended his letter by declaring, "The Islamic Republic of Iran, as the greatest and most powerful base of the Islamic world, can easily fill the vacuum of religious faith in your society."[2] How did we arrive at this point, where a fantastical entity could be so present, so prevalent in political thinking? Why do so many Muslim and non-Muslim political leaders, intellectuals, and religious figures comfortably base many of their arguments and decisions on the idea of the Muslim World without reflecting on the accuracy of the generalization that this term signifies?

Contrary to widespread assumption, the term "Muslim world" does not derive from *ummah*, a concept as old as Islam, which refers to the Muslim religious community. Instead the Muslim world began to develop in the nineteenth century and achieved full flower in the 1870s. Also mistaken is the belief that Muslims were united until nationalist ideology and European colonialism tore them apart. This is precisely backward; in fact, Muslims never dreamed of global political unity *until* the peak of European hegemony in the late nineteenth century, when poor colonial conditions, European discourses of Muslim racial inferiority, and Muslims' theories of their own apparent decline nurtured the first arguments for pan-Islamic solidarity. In other words, the Muslim world arrived with imperial globalization and its concomitant ordering of humanity by race. The racialization of Islam was bound up with its transformation into a universal and uniform religious tradition, a force in international politics, and a distinct object in a discourse of civilizations. Political strategy and intellectual labor made this new reality, and both Muslims and European Christians took part.

The eve of World War I was the high point of perceived global Muslim unity. In the fall of 1914, the sultan of the Ottoman Empire drew on the authority he had cultivated as caliph of the global Muslim community to declare *jihad* on behalf of the

Muslim world. Yet even then there were strong expressions of Muslim loyalty to the Ottomans' enemies: the British, French, Dutch, and Russian empires. Competing Muslim and non-Muslim conceptions of the Muslim world wrought dramatic changes over the next decade. The abolition of the Ottoman caliphate in 1924 inspired self-reflection and debate on Muslim-world identity in an era when modernizing ideologies of nationalism and bolshevism threatened to obviate other political forms.

During World War II, the notion of the Muslim world remained a centerpiece of Great Power propaganda, as both Axis and Allies sought Muslims' support. But afterward, at the peak of decolonization during the 1950s and the 1960s, the Muslim world receded. No successor rose to anchor the Muslim world, as the Ottomans had. Indian independence and the messy partition of Pakistan sapped the influence of Indian Muslims, who, for a century, had been able to sway global affairs by pressuring and cajoling their British overlords. In this period, few journalists and scholars referred to Islam as an explanatory factor in world politics.

But it was not to last. Amid interrelated political events from Arab-Israeli conflicts to the Iranian Revolution, the 1970s and 1980s witnessed a resurgence of pan-Islamic patterns of thinking born in the imperial age. The Muslim world was again seen as a geopolitical unity, even though Muslim societies were by then ruled by more than fifty postcolonial nation-states.

How to explain this resurfacing of century-old tropes during the 1980s despite the radical transformation of the global system? Gone was European imperial hegemony in Muslim societies. Gone was the Ottoman caliphate. And there were all those nation-states. Yet the discourse of Muslim unity survived. It returned through the renewed racialization of Muslims and in the form of post–Cold War Islamist ideologies. The persistence of the geopolitical idea of the Muslim world from its peak in World War I to the present is not an outgrowth of shared history or immutable ideology within Muslim societies.[3] It is, rather, a function of the civilizational and geopolitical narratives concocted in encounters of Muslim societies with European empires, reconfigured according to the exigencies of the Cold War.

The central aim of this book is to demonstrate the origins and understand the appeal of these narratives in which the Muslim world lives alongside the Christian West. I therefore offer a critical genealogy of the idea of the Muslim world, showing how, starting in the late nineteenth century, pan-Islamists and Islamophobes have used the assumption, ideal, and threat of Muslim unity to advance political agendas. Together, and in tension, they created the Muslim world for their own strategic purposes and positioned it in everlasting conflict with the West. I hope that by recovering the imperial context in which essentialized ideas about Islam and the West developed, we will come to appreciate the historical contingency of the Muslim world, to understand more fully the role of religious identities in international affairs, and to reflect on ways in which the overlap of race and geopolitics limits struggles for rights and justice.

◆ ◆ ◆

The idea of the Muslim world is inseparable from the claim that Muslims constitute a race. The distinction of the Muslim world and the Christian West began taking shape most forcefully in the 1880s, when the majority of Muslims and Christians resided in the same empires. The rendering of Muslims as racially distinct—a process that called on both "Semitic" ethnicity and religious difference—and inferior aimed to disable and deny their demands for rights within European empires. Muslim intellectuals could not reject the assumptions of irreducible difference but responded that they were equal to Christians, deserving of rights and fair treatment. The same conception of Muslim unity and difference justified appeals to Muslims as a global community during World War I and World War II. Racial assumptions also ensured that later subaltern and nationalist claims for rights would be framed in the idioms of Muslim solidarity and an enduring clash between Islam and the West, giving rise to the Islamism and Islamophobia of the 1980s and beyond.

It is thanks to this elaboration of both Muslim difference and Muslim unity that contemporary writing, scholarly and otherwise, tends to emphasize Muslim exceptionalism. The assumption is that Muslims, due to their piety and the nature of their faith, naturally resist the liberal international order of independent, pluralistic nation-states. Muslims' attitudes toward politics are presumed different from those of Buddhists, Hindus, Jews, and Christians, whose societies need not be explained by reference to faith tradition or civilizational identity. However, this theory of Muslim exceptionalism is unsupported and unsubstantiated. The Ottoman Empire, Republican Turkey, British-ruled Indian Muslims, Afghanistan, the Saudi Kingdom, Pakistan, postcolonial Egypt, and Iran under the shah ardently supported the imperial and later nationalist world orders. The seeming importance of Islam in the contemporary politics of Muslim-majority societies derives not from theological requirements or a uniquely high level of Muslim piety but from the legacy of imperial racialization of Muslim-ness and from the particular intellectual and political strategies of Muslim resistance to this racialized identity.

The geography and technology of empire were essential to these processes of racialization and resistance in the second half of the nineteenth century. New transportation and communication technologies such as steamships and the telegraph fostered unprecedented levels of connection among Muslims, naturalizing the geopolitical concept of the Muslim world in

Europe and its colonies. The networks enabled by these technologies were the medium of pan-Islamic thought born of confrontation with imperial racism.

Imperial racism, but *not* empire itself. Muslim leaders and thinkers of the nineteenth and early twentieth centuries were not, for the most part, anti-imperialists. Instead they sought fair treatment from the four major European empires: British, Dutch, French, and Russian. These were cosmopolitan arrangements, home to wide-ranging ethnic and religious groups. But racialized legal categorizations shared across European empires, the empowerment strategies of colonized Muslim subjects, and tactics employed in imperial rivalries confirmed rather than challenged Muslim difference, ensuring that Muslims would be a separate class within the imperial whole. The British ruled almost half of the world's Muslims and therefore played an especially important role in guiding the development of pan-Islamic thought. British fears of rebellion and policies of oppression engendered specifically Muslim responses. At the same time, Muslims understood that their vast numbers and the reality of their overwhelming loyalty to the empire allowed them real clout.

Thus Muslim solidarity was of strategic importance. The Ottoman sultans, as the most powerful modern Muslim rulers and overseers of the Muslim holy cities, enjoyed a special position as leaders of the global Muslim community. They used this to their advantage, claiming spiritual sovereignty over Muslims globally and leveraging this influence in political wrangling with the British and other European empires. Seeking a competitive edge by any means available, empires variously used the idea of global Muslim solidarity to weaken their rivals, justify alliances with them, and bolster propaganda campaigns.

The advances of the imperial age led to increased wealth and an intellectual renaissance, including for Muslim subjects of

Christian rule. Printing and steamship technologies enabled
mobility and productivity in Muslim thought and publishing.
Women's rights, education, and economic activity improved.[4]
Yet by the early twentieth century, the categorization of Muslims as an inferior, colored race prone to rebellion against global
white hegemony had provoked paranoia in colonial metropoles,
leading to oppression and Muslim perceptions of their own
victimization.

Late nineteenth-century Muslim intellectuals responded to
the inequalities of racialization with a number of strategies. By
articulating a concept of Islamic civilization, these reformers
sought to elevate the esteem in which Muslims were held and
thereby contest the assertion of racial inferiority—if not racial
difference itself. Pioneers of the idea of Islamic civilization distinguished the values, ideals, and accomplishments of Muslim
societies from Islam as a faith tradition itself but assumed that
the civilization was inspired by the values of the faith. This involved a new focus on a "golden age" of lay Muslim philosophy,
art, and cultural production.

The reformers' goal was to make Islam compatible with modernity. Rebutting the likes of French historian and philosopher
Ernest Renan, who claimed that Islam was incompatible with
modern science, reformist writers argued that Islam was in
harmony with modern standards of reason and progress. The
civilization wrought by Muslims was the evidence. Modernist
reformers emphasized Andalusian Muslim history as a sign of
Islam's contribution to Europe, carving out a place for Averroes
and Avicenna in the global history of science and medicine. Discussion of Islamic civilization in relation to world and European history became a hallmark of intellectual life in every
Muslim society.

But this strategy of contesting inferiority by upholding a narrative of Islamic civilization only reinforced the European ra-

cial discourse in which Muslims were united—and divided from others—by their religion and heritage. Muslim thinking and writing about Islamic civilization created an abstraction linking Mecca to Java and Senegal, Istanbul to Samarkand and Delhi. This narrative of a singular Muslim civilization led to amnesia about cosmopolitan Muslim empires, which could not be reduced to a simplistic civilizational model. Centuries of shared experience with Hindus, Jews, and Buddhists; shamans; Christian Arabs, Greeks, and Armenians; and others were ignored.

Although reformers aimed to elevate the nonreligious characteristics of Islamic history to which non-Muslims could relate as equals, these reformers didn't simply abandon faith. They sought to use it for new purposes, recasting Islam by collapsing its diverse traditions into a singular world religion comparable to Christianity. Its true spirit recovered, Muslim modernists claimed, Islam would be an instrument in the revival of the victimized, declining Muslim world. As followers of a universal religion compatible with science, Muslims would also appropriate and respond to secular European ideologies such as the Enlightenment, social Darwinism, and progress.

In order to bring uniform and systematic meaning to this new world religion, modernist scholars focused strictly on texts from which they claimed to deduce the essence of Islam beyond differences of culture, time, and place. Of course, there has long been a rich Muslim tradition of textual interpretation. Innumerable debates, such as Ghazali's critique of philosophy and Averroes's responses insisting on harmony between revelation and reason, illustrate an enduring struggle to understand God's will by deciphering and arguing about religious texts. But reformers took a novel approach. They discounted vernacular Muslim practices that, historically, were as integral to the meaning of Islam as was textual scholarship. Late nineteenth-century Muslim intellectuals wrote books with essentializing titles such as *The Spirit of Islam, Islam and Progress, The Rise and Decline of Islam, Christianity and Islam,* and *Women's Rights in Islam.* Whereas earlier Muslim scholarship refrained from such generalizations and preserved a polyvocal tradition, these works lumped together diverse Muslim practices and criticized their supposed impurities or simply overlooked them.[5] Muslim societies of the nineteenth century were not actually less diverse than previously, but reformist elites hoped to refashion them as such, fixing the content and principles of Islam in order to create a unity that would empower Muslims.

This process of reformation unfolds in the work of two generations of modern Muslim intellectuals, from Syed Ahmad Khan, Syed Ameer Ali, and Muhammad Abduh to Rashid Rida, Shakib Arslan, and Muhammad Asad. Their ideas inspired unity not only across faith differences but also what had been wide-ranging political and moral agendas. Approaches to slavery provide a case in point. When Ahmet Bey, Tunisia's ruler, banned slavery in the mid-nineteenth century, Muslim scholars justified the ban on the basis of *sharia*. But their reasoning did not reflect a monolithic principle of Islam. It was understood that *sharia* scholars in Egypt and Zanzibar might rule differently. After the Ottomans banned the slave trade, it eventually disappeared in Muslim-ruled states without any universal claims about Islamic rules concerning slavery. Within less than a century, however, Ahmadiyya Muslim missionaries in Europe and America spoke of Islam's categorical ban on racism and slavery, in contrast with Christianity's condoning of racial discrimination.

Thus, in time, the nineteenth-century goal of positioning Islam as enlightened and tolerant—and therefore Muslims as racially equal to their Western overlords—produced the notion of Islam in the abstract, providing the core substance of Muslim reformism and pan-Islamic thought in the early twentieth century. This Muslim modernist strategy to defeat the notion of racial inferiority and articulate Muslim belonging in a universal humanity counterintuitively contributed to a rigid Orientalist conception of Muslims as essentially different from the rest of humanity. Ironically, in both the colonial and postcolonial contexts this assumption further racialized Muslim societies.

Although the historian may distinguish the geopolitical, civilizational, and religious modes of knowledge and discourse inherent in the racialization and reformation of an imagined Muslim world, all were tightly interwoven. Both Christian missionaries and secular theorists such as Renan argued that defects in the Muslim faith itself produced the civilizational decline that legitimized empire. Thus secular Muslim reformers responded by rewriting the history of science and philosophy—typically irrelevant to geopolitics—and theological reformers responded with new religious exegeses. They tried to refute missionary claims and social Darwinism but also, in some respects, embraced them by accepting the narrative of Muslim decline and reinterpreting the Quran and other religious texts to urge believers toward salvation by moral improvement.[6]

This nineteenth- and twentieth-century history helps to reveal falsehoods in today's dominant narratives about politics in the Muslim world—both the politics imagined by Muslims and the politics of Islam imagined by non-Muslims. The literature of Muslim exceptionalism relies on an essentialized notion of Western Europe as nationalist, democratic, and progressive, in contrast with a conservative, antinationalist caliphate born from selective reading of Islamist critiques of Western modernity and redefinitions of Muslim traditions. Both Muslims and non-Muslims often assume that modern Europe created the notion of national sovereignty at the Treaty of Westphalia and that this norm then spread to the rest of the world thanks to the expansion of Eurocentric values projected as universal. Some of today's transnational Islamist political projects and identities claim to challenge Westphalian national borders in the name of the borderless Muslim world.

But this narrative of the encounter between the modern West and the Islamic world is ahistorical and relies on myths of what constitutes the West and the Muslim world. In reality, before and during the colonial period Muslims' political views could be as imperial as Queen Victoria's, as nationalistic as Gandhi's, and as socialistic as Lenin's. In the age when imperialists and reformers were inventing unitary Islam, individual Muslims were anarchists, feminists, and pacifists. They were as modern as their European counterparts. Muslim political visions from the mid-nineteenth century onward, including pan-Islamism, reflect not enduring tradition but rather the particular entanglement of Muslim intellectual history and the shifting international order from the age of empires to that of the contemporary nation-state.

I started researching this topic in 2008, while ruminating on post–September 11 debates about Islam in international affairs. Yet even as late as 2012, I could not have imagined that today there would be a self-proclaimed caliphate in areas controlled by ISIS in Iraq and Syria. ISIS's call attracts and repulses potential followers across the world. Meanwhile Islamophobia in Europe and America insists on categorizing the caliphate's leaders and their Muslim victims as members of the same racial and civilizational unity.

ISIS's caliphate is a caricature, yet it demands acknowledgment of its supposed authenticity. Is today's self-proclaimed caliph, Abu Bakr al-Baghdadi, even aware of the cultural practices of the last Ottoman caliphs, such as Abdulhamid II or Abdulmecid, who enjoyed operas by European composers and, in the fashion of imperial courts, painted portraits of their daughters? Does that so-called caliph know that Muslim rulers once wore proudly the medals bestowed on them by Christian leaders and offered such honors in return? Similarly, the politics of Sunni-Shia division are today presented falsely as fundamental to Islamic life. Do rivals in Syria and Iraq, marshaling ideas of Muslim solidarity against each other, realize that the Shia-Sunni distinction had no political valence in the Eurocentric imperial world of the early twentieth century, when Shia and Sunni both looked to the Ottoman caliph as their spiritual ruler and representative on the world stage?

These dangerous mistakes raise questions that must be approached through nuanced and thorough readings of history. How is it that terms such as *"ummah"* and "caliphate" can signify such different practices now than they did a hundred years ago? What are the narrative and historical links between World War I and the present, today's Muslim question and its imperial past?

In paying close attention to the evolution of Muslim-world narratives over a 150-year period, one sees concepts and epistemologies of the Muslim world transferred from the age of empires to the postcolonial period. Each generation gave new political meanings to these concepts and ways of thinking. Ottoman Sultan Abdulhamid II, Haj Amin al-Husseini of Mandate Palestine, King Faisal of Saudi Arabia, and Ayatollah Khomeini of Iran had different political goals, but they all relied on a similar framework of the imagined Muslim world in relation to the Christian West. Likewise, even though Renan and later scholars such as Arnold Toynbee and Samuel Huntington represent different political sensibilities, they shared the same template of a racial, civilizational, and geopolitical Muslim world distinct from the West. It is in this theater, not of timeless doctrine but of contingent politics and ideas, built by many hands in the late nineteenth century and since renovated repeatedly, that contemporary conflicts play out.

An Imperial *Ummah* before the Nineteenth Century

Tipu Sultan needed allies. It was 1798, and the sultan of Mysore, in southern India, wanted to push the British East India Company out of his territory, but he lacked the forces to do so on his own. When he sought aid from the rulers of France, first the royal court and later the Republic, Tipu spoke of an alliance against a mutual enemy, the British Empire. When he sought the same from Ottoman Sultan Selim III, he did so in the name of Muslim solidarity. In addition to military assistance, the prestige of Ottoman support would help him compete with regional Muslim rivals.

But the sultan in Istanbul was less forthcoming than Tipu hoped. Tipu's language of shared religion and culture could not sway the Ottomans from their strategic interests, allied as they were with Britain and Russia against Napoleon, who had just invaded Ottoman Egypt. Instead, Selim discouraged Tipu's partnership with France and urged peace with the British. When war came to Mysore the next year, shared religion again proved no source of unity: British soldiers conquered and plundered the territory with the cooperation of other Indian Muslim kings, such as Nizam of Hyderabad, who provided troops and munitions.

As Tipu discovered the hard way, the idea of Muslim solidarity was politically impotent. Notions of *ummah* and Muslim-ness existed, but, whatever they meant, it would be almost a hundred years more before they inspired narratives of global Muslim unity along either geopolitical or civilizational lines.[1]

This had been the condition of Muslim empires for more than a millennium. From mid-thirteenth-century Mongolian expansion to the Napoleonic wars, Muslim emperors, kings, emirs, and sultans ruled over hundreds of distinct Eurasian and African dynasties. Muslim rulers fought among themselves, sometimes in alliance with so-called infidels, as much as they fought non-Muslims.[2] Modern advocates of Muslim-world unity, such as the Indian-Pakistani Islamist Abul Ala Maududi and the Iranian revolutionary Ali Shariati, tend to read this period as befits their political interests. Some take a selective approach, glorifying the military achievements of the Ottomans and Mughals in order to inspire a kind of patriotic fervor. Others depict the rulers of cosmopolitan empire as impious, unable to recognize the necessity of empowering a global Muslim community.[3]

These histories assume a shared and invariant Muslim political imagination, albeit one routinely abandoned by self-aggrandizing rulers. The real Muslim political experience from the seventh through the eighteenth century, however, tells a story of multiplicity, contestation, and change, leaving the idea of the Muslim world to emerge later, alongside the later civilizational narrative of the West.[4]

Early Muslim Empires: Diversity and Synthesis

The pre-nineteenth-century notion of *ummah* was deterritorialized. It urged cross-tribal affiliation, shared legal practices, and a collective eschatological vision—the Prophet Muhammad says that, in the hereafter, he will gather his *ummah* from all generations across time—but demanded no specific government or place on a map. Members of the *ummah* neither lived in one land nor were subject to one political authority.

Even when Muslims expanded the territory under their control, the extent of the *ummah* was not necessarily at issue. Populations in Persia, North Africa, Central Asia, and South Asia gradually converted to Islam, but there was no attempt by Muslim rulers to convert all subjects, let alone all of humanity. Muslim theology does not require conversion as a precursor to salvation.[5] Thus the expansion of Muslim dynasties did not involve consistent and aggressive missionary zeal toward people of other faiths, especially fellow People of the Book—Christians and Jews.

It is in part because of this willingness to allow conquered people to maintain their traditions that, throughout history, Muslim-ruled domains were so diverse. Another factor is the behavior of Muslims themselves, who followed multiple spiritual paths, subscribed to various legal schools, spoke many languages, and hailed from diverse backgrounds. Muslims in different parts of the world *were* connected—through education, trade, pilgrimage, politics, and kinship, not just religion and not through collective competition with a non-Muslim other. Yet political loyalties and self-perception were not primarily defined by membership in a global religious and civilizational bloc.[6]

Exchanges among distant Muslims could conceivably have engendered global solidarity. Written texts and oral narratives of the religion circulated widely. *Madrasas* (educational institutions) from India to Morocco used similar textbooks and trained students in the Quran, *hadith* (traditions of Muhammad), law, grammar, and logic. *Sharia,* the legal code, was much respected by its interpreters, and legal scholars held key civic positions across Muslim-dominated lands. Masters were certified to teach particular texts, ensuring a vertical line of connection to disciples across geography.[7] Genealogical trees *(shajara)* of knowledge transmission sketched a transhistorical community of believers and members. For example, Sayyids and Sherifs, grandchildren of the Prophet Muhammad from the lineage of Hussein and Hasan, lived and taught in diverse Muslim societies, linking them to the historical center of Islam. Even Muslims in China, living under the rule of non-Muslim rulers, had multiple generation-long lineages tracing their families to Arabia. Sufis and other groups offered paths of spiritual, social, and personal guidance that might be followed anywhere.

But Muslims were not limited to learning the basic tenets of Islam, notions of filial piety, and stories about the Prophet Muhammad's life. They learned also of Abraham, Moses, Noah, Joseph, Jesus, and Mary, whose moral stories are mentioned in the Quran. Political elites were as familiar with Islamic figures and histories as they were with Alexander the Great and Genghis Khan, Persian fables and Hindu stories. Many tales beloved by Muslims, such as *Dede Korkut, Shahnameh,* and *Saif al-Muluk,* cannot be traced to religious texts. Love stories, such as *Layla wa Majnun,* were as well known to Muslims as were their religious legal codes. Prince Saif al-Muluk's love affair with the fairy Badrul Jamal, Qays's unrequited and untamable desire for Layla, *Shahnameh*'s legendary Persian kings—these belong to a world without civilizational and geopolitical borders. Some of the Muslim heroes in *Dede Korkut* fall in love with infidel women, praising their virtues. Muslim doctors and mathematicians similarly were exposed to sources outside Islamic tradition and were proud of the disciplinary lineage connecting them to ancient Greeks and Egyptians and never made the simplistic binary distinction between East and West.

Interpretations of religious texts and practices differed in local languages and contexts.[8] Even within a textual legal tradition there was room for many voices and interpretations, preventing any one person from speaking on behalf of the Muslim world and universal Muslim faith.[9] It is because the lands where Muslims lived were so varied that travelers sought scholarly and spiritual knowledge throughout them. On their journeys, they shared a cosmopolitan tradition of learning. They also noted stark differences between far-flung Muslim communities, despite the shared faith tradition. Because there was no central, church-like institution to bind Muslims, there was also no distinction between orthodox and heterodox practice.

Muslims were spread across a vast range of political entities, which treated Islam in their own ways and furthered its development along different trajectories. Muslims lived in lands legally classified as Darul Islam, realms of Muslim authority, where one could practice faith freely under the protection of a Muslim ruler, and Darul Harb, hostile places, where a Muslim lacked legal protection and safety. There were also Darul Aman, lands of peace, where Muslims practiced freely, though they did not rule. Muslims in China, for instance, mostly lived under the rule of non-Muslim monarchs, but they did not consider Chinese empires lands of war and in fact served these empires. Many preferred Chinese rule to the alternatives. Conversely, Muslim dynasties in India ruled over populations in which Muslims were a minority and had to adjust their legal distinctions accordingly. But these were theoretical distinctions, far removed from practice. There was no effective binary of Muslim and non-Muslim lands, which makes sense since *ummah* described a faith community, not a geopolitical unity.

Where Muslims did rule, political elites made alliances with non-Muslims against other Muslims, just as European Christians allied with non-Christians, which was forbidden in theory but common in reality.[10] Not only did Christian rulers make alliances with Muslim rulers but Crusader kingdoms eventually had to tolerate the religious practices of Muslims under their authority.

Muslim rulers did expect subservience from Christian subjects and instituted practices, such as distinguishing Muslims' and Christians' clothing, that may seem to affirm rigid boundaries between Darul Islam and Darul Harb or between Islamic and Christian. But while distinctions were made between Muslims and non-Muslims, Ottoman, Safavid, Mughal, and Moroccan rulers also gave Jews, Greeks, Hindus, and Armenians important positions in trade, diplomacy, and government bureaucracy, suggesting that group borders were porous.[11] Muslim corsairs in the Mediterranean called their piracy a "sea *jihad*" but also cooperated with non-Muslims and shared the culture of Christian pirates, which facilitated frequent conversion from one faith to another. A significant portion of the sixteenth-century Ottoman navy comprised Christian-born Mediterranean sailors who spoke the same language as their adversaries.[12] Given the diversity of premodern Muslim identities in theory and practice and the amount of Muslim-Christian cross-pollination, we cannot locate the seeds of the modern division between Islam and the West in Muslim-Christian relations of the medieval period.

Early Muslim political life also demonstrates that the notion of a caliphate, like that of an *ummah,* cannot sustain contemporary claims of Muslim unity. The original caliphate formed in the relatively small community of early Muslims in Medina after the death of Prophet Muhammad in 632. It was not long before internal tensions and outside influences were felt.

Traumatic intra-Muslim violence culminated in the killing of the Prophet's grandson Hussein and his companions by the Umayyad caliph Yazid in the Battle of Karbala (680). By the end of the century, the Umayyad Dynasty had incorporated imperial practices from Byzantine and Persian traditions. Rulers lived in luxurious palaces and adopted institutions and talent from other empires. Whereas the earliest caliphs believed they represented the deceased prophet, some pro-Umayyad interpreters suggested that caliphs represented God, as in the Byzantine style. Within just two generations, the caliphate was being reinvented.

Both the Umayyad (661–750) and Abbasid (750–1258) dynasties claimed to champion the ideals of a single Muslim caliphate, yet both exhibited the characteristics of diverse, large-scale empires. They didn't rule a unity of Muslims but attempted to maintain nominal control of many peoples in distant locales pressing different agendas. After the Abbasids lost political authority in the tenth century, three centuries of Muslim sultanates and dynasties with powerful armies—such as the Seljuks, Ghaznavids, and Shia Buyids—protected the weak caliph in Baghdad in return for his recognition of the legitimacy of their kingdoms. The legal and political theory of the caliphate evolved over this period, but it never fully embraced the reality of competing power centers across Muslim societies.

The powerless Abbasids were finally defeated by the Mongolian Empire in 1258, though some descendants of the Abbasid Dynasty continued to claim the title of caliph without holding any political responsibility. Even though the Mongol rulers of Muslim lands did not claim to be caliphs, they did respect Muslim legal and moral norms, a means to establish their legitimacy among the Muslims they conquered.

The synthesis of Mongolian and Muslim political traditions at the turn of the fourteenth century reshaped the meanings of *ummah,* Darul Islam, and the caliphate, creating a lasting imperial legacy. One source of that synthesis was Ghazan Khan (d. 1304), a ruler of the Ilkhanid house of the Mongols, who was raised as a Christian but converted to Islam just before taking power in 1295. Both Ghazan Khan and his Muslim-Mongol, successor Öljeitü (r. 1304–1317), sought to expand from Persia by conquering Mamluk lands in Syria. But how to convince the defeated Muslim populations of Iran and Iraq to fight for Mongol armies, or Muslims in Mamluk lands to submit to Mongol rule? Ghazan Khan adopted the title padishah al-Islam (king of Islam) and argued for the necessity of his war against Mamluks, noting that they violated various Muslim moral and legal norms in their invasion of the Mongol-ruled city of Mardin. Ghazan Khan also appealed to Muslim sentiments with a declaration of peace and protection read at the Umayyad Mosque of Damascus in 1300, after his military victories. He tried to send a caravan of gifts and charity to Mecca to bolster his image as a Muslim monarch, but the city's Mamluk rulers prevented it.

In the eyes of Syrian Muslims, Ghazan Khan and later Ilkhanid rulers could be legitimate rulers as long as they offered decent treatment. They promoted order and stability and extended the prestigious dynastic lineage of Genghis Khan. There was little reason to fight against these Mongols, who were not only Muslims themselves but also allowed their populations to practice their religion and laws.[13]

The Mamluk Dynasty remained a rival, however, and tried to resist the emerging synthesis of Muslim and Mongol traditions in the hope of undermining popular support for the Ilkhanids. One might say they initiated a public relations campaign, inculcating a narrative of Muslim unity against foreign aggression. Thus Ibn Taymiyyah (1263–1328), a Mamluk jurist, issued three anti-Mongol religious opinions *(fatwa)* explaining why it was legitimate to fight against the Ilkhanid armies despite the

conversion of their king and the presence of large numbers of
Muslim soldiers in their ranks. By analogy to Muslim criticism
of the Christian representation of Jesus as the son of God, Taymiyyah challenged the Mongol view of Genghis Khan as a sacred
human being. Taymiyyah condemned the Mongol government's
tolerance of religious diversity within a relatively neutral state.
And he ridiculed the fact that Ilkhanid Mongols granted religious freedom and autonomy to shamans, Christian monks, and
Muslim scholars alike, irrespective of the truth or falsehood of
their tradition.[14]

Over the next six centuries, major Muslim-ruled empires in
Eurasia inherited the syncretic legacy of Ghazan Khan without
rejecting the juridical textual tradition of scholars such as
Taymiyyah. As long as a just ruler protected the security of his
subjects and allowed the private practice of *sharia,* it did not
matter how that ruler came to power. Taymiyyah's and other jurists' writing on good governance could have inspired some
Muslim officials, but no dynasty governed a society based on
strict textual interpretation. There were no fundamentalist
kingdoms following Muslim juridical rulings to the letter.

It was Tamerlane, a Sufi Muslim proud of his descent from
Genghis Khan and the Prophet Muhammad, who best symbolized the synthesis of Mongol and Muslim political visions. That
Tamerlane and his successors boasted of this lineage and considered Genghis Khan's multiethnic empire a model—even
though this empire invaded and destroyed the capital of the Abbasid caliphate—was indicative of new imperial visions. One of
Tamerlane's most important legacies is his emphasis on *yasa,*
the law of the state, as distinct from *sharia.* This did not entail
a rejection of *sharia,* but it did help to legitimize the kind of universal empire that ruled diverse subjects.

There were significant differences in the governance practices
of the Mughal, Safavid, and Ottoman empires, as well as changes

over time within each empire, yet all of these inherited the universal visions of Ghazan Khan and Tamerlane. Muslim monarchs after the fifteenth century—such as the Safavid Shah Ismail, Suleiman the Magnificent of the Ottoman Empire, and the Mughal ruler Akbar—were no less Muslim than were the Abbasid caliphs, but they embraced a *political* vision significantly different from that of the caliphates in the first three centuries after Muhammad.[15]

Mughal and Ottoman elites built their empires on the basis of inherited practices of kingship as well as their own innovations. They may have been exposed to written theories of ideal Muslim political order, but there was never a consensus among scholars on what that ideal would look like, and there were no political parties or ideological movements to articulate political systems in harmony with religious texts.[16] One of the starkest examples of cosmopolitan Muslim political practice was in the Mughal Empire in India, whose elites perceived the body of the king as sacred, similar to a Sufi saint. This supported a kind of messianic understanding of kingship, according to which Mughal rulers provided justice and order for all the subjects irrespective of religious affiliation.[17]

The meaning of the caliphate changed still further under the Mamluks and Ottomans. In the fourteenth and fifteenth centuries, the Mamluk Empire hosted in Cairo the rump Abbasid caliph—who claimed religious but not political authority—and protected the Muslim holy cities of Mecca, Medina, and Jerusalem. The attending prestige benefited the Mamluks in their diplomatic correspondence with other monarchs, though they never claimed to create an *ummah* under a single caliph.[18] In fact, the sheltering of a powerless, symbolic caliph was a violation of all earlier writings on the theory of caliphates.

The entrusting to the Mamluks of the holy sites and the caliph did not dissuade the Ottoman Empire from invading Egypt in 1517, precipitating the end of one important Muslim kingdom at the hands of another. Contrary to legend, the Ottoman sultan Selim did not try to inherit title to the caliphate. Instead, once the Ottoman Empire took over the protection of Mecca and Medina, Selim created a new legitimizing title for himself: servant of the Two Holy Cities. Further muddying the easy narrative of succession, the Ottomans hosted the last Abbasid caliph, Mütevekkil III, in Istanbul for about a decade. Mütevekkil returned to Cairo still claiming to be caliph, without any objection from the Ottoman rulers.

As the Abbasid caliphate gradually faded away, the Ottoman sultans, the most powerful Muslim rulers, came to be seen as the most legitimate heirs to the caliphate.[19] Yet Sultan Selim and his son Sultan Suleiman—who expanded the Ottoman realm to the Arab Middle East, Europe, and Egypt—primarily called themselves shah and khan. Various Ottoman sultans after Selim proudly used the title of caliph in addition to their sovereign titles of khan and padishah (shah), but never alone.[20] Meanwhile, an Ottoman sultan could claim to have inherited the Roman Empire and use the title Caesar without fear of contradicting the imperial legacy of Mongolians and Muslims.[21] In an empire ruling over a large and diversely populated area, legitimacy sprang from many sources.

Tellingly, Muslims outside Ottoman lands rarely described the sultans in Istanbul as the singular caliphs of the *ummah*.[22] Many smaller-scale sultanates tried to claim the caliphate title for their own political purposes. In the sixteenth century, Moroccan sultan Ahmad al-Mansur, little concerned with the Ottoman sultan's claim to the caliphate, declared himself caliph and allied with Britain against Habsburg Spain.[23]

As we have seen, the absence of a Muslim political order based solely on notions of caliphate or *ummah* did not prevent the transmission and sharing across empires of customs, rules, and values mainly deriving from Muslim legal and faith traditions. For example, there was an understanding that Muslims had a right to travel to Mecca, though the ratio of Muslims who could perform pilgrimage was rather low before the nineteenth century. Interpretations of *sharia* were more or less respected by all Muslim rulers in commercial and civil life, even though room for local differences in application was taken for granted. In times of military conflict among Muslim rulers, shared laws and principles governed the conduct of war and treatment of prisoners and civilians. Thus an Ottoman prisoner of war in Cairo and a Mamluk prisoner in Ottoman lands could appeal to *sharia* for better treatment.[24] Even if Muslim societies across three continents did not form a single economic, legal, or political system, there was a "community of discourse" in which similar notions of legal legitimacy and moral propriety were shared.[25] Vernacular adoptions of Muslim faith were more common than its textual and elite interpretations.

And yet we should not emphasize too greatly the density and causal effects of these intra-Muslim connections. Naturally, Bosnian Muslims had more cultural and trade links with Eastern European Christians than with Southeast Asian Muslims. Chinese and North African Muslims were more closely connected to their neighbors and regional empires than to each other. In the Mediterranean, southeastern Europe, the Caucuses, South Asia, and Southeast Asia, Muslims always lived together with non-Muslims, imbibing a local brew of politics, culture, economics, and daily life. Muslim-majority port cities of the southern Mediterranean were full of non-Muslim merchants, residents, and even neighborhoods, while in many South Asian cities, Muslims tallied second to the Hindu majority. One could find similarities among Muslims from Africa to East Asia, but diversity and difference would be as stark and important as commonalities and connections. More importantly, shared religious knowledge and practices never meant and implied a political unity and solidarity across the globe.

Through all this complexity and change, some notion of *ummah* as an abstract religious term and ideal persisted. But its permutations were many and endlessly varied. The writings of two Muslim travelers, one from the fourteenth century and the other from the seventeenth, provide enduring portraits of this diverse world, devoid of notions of civilizational and geopolitical unity.

The Muslim scholar and explorer Ibn Batuta (1304–1368) is famed for his extensive travel across Muslim and non-Muslim lands. To some, his journey, recorded in the *Rihla,* illustrates the diversity and ambiguity of the Muslim political experience after the Mongol destruction of the Abbasid capital in Baghdad. To others Batuta's world is a model of unified, borderless Muslim societies.[26] But what did Batuta think? Did he perceive a Muslim world in his travels?

According to the *Rihla,* Ibn Batuta traveled seventy-five thousand miles, from North Africa to the Middle East, Anatolia, India, and China, crossing the domains of kings, sultans, and emperors. And everywhere he visited, the Arabic language connected Batuta to educated local Muslims. He also interacted with more than ten different Muslim sultans, some of whom he served as an ambassador and judge.

The cosmopolitan space in which Batuta traveled was limiting, though. His reliance on Arabic, the language of educated Muslims, restricted his understanding of and access to vernacular Muslim languages and literatures as well as Hindu, Buddhist, Confucian, and Christian traditions. Batuta did visit many non-Muslim sites and converse with non-Muslims, but the stories he tells of them lack the kinds of detail he marshals when describing interactions with the few non-Arab Muslims he met who could speak Arabic.[27] Perhaps because transnational Muslim networks coexisted so fluidly with other people and practices, Batuta never makes a simple distinction between the world of Muslims and the world of non-Muslims, between Islam and Christianity, or Islam and the West. He did not have a concept of threatening, alien civilization, be it Christian, Hindu, or Buddhist. In fact, for Batuta there was no abstract and globalized concept of a Muslim civilization.

A later traveler, the Ottoman Evliya Çelebi (1611–1682), reinforces the sense of diversity that Batuta found in Muslim lands. About three centuries after Batuta, Çelebi confined his travels to the domains of the Ottoman Empire, in whose service he worked. But more than 40 percent of the occupants of the empire were non-Muslim, and Çelebi's journal offers a detailed and sympathetic account of their cultures, languages, and histories. He takes obvious pride in the diversity of people living peacefully under the protection of a Muslim sultan ruling over such expansive territory. He is curious about unfamiliar customs and describes for readers the singers and entertainers of Bursa, Mecca's dancing Abyssinian slave women, Albanian Muslims' public displays of affection between two male companions. Though he recognizes that some in Istanbul might find these practices disgraceful, he makes sure readers understand they were normal and acceptable for Muslims elsewhere.[28]

Çelebi knew Ottoman Turkish, Arabic, and Persian, but he went beyond these major Muslim languages and made an effort to learn the local tongues and tales of southern Poland, Romania, and the Caucasus. He was fascinated by vampire stories as well as the poetry of local Muslims and Christians. He wrote observantly about the architecture and scholarship of regions irrespective of their inhabitants' religions. He saw no contradiction between his piety as a Muslim who memorized the Quran and his respect for non-Muslim cultures.

Though Çelebi was conscious of belonging to the privileged Muslim elite, he saw non-Muslims as part of the Ottoman imperial order. The "other," for Çelebi, was not Christendom or the West but specific empires, such as the Habsburgs and Safavids.[29] He was not, in this regard, an exceptional cosmopolitan. His unrelated contemporary Kâtip Çelebi (1609–1657) wrote extensively about the different empires and geographies of the world and was aware of the European sea voyages and writings on East Asia and the American continent. Although both of these Age of Exploration writers could have drawn on increasing knowledge of distant lands, neither made geopolitical distinctions between the Muslim world and the West—nor did fellow Ottoman scholars of the era.

To be sure, cosmopolitan empires were still full of prejudice. One can find all kinds of derogatory remarks and stereotypes in Muslim writings about Christians and Hindus. Similarly, European Christians attacked Muslims with dehumanizing associations and symbols. As Nabil Matar notes, British writers repurposed terms of abuse applied to native Americans in the Western Hemisphere—for example, accusations of bestiality and sodomy—to describe Muslims they encountered in North Africa and South Asia.

But there are two important distinctions between this sort of religious prejudice and the terms of late nineteenth-century racialized geopolitical competition between the Muslim world and Christian West. First, even when pre-nineteenth-century Muslim writers distinguished Muslim lands from others, they had no concept of Muslims the world over unified in civilizational and religious unity against a common enemy. For example, Hasan Kafi al-Akhisari, a sixteenth-century Ottoman author of political treatises, used the term "Islam *memleketleri*" (Muslim countries) to refer to lands inhabited by Muslims, but, in doing so, he did not imply a geopolitical and civilizational unity in relation to the putative unity of the Christian West.[30] Second, in spite of prejudice, concepts of universal justice prevailed in Muslim empires. As Akhisari argued, an unjust Muslim monarch is no better than a just non-Muslim one.

Conflicts of Empire, Not Civilization

Evliya Çelebi died just a year before the second Ottoman Siege of Vienna in 1683, so he did not witness that critical Habsburg victory. Today this siege is remembered in countless books and popular culture as the ultimate symbol of a perennial conflict between Islam and Christendom. Anders Breivik, the Norwegian terrorist who committed mass murder at a Labor Party youth camp in July 2011, wrote of the Battle of Vienna's historical significance in a manifesto titled "2083: A European Declaration of Independence." As Breivik sees it, European Christians stopped a Muslim attack in 1683 and should, by the time of the four hundredth anniversary, be prepared to expel all Muslims from the continent.

In reality, however, the siege in 1683 and other Ottoman-Habsburg conflicts were primarily confrontations between empires, not rival faiths or civilizations. True, Muslim-ness was an important aspect of identity in the Ottoman Dynasty, and Catholicism was equally important for Habsburg self-perception and international legitimacy.[31] Texts and speeches detailing Ottoman-Habsburg rivalry make frequent reference to "holy war," with both sides marshaling religious language against infidels. But contemporary references to the Siege of Vienna as a clash between Islam and Christianity are oblivious to the fact that the Ottomans fought this war in support of Protestant Hungarians. There were Christian soldiers and allies fighting on the Ottoman side. Meanwhile, the Ottoman's Muslim rivals, such as the Safavid Empire, did not consider the Habsburgs their enemies simply because they were at war with other Muslims. And after the Ottoman defeat, the Muslim elite of the empire did not ostracize their Christian subjects. In fact, the 1699 Treaty of Karlowitz, which brought an end to this period of Ottoman-Habsburg war, was drafted by Alexander Mavrocordatos, a Greek Christian bureaucrat of the Ottoman Empire.[32]

In the course of centuries of wars against Catholic Habsburg enemies, Ottomans were often allied with Christians, such as the French. In the eighteenth century, the Ottomans fought Russia and the Habsburg Empire in order to maintain the integrity and sovereignty of Christian Poland for strategic reasons, not for any Muslim cause. *Jihad* may have been part of the language in some of these conflicts, but the logic of Muslim friend and Christian enemy did not apply.

The same was true during the sixteenth-century Ottoman-Portuguese conflict in the Indian Ocean. The Ottomans made much of their enemy's Christian religion and sought alliance with Muslim sultanates in the Horn of Africa and Indian subcontinent. Yet the Portuguese had their own Muslim allies, and some Muslim rulers resisted cooperation with the Ottomans. The Ottoman moment in the Indian Ocean did not last into the seventeenth century, and once the Portuguese threat to Muslim traders there was averted, the Ottomans stopped intervening.[33]

In the eighteenth century, when European imperial powers expanded into Eurasia, Muslim rulers of Iran, Afghanistan, Central Asia, and India did not turn to pan-Islamic solidarity but instead sought their own aggrandizement at each other's expense. Even as Europeans were marching to their doorsteps, Muslim rulers didn't imagine a Western threat to a shared Muslim world. They were pursuing their independent interests.

The Mughal Empire was weakened and divided not by European empires but by the Persian Muslim ruler Nader Shah's devastating 1727 invasion. Soon after Nader Shah's victories, Persia came under the domination of the Afghan Durranis. When Russia expanded into Muslim-majority Persian territories of the Caucuses, the Ottoman Empire stood by, indifferent.[34] There were no calls for solidarity against the Russians from Indian or North African Muslims. The British East India Company had the support of Muslim maharajas and sultans as well as Muslim soldiers in their war with Mysore.[35]

On some occasions in the eighteenth century, one does find references to a general Muslim solidarity, especially under circumstances in which Muslims felt their religious freedom was threatened. For instance, toward the end of the century, Indian Muslim scholars began to refer to the sultan of the Ottoman Empire as a potential protector of their religious practices and values. Similarly, in diplomatic correspondence with the Ottomans, Central Asian Muslim khanates called for solidarity against Russian imperial expansion.[36] But these appeals were inconsequential. Muslim networks of education, religious fraternity, trade, and pilgrimage thrived in the eighteenth century without protection by a single Muslim empire or alliance of Muslim polities. Politically diffused, these networks were powerless against European maritime and land empires intervening in Malacca, Java, Bengal, Crimea, the Caucuses, and East Africa and never coalesced into any kind of world solidarity.

The Russian annexation of the Muslim Crimean khanate provides a case in point. After annexation, Ottoman jurists debated the religious and legal obligations of Muslims living under Christian rule.[37] The Küçük Kaynarca Treaty of 1774 partly diffused the debate by giving Ottoman sultans rights over Muslims in Russia in return for Russian rights over Orthodox Christians of the Ottoman Empire. But the treaty recognized Ottoman protection only of Crimean Muslims, not all Muslims globally. And the sultans rarely used their powers to interfere in the affairs of Muslims in the Russian Empire. Legal wrangling about the rights of Muslims living under the Christian rules, or the freedom of enslaved Muslim soldiers captured by Russian forces aside, the Ottoman jurists did not concern themselves with universal notions of Islam. They didn't pay attention to how Indian, Chinese, or Malay jurists dealt with their religious duties under the rule of Christian monarchs.

Meanwhile, diverse strains of vernacular, sufi, and textual Islam continued to spread during the eighteenth century. The Naqshbandi Sufi order demonstrated the reach of Central Asian practices, which passed via India to Ottoman Arabia, Anatolia, and Africa. Ottoman followers of Mawlana Khalid Baghdadi (1776–1827) expanded Naqshbandi Sufi influence among elites and common subjects across the empire, from Istanbul to Kurdistan, the Levant, and the Balkans. Other Sufi orders, such as the Khalwatiyya, Tijaniya, Sammaniyya, Sanusiya, and Salihiyya, spread in Ottoman North Africa and in sub-Saharan Africa, ruled by its own clutch of sultans.

Overlapping with these Sufi networks, and sometimes in tension with them, there emerged multiple movements for seemingly puritanical renewal. Three leading renewal advocates— Shah Wali Allah of Delhi (1702–1763), the Najdi Muhammad Ibn Abd al-Wahhab (1703–1792), and the Nigerian Uthman dan Fodio (1755–1816)—are often considered originators of pan-Islamism. But such calls for puritanical reform are not unusual in the history of Muslim religious thought—they arrived in the thirteenth and sixteenth centuries as well—and these disparate three were not especially concerned with the global situation of Islam or an imagined Muslim world. They didn't respond to European empires encroaching in the Indian Ocean and on African coasts. They didn't elaborate pan-Islamic ideas about the Western threat or attempt to formulate an essentialist global Islam. They also did not have any global impact. There is no proven connection among these revivalist scholars, suggesting that their ideas and influence should be understood in their particular contexts of West Africa, Arabia, and South Asia.[38]

The Myth of the Napoleonic Turning Point

Like the Siege of Vienna before it, Napoleon's invasion of the Ottoman province of Egypt in 1798 is often depicted as a transformative experience in the history of Europe and the Muslim Middle East. Some see it in even more grandiose terms, as an instance of the clash between the West and the Muslim world—a traumatic and galvanizing moment of awakening in traditional Muslim societies, which gained new appreciation for the military power and revolutionary ideologies of Europe.

Yet again, the details indicate otherwise. Napoleon did not invade Egypt as a Christian or a white monarch bringing Western modernity to the backward Muslim world. One of his goals was to reach India to help Tipu Sultan, his Muslim ally, resist the British. There also was no pan-Islamic response to Napoleon; his arrival in Egypt, like other late eighteenth-century European invasions of Muslim societies, produced no visions of Muslim-world identity.

That said, Napoleon's expedition to Egypt departed in revealing ways from earlier European imperial activities.[39] It was Napoleon, not the Egyptians or Ottomans, who tried to appeal to an abstract notion of Islam. He presented himself as a friend of Muslims and even the Ottoman sultan, come to Egypt to eliminate the tyranny of the Mamluk aristocracy, who effectively ruled hundreds of miles from Istanbul.

Napoleon was not interested in asserting European superiority or striking a blow against the Muslim world for Christian civilization. Indeed, so eager was he to endear himself to the Muslim population that his officers asked Egyptian clerics whether his conversion to Islam would legitimize his rule.[40] It seems that a segment of Egyptian Muslims was willing to accept such an arrangement.[41] We do not know what the French public would have thought of their revolutionary general had they known that Muslim clerics were contemplating the terms of his conversion, but Napoleon himself saw no contradiction between his desired roles of protector of Muslims in Cairo and revolutionary republican in Paris.[42] The several hundred Arabs who returned to France with him did not have to make a choice between their Arab, Muslim, and French identities, either, until the new round of French imperialism, beginning with the invasion of Algiers in 1830.[43]

The Ottoman response to the French invasion of Egypt was a classic imperial strategy, welcoming assistance from Christian powers and innocent of any religious or civilizational quarrel. The Ottomans partnered with the British against France and even secured an alliance with the Russian Empire, despite their frequent eighteenth-century conflicts. The erstwhile enemies pursued successful joint naval operations against France in the Ionian Islands.[44] It was under these conditions that the Ottoman refused to aid Tipu's war with the British in Mysore.

The diplomatic dance between Mysore and the Ottoman Empire exemplifies the complexity of eighteenth-century Muslim cosmopolitanism. Tipu's letters to the Ottoman sultan illustrate his own hybrid legitimacy as a Muslim ruler within the diverse, Persian-inflected Mughal imperial tradition, long declining and besieged by the British. Though Tipu was firmly grounded in Muslim political vocabulary, his correspondence also reveals similar comfort with Turkish and Persian imperial traditions and strong awareness of global imperial currents.[45] He was respectful of the Ottoman sultan, whom he once addressed as caliph, in part because a major Muslim emperor's endorsement would have empowered the sultan of Mysore against other Muslim leaders in south Asia. Yet the Ottomans were in no position to help, given their alliance with the British against the French. And they were loath to enter the intricate political landscape of south Asia, where various Muslim and Hindu states interacted with the nominal Mughal emperor in Delhi and the powerful British East India Company centered in Bengal.

The Ottomans' choice paid off, as their forces eventually drove Napoleon from Egypt with the help of the British Navy, which destroyed French Navy off the coast of Egypt.[46] Sultan Selim III created a new honor, the Order of the Crescent, for the commander of British naval forces, Admiral Horatio Nelson, who proudly wore the medal on his uniform and used the title in diplomatic correspondence. Nelson's membership in the Order of the Crescent appears even on his gravestone, indicating a kind of imperial universalism across Christian and Muslim religious identity markers.

Meanwhile, after Tipu's death in defeat at the Battle of Seringapatam in 1799, a victorious interfaith army of Christians and Muslims plundered his palace and his city. Twenty years later, the Ottomans would also refuse protection to Emir Haidar of Bukhara, now in Uzbekistan, who feared Russian expansion. Responding to the emir's entreaties, the Ottoman government advised that the caliph provided spiritual protection to all Muslims but implied that it need offer neither military nor political protection. The caliph's political aid would be dispensed selectively and strategically—not according to any notion of Muslim solidarity.

◆ ◆ ◆

The complex relations among revolutionary France, the Ottoman Empire, its province of Egypt, and the Mysore sultanate suggest that what emerged decades later—clear-cut and hardened borders between the Christian West and the Muslim world—was not inevitable. At the turn of the nineteenth century,

Muslim polities behaved in the mold of dynasties and empires that had been developing for a thousand years.

The geographical area where Muslims lived, extending from Mali and Nigeria to Southeast Asia, was too broad and disconnected to support a single political system. Approximately thirty dynasties ruled Muslim societies around 1800, and they were far from united. The Sharifian Alaouite Dynasty in Morocco, Qajar Dynasty in Persia, Bornu Empire in the Niger area, khanates of Khiva and Kokand in central Asia, and sultanates of Banten and Aceh in Southeast Asia were just a few of the non-Ottoman Muslim rulerships with significant state-building traditions. And some territories officially under Ottoman rule, such as the North African beys of Tunis and Tripoli, were autonomous.[47] Powerful Muslim dynasties could be challenged and weakened by other Muslim dynasties.[48] And while transportation and communication technology did enable much interconnection among Muslim scholars and elites, there was not yet a sense of global Muslim public opinion, let alone any shared narrative of Muslim history and political experience. Muslim networks did at least as much to spread diversity as enforce uniformity.

Within seventy-five years of Napoleon's invasion of Egypt, there would emerge a strain of Muslim public opinion connecting across imperial lines, but this development itself followed a crooked line. Between the Napoleonic Wars and the 1870s, the political energy of Muslim societies was mainly devoted to strengthening existing Muslim dynasties and empowering the Muslim subjects of non-Muslim monarchs. As European powers expanded in Asia and Africa in the first half of the nineteenth century, the Muslim world was still a long way off. Far from an enduring global heritage, pan-Islamism was not the first or natural response even to the new imperialism.

Reinforcing the
Imperial World Order

(1814–1878)

In the first half of the nineteenth century, when European empires gained more military, legal, and political power over Muslim societies, the Muslim world was nowhere to be found. Empires, not civilizations, remained the principal agents of political history. In the late 1840s, Mirza Asadullah Ghalib and Syed Ahmad Khan, two prominent Indian Muslim intellectuals, could weigh the merits of the British and Mughal empires without allowing religious sympathy to dictate their preferences.[1] Indian Muslims imagined their political future under Queen Victoria, and many Balkan Christians accepted the rule of a reformist Muslim sultan in Istanbul. The Ottoman Empire was a de facto member of the European club of empires, with assurances of its sovereignty over millions of Christians.

Empire demanded that different ethnic and religious groups coexist under a ruler who may not share their language, heritage, and beliefs. In the first half of the nineteenth century, this political ideal was reaffirmed and bolstered by claims on behalf of empire as an agent of progress and civilization. Whether led by Christians or Muslims, empires were expected to deal with each other on equal terms, as sovereign entities with the same rights and obligations in the international arena. In reality, the imperial system was full of inequality, but many empires aspired to universality and tolerance of difference. Throughout the nineteenth century, major world powers worked to preserve the imperial system by promising a degree of equality at home and prioritizing strategic alliances above ethnic and religious solidarity.

The racialization of Muslim-ness, a process that unfolded between the 1820s and 1880s alongside racialization of blackness and Asian-ness, challenged the imperial balance. In 1875, just a few decades after Ghalib and Syed Ahmad Khan debated the virtues of imperial masters, Edward Blyden, a black Protestant in West Africa described as the "father of pan-Africanism," wrote an influential article titled "Mohammedanism and the Negro Race."[2] Here "Muhammedanism" denotes a racial category, akin to "Negro." What is more, in Blyden's telling, the futures of Muslims and black-skinned people all over the world are distinct from those of the white Christian race. Blyden's writing is representative of a consciousness that had built over two generations—a consciousness of racial and geopolitical unity and difference coexisting with, but also contradicting, imperial loyalties and realities.

One cannot sufficiently emphasize the historical novelty of this consciousness. Previously, Ottoman Muslims had seemed very different to their Russian, Greek, and Serbian enemies than Muslim subjects had to their Dutch or French overlords. Political circumstances dictated that some Muslims were conquerors, some were loyal to Christian-ruled empires, and some were insubordinate. In these conditions, it made little sense to collapse the world's Muslims into an undifferentiated group.

However, with changing circumstances in the second half of the nineteenth century came the othering and racializing of Muslims in European metropoles and within Muslim societies themselves. The conjuring of a global Muslim erased differences between Muslims from Bulgaria to Nigeria and Malaysia. Ottoman suppression of Balkan rebellions contributed to European demonization of a Muslim enemy, a tyrannical sultan lording over Christians. Yet anyone could see that Christians ruled Muslims all over the world. In this context, British policies toward the Ottomans became a crucial test of Muslim loyalty in India, effectively linking the politics of South Asian Muslims to turbulence in Ottoman-ruled Southeastern Europe.

As the nineteenth century progressed, relationships between Muslim societies and Christian rulers and neighbors increasingly broke down along lines of religious difference once submerged by the logic of empire. Consider the fez, that red felt hat with the tassel. In the 1820s, the Ottomans began requiring all their bureaucrats to wear tight, European-style clothing and fezzes, imported from the traditional garb of Orthodox Christian Greeks. The fez law was part of a larger set of modernizing reforms intended to foster and assert equality among Ottoman subjects and overcome markers of rank and religious affiliation. If Turkish, Armenian, and Greek bureaucrats all wore the same clothes, one could not distinguish their religious background by their appearance: all would be called Ottomans. By the 1890s, Muslim reformers all over the world had adopted the fez to demonstrate the compatibility between their faith and modern progress. But Europeans saw in the hat a symbol of enemy Islam, not a Muslim version of cosmopolitan modernity. The fez as a symbol of cosmopolitan imperial identity ended up becoming a symbol of global Muslim identity within half a century.

The aesthetics reflect the politics. By the early 1870s, Indian Muslims following the European debate on the "barbarous" Ottoman crackdown against Christian insurrection themselves felt the sting of insult. As Christians demanded national independence from the Ottomans and more Muslim societies fell under Christian rule, the parity of empires was lost, with Muslims increasingly understood as, and understanding themselves to be, a separate and marginalized class of imperial subjects. Many Muslims wondered why Christian rulers in their empires could celebrate national self-determination of Greeks and Bulgarians, yet they themselves had to submit to foreign control. These contradictions within the imperial framework were at the root of the emerging Muslim-world consciousness. The ruins of the imperial balance—not any classical theory of caliphate—were the foundation of the modern conception of Muslim unity.

The imperial system destroyed itself. Imperial universalism resisted the logic of racial separation and hierarchy, yet imperial elites became invested in the discourse of innate difference. To do so was not only expedient—difference and solidarity were useful tools in domestic and foreign policy, in securing legitimacy and building alliances—but also in keeping with new liberal values that would sacrifice the old system of empires in the name of humanity and civilization.

It was neither the shared history nor an immutable tradition of Muslims that built the Muslim world. Rather, the source lies in the accumulated impact of contingent policies, conflicts, and ideologies of empires from the 1820s to the 1870s.

Reforming Empire

The path to racialization and conflict between Islam and the West was not straightforward. Between the 1815 Congress of

Vienna and the Ottoman-Russian wars of 1877–1878, dynastic states sought to consolidate the imperial system through reform at home and respect for allegiance and sovereignty abroad. Collectively, the empires would legitimize each other in the eyes of their respective subjects.

Contacts between Christian and Muslim elites provide a revealing portrait of the imperial framework. One of the most significant of these contacts was Ottoman sultan Abdulaziz's 1867 tour in Europe, where he was welcomed with utmost ceremonial respect by the rulers of the French, British, and Austro-Hungarian empires and by the kingdoms of Belgium and Prussia.[3] In London, ministers representing Sultan Abdulaziz and Queen Victoria discussed matchmaking between Crown Prince Murad and a British princess in order to cement strong ties between the two empires.[4] The crown prince danced in public while Abdulaziz and Victoria discussed Christian and Muslim understandings of polygamy. The sultan also accepted membership in the Order of the Knights of the Garter in a ceremony at St. George's Chapel. The Ottoman delegation noted the presence of Indian Muslims loyal to the queen at a reception hosted by the East India Company but did not find this unusual. After all, the Ottomans had many faithful European Christian subjects; Kostaki Musurus Pasha, the Ottoman sultan's ambassador in London and one of his favorite bureaucrats, was a Greek Christian.[5]

It was not only Ottomans who forged relationships with European leaders on the basis of interimperial cooperation and the primacy of imperial over religious identity. In 1846 Ahmed Bey of Tunis became the first Muslim ruler to visit Paris. Egypt's Khedive Ismail accompanied Sultan Abdulaziz in 1867. In 1879 Abu Bakar, the maharaja of Johor (Malaysia), traveled to England, the metropole. Qajar (Persian) shahs made trips in 1873 and 1878. Persian shah Nasiruddin was also inducted into the Order of the Garter, confirming an international system in which rulers recognized each other by bestowing medals and honors. Muslim monarchs proudly wore their medals, some, such as the Order of the Garter, decorated with crosses.

During the opening of the Suez Canal in 1869, the Fez-wearing Egyptian Khedive Ismail hosted more guests from European royal houses than from Muslim dynasties. He later declared that Egypt, then an autonomous vassal of the Ottoman Empire, was becoming part of the European imperial order thanks to transportation fostered by the Canal. Khedive Ismail commissioned Giuseppe Verdi's opera *Aida* to celebrate the opening of the Canal. It was first performed in Cairo in 1871.[6] French sculptor Frédéric Auguste Bartholdi, who designed the Statue of Liberty in New York Harbor, planned a similar statue of an Egyptian peasant women holding a torch of liberty at the mouth of the Canal.

In 1869, Syed Ahmad Khan, one of the most influential Indian Muslim reformists, visited London in an effort to strengthen his commitment to British-Indian Muslim identity.[7] And at Anglo-Muhammadan College in Uttar Pradesh, Khan introduced the fez to his Indian Muslim students out of respect for an Ottoman monarch ruling a mixed population of Christians and Muslims. Khan, who would be knighted in 1888, believed that the British queen could rule over a diverse empire of Muslims, Hindus, and Christians. An Ottoman-British alliance would allow Indian Muslims to maintain loyalty to Queen Victoria while respecting the caliph as protector of the holy cities.

The Ottoman traveler and religious scholar Abdurrahman Efendi reinforced the global quality of the imperial framework when he made a three-year visit to Brazil beginning in 1866. At the time, he compared the Ottoman Empire to the Brazilian "empire" under the Portuguese ruler Dom Pedro II (1831–1889). He placed the Ottoman higher in rank, but the point is that, to Abdurrahman Efendi, the world was ordered not by faith, language, tradition, and geography but by empires ruling vast areas containing diverse subjects.[8] Later, Pedro visited Istanbul on his European tour as a guest of the Ottoman sultan.

This cosmopolitanism should not be confused for the pro-Western illusions of alienated Muslim elites. There was no questioning the Muslim credentials of the Ottoman sultan, Tunisian dey, and Egyptian khedive, or of Syed Ahmad Khan. Nor were cosmopolitan elites misguided in believing themselves members of an imperial world order. Muslim rulers were fashioning their own version of imperial modernity. There certainly were contemporary critiques of Muslim kings' strategies and reforms. But these critiques did not challenge imperial legitimacy, nor did they argue that traditional Islam was at odds with the reforms. Imperial reforms were not necessarily identified with secularism and pro-Westernism.[9]

The Ottoman reform process, called Tanzimat, took off even before Grand Vizier Mustafa Reşit Paşa's Gülhane Imperial Edict of 1839. The goal was to ensure equal treatment of all imperial subjects, irrespective of their religious and ethnic differences, and, in doing so, better secure the empire's place in the concert of Europe, thereby also strengthening European imperial norms. Conveying strong support for the universalism of empire, the edict noted that freedom and equality across faith traditions were assured by both *sharia* and existing civilized norms.[10] Ottoman rule had always included civil law, known as Kanun, itself derived from the Mongolian *yasa* tradition. Thus the edict's reference to *sharia* was intended as much to justify the guarantee of equal rights as to indicate harmony between civil and Muslim law. Tanzimat would inspire similar reforms in Egypt, Tunisia, and Iran. Meanwhile, the Russian, French, Dutch, and British empires practiced their own modes of tolerance toward Muslim subjects, as befit their strategies of rule.

This ideal of imperial inclusion was never perfectly realized, and there were varying degrees of discrimination and privilege in lands shared by Muslims and Christians. But the ideal itself allowed subjects of different empires to appeal to law and principle in demanding their rights from the imperial center. It also welcomed allegiance across potential barriers of identity. Successive Ottoman governments included prominent and influential ministers and bureaucrats of Greek and Armenian backgrounds. Cosmopolitanism made room for men such as the Maronite Lebanese Ahmad Faris al-Shidyaq (1804–1887), a Protestant convert who served the Ottoman Empire as a journalist in the 1860s and 1870s. After a long career translating the English Bible into Arabic and working in the Parisian Socialist movement, Al-Shidyaq published *al-Jawaib,* a pan-Ottoman journal in Arabic.[11]

Imperial self-strengthening reform had its intellectual foundations in a Muslim interpretation of the idea of civilization. Not civilization as in separate cultures of people—specific groups with their distinctive religious ways, politics, and traditions—but civilization as in a cultivated way of life accessible to all humanity: to be civilized and live in a civilized polity. Ottoman elites adopted this notion from Europeans during the 1830s and coined their own term for it: *medeniyet.* By the 1850s, the meaning of *medeniyet* had solidified through references to the "civilized nations," the "civilized world," and the "progress of civilization." Ottoman elites, no less than the cream of Christian empires, believed in the existence of a single world civilization marked by progress, better governance, and prosperity.

Muslims who adopted the European concept of civilization understood and embraced its controversial politics. Munif Pasha, an 1860s Ottoman bureaucrat, blamed Chinese losses in the Opium Wars on the Chinese Empire's supposedly low level of civilization. How else to account for defeat at the hands of much smaller British armies? In an 1871 article, the influential Ottoman journalist, playwright, and reformer Namık Kemal asked, "Are these uncivilized [*gayri-mütemeddine*] nations able to preserve their freedom against so many civilized nations?" By resisting the "lessons, teachings, machines, progress, [and] innovations" of civilization, Kemal wrote, "one would lose his freedom and come under the authority of a foreign power—something that is in no way suitable for human dignity." To him, Indians and Algerians, subjects of European control, were too backward to maintain their freedom.

Although Kemal and his ilk were committed to the European concept of civilization, they didn't necessarily emulate Europeans:

> Just as we needn't skewer kebabs in Chinese fashion to be civilized [*temeddün*], we need not imitate blindly European dance or marriage principles. . . . Our hope is this: That if appropriate action is taken, given the principles of the Islamic [*sharia*] and the situation and our people's extraordinary ability that we have to hand, [in the] Ottoman lands—which in the times of the Ancient Egyptians, and Chaldeans and the Jews and Iranians and Arabs, and Greeks were six or seven times greater in terms of places of intellectual instruction and were centers from which progress was transmitted—through [our] illustrious deeds it will be possible to bring about a civilization in a way that will evoke the world's admiration.[12]

Note that even as Kemal rejects mimicry, he draws no distinction between the Muslim world and the Christian West. Ottoman elites believed they could maintain a degree of difference while empowering their empire through the model of civilization cherished and projected by their European counterparts.

The idea of civilization was also strategically important. In 1848 the Ottoman sultan gave protection to Hungarian and Polish revolutionaries, including Hungarian leader Lajos Kossuth, seeking freedom from the Austro-Hungarian Empire. In doing so, the sultan gained respect from English liberals, who opposed the Austro-Hungarians' ally, Russia. Eventually the revolutionaries were defeated and exiled, but, after leaving their temporary residence in Istanbul, they were welcomed in England by circles surrounding the likes of John Stuart Mill and Giuseppe Mazzini, confirming a climate of public opinion favoring the Ottomans against the Russians. Close ties paid off for both parties. The Ottomans benefited from British aid in the Crimean War (1853–1856), and the Ottoman elite backed the British against Muslim and Hindu fighters during the 1857 Indian Rebellion.

The Ottomans were hardly the only Muslim reformers drawing inspiration from civilized Europe. In Egypt, the second most powerful autonomous Muslim polity under Istanbul's sovereignty, Muhammad Ali Paşa combined European fiscal and military methods with his knowledge of earlier Muslim and Ottoman examples.[13] With stronger military power, Muhammad Ali expanded Egyptian rule in the south and in 1822 placed Sudan nominally under Ottoman rule.[14]

Around the same time, the Abu Saidi rulers of the Omani sultanate of Muscat exhibited their own ambitions within the imperial order by incorporating Zanzibar Island and the coastline of Mombasa into their kingdom.[15] Later, Zanzibar's sultan Barghash bin Said (r. 1870–1888) was known to follow the world news closely, asking his personal assistant to summarize the content of British papers for him on a daily basis. His self-strengthening projects were in line with Tanzimat reforms and included construction of telegraph stations, public clocks, and a tram system. In 1880 Zanzibar established the Sultanate Press and would go on to promote Arabic publications.[16]

Tunisia, too, showed remarkable energy for self-strengthening reform. This included the drafting of a constitution under the leadership of the Circassian-born grand vizier Hayreddin Pasha.[17] Hayreddin was convinced that a parliamentary government and modern European ways were compatible with the Muslim and Ottoman political traditions in part because Tanzimat-style reforms derived from the universally applicable notion of civilization.[18] Thus when Tunisian authorities abolished the slave trade, they did so on the basis of both Muslim legal arguments and global antislavery discourses.[19] During this process of reform, Ottoman and Egyptian authorities also banned the slave trade, without making any grand claims about "Islam and slavery." Slavery itself gradually disappeared from Ottoman Turkey and Egypt by the early twentieth century without having any ideological or religious movement akin to abolitionism. Pragmatic and ethical state policies, new moral ideas about human equality as well as the capitalist labor market ended slavery in modernizing Muslim societies, all without any grand claims on behalf of the Islamic world and the Western world.[20]

One can go on and on. The mid-nineteenth century was a time of self-strengthening in Qajar Persia, Morocco, Afghanistan, the Central Asian khanates, and Indian princely states, as well. Often, reform leaders in these areas knew what was happening under the reign of other Muslim monarchs and in Europe.[21]

Reformist Muslim rulers did not see themselves as victims of European expansion but as beneficiaries and active agents of new governance practices. And public opinion was largely on their side, thanks in part to the long history of diversity within and among Muslim societies. For example, the Ottoman government received scholarly endorsement for the abolition of *jizya*—special taxes on non-Muslims—in 1856. Muslim elites saw equal citizenship of Christians and Jews as a legitimate reinterpretation of Ottoman governing tradition in harmony with the changing conditions of the time and the needs of the empire. Those Muslims who disagreed with aspects of reform did not base their critiques on ideals of Muslim-world destiny or monolithic universal Islam. *Jizya* was never to be reintroduced or even mentioned by any of the late Ottoman ideological camps.[22]

The implementation of extraterritoriality—a common legal arrangement whereby imperial subjects would be exempt from local law while abroad—also did not initially offend many Muslims and Ottoman elites. Legal pluralism was an accepted practice in early modern and modern imperial governance. In Tunisia, for example, reformist rulers allowed their subjects recourse to diverse legal practices, ranging from embassy courts to Jewish Talmudic law and *sharia*, depending on the merits and parties of each case.[23]

Just as reformist Muslim elites did not see themselves as victims of Europe, they also didn't see themselves as outsiders seeking entry into European society. They were contributing to the development of a new Euro-Mediterranean imperial order, and many leading Europeans welcomed their effort. For example, British foreign secretary Lord Palmerston supported the Tanzimat reforms, confidently asserting, "There is no reason whatsoever why [Turkey] should not become a respectable power" within ten years of peaceful reorganization and reform.[24] The Austrian prince Metternich was more conservative than Lord Palmerston, but he agreed that the Ottoman Empire was part of the European imperial system. Both talked about Christian superiority over Islam and other religions and made derogatory remarks about Muslims and Ottomans. But they did not argue that European imperial society needed to exclude the Ottoman empire, nor that Christians must be ruled only by other Christians.

Thus from the perspective of both Muslim and Christian elites, much of the nineteenth century was a period of imperial entrenchment, diplomacy, and strategy. The Ottomans continued to respect their allegiances above shared religion and tradition. In the 1840s and 1850s, when Caucasian Muslims just beyond Ottoman borders were resisting Russian imperial expansion, the Ottomans provided their fellow Muslims no support, even though the Ottomans and Russians were longtime enemies. Upon defeat and incorporation into the Russian Empire, more than half a million Caucasian Muslims immigrated to Ottoman-controlled territories in what should be considered one of the first modern cases of ethnic cleansing.[25] But Muslims also integrated into Russia, as the imperial framework demanded: it was accepted that the Russian czar could rule over Muslims and give them their religious rights, just as the Ottoman sultan could rule over Christian subjects.[26]

Nationalism and Religion

One critical, and perhaps surprising, source of inspiration for globalized Muslim identity was nineteenth-century Christian nationalism. European support for Greek, Serbian, Romanian, or Bulgarian independence from Ottoman rule disrupted imperial norms. Muslims living under the rule of different Christian monarchs closely followed Christian nationalist revolts against their Ottoman rulers, which proved formative in the politicization of Muslim-ness.

Christian liberation in southeastern Europe came just as European empires were ramping up colonization of Muslims in Africa and Asia, creating racializing asymmetries that threatened the imperial framework. Thus when conflicts—the Greek War of Independence, the French invasion of Algeria, the Crimean War, and the Indian Rebellion—tested imperial cosmopolitanism, the Great Powers retrenched further, reformulating imperial logic in still more universalistic terms. That such retrenchment occurred, though, speaks to the tension facing the imperial system after the 1820s.

One of the most significant sources of that tension was the Greek War of Independence, beginning in 1821. Greeks had lived under Ottoman rule for almost four hundred years, in diverse populations comprising Christians and Muslims of different ethnicities.[27] Greek elites were the most privileged Christian denomination of the Ottoman Empire, and during the early nineteenth century, some Greek families were further empowered within the Ottoman bureaucracy.[28] But these elites also forged educational and cultural networks in across Europe and Russia and, through them, imbibed Enlightenment ideas of nationalism, liberty, and resistance to tyranny, as well as romantic notions of Greece's place in the history of Europe and Russian arguments for freedom of Orthodox Christians from the sultan.[29] It was not unusual for Ottoman subjects to complain of despotic rule; after all, even Muslim subjects had legitimate complaints against the empire. But Greek nationalists didn't just want better treatment within the empire; they wanted a separate Greek state.

The early Greek revolt, which started in the Danubian Principalities (modern Romania) with Russian support, quickly turned into a conflict between Christians and Muslims. In southern Greece, Muslims were seen as representatives of Istanbul and were massacred for that reason.

The Ottoman elite seemed unable to understand the novel, nationalist quality of the revolt. Sultan Mahmud II punished loyal Greek bureaucrats and diplomats by removing them from key administrative positions, a move that would only inflame Greek nationalist sentiment. More significant, the sultan also ordered the execution of Patriarch Gregory V of Constantinople, whom he accused of failing to assure the loyalty of Greek Christian subjects. In fact the patriarch had condemned the Greek nationalists, and there was no proven link between the revolt and the patriarchy, despite the nationalists' strong Orthodox Christian language and the participation of local priests in their ranks.[30] The execution of the patriarch again reflected the confusion of the sultan, who was attempting to quash an unprecedented national rebellion using the imperial playbook. News of the patriarch's execution confirmed the image of the tyrannical Muslim sultan and encouraged international Christian sympathy for the Greek nationalist cause.

At first, with the help of Ibrahim Pasha of Egypt, the Ottomans managed to suppress the Greek revolt. However, the Greek nationalist struggle soon received tremendous support from British, French, American, and Russian elites.[31] This spectacular public-opinion victory was captured in the poetry of Lord Byron, who became a symbol of white, Christian, European solidarity when he financed the Greek cause and soon after died in Greece en route to a military engagement.

There was, of course, a multiplicity of views among white Christians. In the novel *Anastasius*, Byron's contemporary Thomas Hope depicts an Ottoman Empire ensuring its subjects' freedom.[32] The Scottish diplomat David Urquhart initially supported Greek independence but then became an equally strong supporter of the Ottoman Empire and Ottoman-British alliance, praising the tolerance of Ottoman rule over diverse subjects, including Christians.[33]

On balance, however, the Greek rebellion helped catalyze a shift in European public opinion against the Ottomans. European empires mobilized in support of Greek nationalism, despite the antinationalist principles of the Congress of Vienna. The resulting diplomatic and military intervention was a decisive factor in Greek independence. It was in this context that Czar Nicholas I (r. 1825–1855) strengthened the Russian claim to protect Orthodox Christians in the Balkans, thereby buttressing Orthodox Christian nationalism under the rule of the Ottoman Empire and further upsetting the imperial framework.

It would be wrong, though, to understand the Greek revolt as an end to Muslim-Greek coexistence within an imperial framework. Greek independence was not so much a historical turning point as an early stage in the unraveling of an imperial system still largely intact. When the Ottoman Empire recognized Greek secession and independence in the London Protocol of 1830, it was home to almost as many Greeks as the new kingdom of Greece itself. Soon after independence, the Greek National Assembly elected Prince Otto of Bavaria as King Otto I of Greece, muting the nationalist blow against the prevailing imperial order.[34] The Ottoman Empire also made a point of keeping strong ties with loyal Greek subjects, such as the diplomat Kostaki Musurus, who was ambassador to Athens between 1840 and 1848. Musurus's devotion to the Ottoman Empire was so strong that Greek politicians accused him of betraying the Greek nationalist cause, provoking a failed attempt on his life in 1848.

The larger program of European imperial law and relations also survived Greek independence. The Ottoman Empire and the kingdom of Greece were treated equally in diplomatic circles. When the king of Greece offended Musurus at a party, Musurus left Athens and did not return to his post until the Greek government officially apologized. Musurus's would-be assassin was a Greek who carried an Ottoman travel documents, and upon diplomatic request from Istanbul, Greece handed him over to Ottoman authorities for punishment.[35] Unequal treaties between European empires and "backward" or "uncivilized" non-European polities would come later. In the years after Greek independence, European international law—if not always public sentiment—still did not make these racialized distinctions.

Around the same time as Greek independence, another European project shook the structure of the imperial system. The French invasion of Ottoman Algeria, just as Europeans were urging Christian self-determination, made for a blatant contradiction.

Initially the French made quick work of Ottoman forces, but Algerian Muslim resistance was stouter and longer-lived, mainly under the leadership of the cosmopolitan Sufi emir Abdelkader al-Jazairi (1808–1883).[36] Abdelkader led a *jihad* against the invading French forces in Algeria, with the goal of creating a state in western Algeria. But eventually Abdelkader too fell. He and his forces surrendered in 1847.

While armed resistance was ongoing, some Algerian intellectuals appealed to the same universal values of enlightenment, nationalism, and liberty that had inspired white Christians to support the Greeks against imperial oppression. In 1833 the scholar Hamdan Khodja reached out to French public opinion with an anti-imperial tract, in French, arguing that destruction of Muslim lives and institutions conflicted with the noble universal values France espoused. Using the language of French liberals, he brought up the French defense of Greek, Belgian, and Polish nationalisms and asked why the French could not similarly support a national, self-governing Algeria that would be a friend of France and a model of civilizational progress.[37]

The contrast between Greek liberation and Algerian colonization established a pattern. White European Christians tended to support struggles for Serbian, Romanian, and Bulgarian independence from the Ottoman Empire, all while Muslims in Central Asia, North Africa, and South Asia were colonized by Russia, France, the Netherlands, and Britain. Some Indian

Muslims under British rule understood these events in the same terms as Khodja. They supported the Ottoman Empire's right to suppress Christian insurrections in Crete and Bulgaria and asked the British government to back the Ottomans. But their wishes went unfulfilled. In Europe, the nationalist imagination, fueled by racialized perceptions of religious difference, was making inroads.

Even the most imperial of mid-nineteenth-century wars, the Crimean War, emerged from religious dispute. The war was precipitated by Russia's demand for recognition as the protector of Ottoman Orthodox Christians and for additional privileges for Orthodox Christians in Ottoman-ruled Jerusalem. But after the initial Russian naval victory against the Ottomans at Sinop in 1853, imperial order asserted itself: Britain and France, later joined by the kingdom of Sardinia, declared war on Russia in March 1854 in support of the Ottoman Empire.[38] This exceptionally bloody war, in which improved military technology brought massive casualties, ended in Russian defeat.

The Ottomans took great pride in victory. From their perspective, the Crimean War was a conflict purely in the imperial mold. No *jihad* was declared. For British and Ottoman elites, this was a case of civilization defending itself from Russian barbarism. During peace talks at the Congress of Paris, the Great Powers proclaimed the Ottoman Empire's membership into the concert of Europe, thus assuring its sovereignty and equality in inter-imperial order. The Ottoman sultan agreed to improved conditions for Christian subjects. In other words, the peace agreement attempted to secure the imperial status quo in Europe, with the Ottoman Empire firmly included. Inclusion in this system of universal imperial civility is precisely what the Ottomans wanted, as they demonstrated by, for instance, protecting Christians from Muslim attackers during an 1860 Damascus riot.

Just a year after the conclusion of the Crimean War, the Indian Rebellion in 1857 further tested the imperial framework. And once again, when the conflict ended, the triumph of imperial logic was confirmed, even as the increasing importance of religious identities was undeniable.

The British Empire's expansion in India, which was still nominally under Muslim Mughal rule, was piecemeal. For much of its history, the British East India Company relied on indirect rule and tributary alliances with Indian princely states. That meant it needed local cooperation, which it found from great numbers of Hindus, Muslims, and Sikhs, including religious scholars and military officers.

Despite this success, rebellion broke out on May 10, 1857. The first major act of the revolutionaries was to restore the elderly Mughal emperor Bahadur Shah, demonstrating the continuing power of imperial legitimacy.[39] Many Muslim scholars issued calls for *jihad*, and many Hindus similarly justified their revolt on the basis of religious ideals. Notably, calls for *jihad* were directed only at the British, not Hindus, suggesting an inclusive vision of empire respectful of both Hindu and Muslim traditions. Hindu-Muslim unity during the 1857 rebellion was impressive and speaks to the historical contingency of mid-twentieth-century Muslim-Hindu divisions.

While there were also calls for Muslim solidarity under the banner of the Mughal emperor, the rebellion did not attract support from other Muslim dynasties and was quelled within two years. The Ottoman Empire backed their British ally and sent aid to British war victims. This loyalty should not be surprising, given Ottoman-British cooperation during the Crimean War. The imperial alliance was beneficial for both; the British had often referenced their friendship with the Ottoman caliph to justify their rule in India.[40]

With the rebels defeated, the Crown took direct control of possessions in India, and later on Queen Victoria was declared as Empress of India. This was the sort of direct rule and responsibility that empires hoped to avoid. The British press associated the 1857 rebellion with Muslims, inspiring suspicion of Muslim disloyalty and books such as William Wilson Hunter's *The Indian Musalmans: Are They Bound in Conscience to Rebel against the Queen?* (1871).[41] British colonial officers openly discussed whether Muslims, as opposed to Hindus, could be loyal subjects of the empire. Muslim intellectuals debated the same question.

Syed Ahmad Khan believed the answer was yes, Muslims could be equal and loyal. One of the most influential Muslim leaders in India, Khan formulated a modernist Muslim identity that embraced British imperial rule. But he was not a mere lackey for the Crown. He also contested the anti-Muslim discourses of British missionaries and colonial officers. In significant ways, Khan embodied the project of imperial universalism, trying to make the British Empire more inclusive by asserting his Muslim identity under the umbrella of a Christian monarch, Queen Victoria. Thus in 1875 he established Muhammadan Anglo-Oriental College to create a new Indian generation both Muslim and British. He hoped that the students, mostly children of Muslim provincial elites, would serve the empire in India while empowering Muslim communities. In the 1880s, when British and Ottoman geopolitical interests began to diverge, Khan argued that Indian Muslims were bound by their religious duties to obey their Christian rulers, not the caliph in Istanbul.[42] (This was the kind of loyalty Ottoman elites themselves could understand, per the logic of empire, and had expected from their Orthodox Christian subjects during their conflict with the Russian Empire.) Khan was not alone in his opinions; the majority of Sunni scholars in British India found ways to institutionalize Islamic education and scholarship while presenting British rule as legitimate within the Muslim legal tradition.[43]

Khan and others promoting Muslim equality within the empire faced significant obstacles from Christian missionary activities, which increased dramatically among Indian Muslims in the mid-nineteenth century. Even though British colonial officers did not officially endorse missionary activities, in most cases Christian missionaries benefited from the political capital and protection of the empire. They embedded their theological claims in imperial and racial hierarchies by portraying European imperial hegemony and scientific progress as signs of God's favor to Christians. Muslim scholars rebutted missionary arguments with their own polemics. The era's improved communication and transportation technologies were essential in spreading these arguments throughout Muslim societies, initiating what turned out to be a novel tradition in which Islam was positioned as a universal and global religion that could respond to the challenge of missionary Christianity and its claims of Muslim inferiority.

The story of one Indian Muslim scholar's engagement with missionary Christianity illustrates how Muslim identity started to become universalized in response to the narrative of racialized inferiority emanating from Europe. Before the 1857 rebellion, Rahmatullah Kairanwi was well known for a debate held in Delhi with the German evangelical missionary Carl Gottlieb Pfander. Relying in part on modern European biblical criticism, Kairanwi challenged the authenticity of Christian scriptures and reiterated Muslim rejection of the Trinity.[44] The debate lasted two days, with each side claiming victory. Pfander later traveled to Istanbul, where he again bragged of the outcome.

Ottoman sultan Abdulaziz was disturbed by Pfander's boast and wanted to know Kairanwi's version of events. The sultan invited him to Istanbul and funded the publication of his book, *Izharul Haq*, in which he clarified his arguments about the singular truth of Islam. Published in Arabic in 1864, *Izharul Haq* was widely circulated. For example, Blyden noted in his 1875 essay that "West African Mohammedans at Sierra Leone" read and discussed the book.[45]

It is tempting to believe that, with *Izharul Haq,* modern notions of universal Islam had come of age. After all, here was the Ottoman sultan financing the publication of a text arguing for the superiority of Islam over a globalized missionary Christianity. Yet Sultan Abdulaziz was also a strong believer in Tanzimat, committed to sustaining an empire a third of which was Christian. In the 1860s, the binary of Muslim world and Christian West was not yet established, but the mixture of religion, empire, and race was becoming more complicated as it was becoming globalized. That a European Protestant missionary in British India could unsettle the sensitive balance of the Ottoman Empire centered thousands of miles away demonstrates not just the power of new technologies of movement and communication but also the weakened state of the imperial framework after decades of intensifying ethnic and religious tension.

Empires Overcome by Race and Geopolitics?

The years 1873 to 1883 saw a considerable deepening of networks associated with new transnational Muslim modernist and imperial sensibilities. One example came at the beginning of that decade, when the sultan of Aceh sent an envoy to Istanbul to request Ottoman protection against a Dutch military assault.[46] While in Istanbul, the Acehnese met representatives of the Kashgar Emirate of Eastern Turkistan and the Central Asian emirates of Khiva and Bukhara, who were also seeking Ottoman military and diplomatic support. Both Acehnese and Kashgari delegations similarly asked for help from the British Empire, seen as an ally of the Sultan Caliph in Istanbul. Ottoman support for distant Muslims had never been a sure thing, but a burgeoning and very active Muslim press in Istanbul pushed for the government to support Aceh, and the sultan himself liked the idea of increased prestige among Muslims globally.[47] Ultimately, he was able to do little, thanks to Dutch protests. The sultan did award the Kashgari envoy a state medal, diplomatic recognition, and financial support, but he refused military aid and advised the Kashgaris not to get into quarrels with Russia and China.[48]

The Aceh and Kashgar meetings were not only opportunities for the Ottoman elites to build prestige among Muslim societies. They also inspired Ottoman curiosity about Muslims in different parts of the world. Namık Kemal noted with a hint of irony that, during the 1870s, the Ottoman public began to agitate for solidarity with the Muslims of western China, of whom they had little knowledge twenty years earlier.[49]

There were Blyden's writings on the global Muslim race, too, around this time. And recognition of transnational Islamic identity also became apparent in British and Dutch espionage. The British Foreign Office wanted to figure out whether the Ottomans were instigating Muslim religious and political revival within the queen's empire. In consultation with Dutch officials, the Foreign Office produced almost thirty reports collected by consulates in various Muslim-majority cities. The British concluded that there was no organized pan-Islamic movement, but their fears were not entirely without basis. The Foreign Office did note that Muslims seemed to be developing greater awareness of global affairs due to the new journalism, which provided daily news about distant places via telegraph lines. While some British and Dutch colonial officers worried about the potential rise of a pan-Islamic response to their colonial administration over Muslims, the Russian Empire's pan-Slavic policies toward Christian populations of the Ottoman Empire became an inspiration for early pan-Islamist ideas among Muslims themselves.[50]

A turning point was the Ottoman-Russian War of 1877–1878. The conflict featured a full mobilization of Muslim and Christian identities globally, with the racialized distinction between Muslims and Christians overshadowing imperial logic. Russia appealed to Orthodox Christian solidarity and the symbol of the Hagia Sophia, ruled by Muslims. The Ottomans called for *jihad,* even though their goal was to retain control over Bulgarian, Romanian, and Serbian Christian territories.

Russia was not the only source of support for Balkan independence. As in the case of Greek independence almost fifty years earlier, English liberals, represented by William Gladstone, backed secession in the name of saving Christian populations from Muslim oppression.[51] From an imperial perspective, Gladstone's position was irrational: his own empire ruled more Muslims than Christians, yet here he was arguing for religious and ethnic separation. Benjamin Disraeli, Gladstone's rival, maintained the imperial view, sympathetic to Ottoman territorial integrity as long as the empire granted its Christian subjects liberty.[52]

Gladstone's staunchly anti-Muslim rhetoric—he called Ottoman Muslim elites an "anti-human specimen of humanity"— reflected a broader trend toward geopolitical debate on the basis of nationality and race as opposed to imperial strategy. Gladstone tried to be careful about generalizing his anti-Ottoman rhetoric to all Muslims, instead distinguishing Turks from Indians and noting that it was not "Muhammedanism" alone but its mixture with the Turkish race that created Ottoman despotism. Yet his name soon became associated with anti-Muslim racism among Indian Muslim intellectuals and beyond. A new breed of European and American journalists followed the Russian-Ottoman War closely and reported it with pro-Christian and anti-Muslim bias.[53]

Still, some segments of the British public wanted to continue the imperial alliance with the Ottomans. The most energetic supporting that camp were Indian Muslims, who mustered unprecedented levels of humanitarian sentiment on behalf of Muslim victims of Christian nationalism and Russian aggression, offered financial aid to Muslim refugees, and engaged in political activism to benefit the Ottomans. They argued that the queen's Muslim subjects had a special relationship with the Ottoman caliph and that turning back the Russian invasion was in the British Empire's interests. Some British officers, including the ambassador to Istanbul, Henry Layard, and the viceroy of India, Robert Bulwer-Lytton, agreed. It was Layard and Bulwer-Lytton who suggested and then facilitated an Ottoman mission to Afghanistan to request Afghan assistance against the Russians.[54] These British imperial officers were imagining a Muslim unity under joint Ottoman-British leadership against Russian expansion to the south. The Afghan king refused to fight the Russians, as suggested by this British-supported Ottoman delegation, noting that it was the British that had just invaded Afghan territories.

Overall, however, British policy toward the Ottoman Empire shifted from alliance to neutrality, partly under the influence of Evangelical Christian propaganda. Gladstone's emphasis on Christian oppression by the Muslim sultan won the day. Without British military and diplomatic support, the Ottomans lacked the resources to overcome their Russian enemy. At the same time, it became clear to the Ottomans that Britain's Muslim subjects in India were on their side, the *Muslim* side.

With the war lost, most of the Christian-majority Balkan provinces gained independence. Christians, once more than a third of the Ottoman Empire, now accounted for just a fifth of the population.[55] The sultan began to emphasize his religious bona fides in order to encourage internal solidarity. Islam became a source of national identity, as Christianity had in European empires and territories once under Ottoman rule. In European discussions of the "Eastern Question," the Ottoman Empire was now a Muslim despotism unworthy of alliance and in need of further division. The depiction of the Ottoman Empire as the sick man of Europe, better off dismantled, extended the racialization of colonized Muslims to the last major independent Muslim-ruled dynasty.

In 1881 and 1882, when the former Ottoman provinces of Tunisia and Egypt were absorbed, respectively, into French and British protectorates, the Muslim press and Muslim public opinion became more vocal about the subjugation of Muslims by Christian empires. The seeds of pan-Islamism brewing in the Ottoman Empire and British India since defeat at the hands of the Russians gave its first fruits. In 1884 the first pan-Islamic magazine, *al-Urwat al-Wuthqa,* was published in Paris by Jamal ad-Din al-Afghani and Muhammad Abduh. The contents were highly anti-British and anti-imperial.[56] This magazine's anti-British content was already indicating that the idea of Muslim world unity, which initially meant Ottoman-British alliance against Russia, could turn into an anti-British argument in the aftermath of the British invasion of Egypt. Yet Pan-Islamism did not remain consistently anti-British, even in the 1880s.

The lives of al-Afghani and Abduh testify to the time in which they lived: a period when imperial and transnational Muslim identities coexisted. Their biographies don't fit in any neat categories; they held anti-imperialist, pan-Islamic views and yet collaborated with empires. Their magazine was published at the heart of the French Empire, which had conquered another North African Muslim area. They often self-censored their criticism of French imperialism in North Africa while saving their venom for Britain, which was politically convenient for their French hosts. Yet they could soon begin to talk to British colonial officers and suggest their support for several British imperial projects. Al-Afghani praised the pan-Islamic implications of the Mahdi rebellion in Sudan and yet offered to serve as a mediator between the Mahdi and the British. Al-Afghani was much less pan-Islamic before the mid-1880s. In Egypt, he was close to

Khedive Tawfik until the late 1870s, and, had the imperial balance been maintained, he may have remained committed to Egyptian self-strengthening. In spite of his anti-imperialism, Abduh returned to Egypt in 1888 and worked under the aegis of the British protectorate. When he died in 1905, the only obituary published in Istanbul was carried by the pro-British social Darwinist magazine of the Kurdish physician Abdullah Cevdet, not in anti-imperialist circles.

Both Al-Afghani and Abduh remained close to British aristocrat Wilfrid Blunt, who exhibited some sympathy for Egyptian claims to independence from Britain but was at the same time a firm believer in empire in India and in Britain's status as the greatest Muslim power in the world.[57] For Abduh and al-Afghani, geopolitical and racial ideas of Muslim-world solidarity could coexist in complex ways with the reality of Christian-dominated imperial governance.

◆ ◆ ◆

Despite the assertion of a universal imperial vision throughout the nineteenth century, the particular character of imperialism in the Muslim societies of Africa and Asia led to the racialization of Muslims by the early 1880s. This is the foundation of the idea of the Muslim world. The theaters of Muslim racialization were everywhere. Muslim subjects in the Russian Empire had varied legal status, yet all were defined as Muslims. The Dutch and French empires made legal distinctions between white citizens and Muslim subjects; full equality was almost impossible for Muslims to achieve. The British Empire practically gave a new legal status to 40 percent of the world's Muslim population by codifying *sharia* for personal and family law and implementing it among Muslim subjects. In territories from Nigeria to Malaysia, British Muslims were subjected to special scrutiny

with respect to loyalty. Muslims contested these imperial practices on the basis of not just their own experiences but also those
of other Muslims.

In that context, the Ottoman Empire's reforms and struggle
to maintain the logic of empire amid mounting Christian
nationalism—within its borders and supported by other European powers—take on an ironic cast. Even though the Ottomans
did their best to uphold the universalism of the Concert of Europe, they became identified with a distinctive Muslim-ness in
both European metropoles and Muslim colonies.

There were no hegemonic and monolithic narratives of Islam
versus the West in the first half of the century, as attested by
British support for Ottoman Muslim rule over Christians. Yet
by the 1880s, such narratives had grown strong enough that they
could not be ignored. Imperial visions were not fully defeated;
certainly empires themselves were not. But they needed to
accept the new reality of race and develop tools to deal with its
political power. When, in a speech in 1883, Ernest Renan proclaimed Muslims members of the Semitic race incapable of
producing progress and science due to their fanaticism, the glo-
bality of Muslim modernist response to this racial inferiority argument was already indicating a significant rupture in the way
the Muslim world became imagined in the new Eurocentric imperial world order.

Searching for Harmony
between Queen and Caliph
(1878–1908)

The three decades after the Ottoman defeat at the hands of the Russians in 1878, in a war that saw the British Empire abandon their longtime Ottoman ally in response to deepening anti-Muslim sentiment at home, were a time of paradox and transition. From the ashes of the old, universal imperial system arose a new style of empire starkly inflected by race, the borders of which were drawn along multiple lines—not just physical features of human bodies but also religion and perceptions of shared history and political loyalty. During this period, colonial rulers' views of Muslim subjects as members of a single civilization and race solidified. Muslim subjects embraced this racial identity for various political purposes of their own.

Muslim intellectuals of this era trumpeted pan-Islamic ideas and increasingly looked to the Ottoman sultan as caliph and leader of a global Muslim community. When convenient, the sultan took advantage of his new role as Islam's international representative. At the same time, he worked to win over restive Christians within the empire and restore as much of the previous order as he could. Meanwhile, the pan-Islamist push for Muslim unity and modernity contested the European Christian narrative of inferiority, but it did little to overcome and defeat racialization itself. Pan-Islamists pressed antiracist and anti-imperialist agendas even as they accommodated the fact that 70 percent of the world's Muslims were governed by European Christians.

The Cairo pan-Islamic congress of November 1907 illustrates these overlaps and tensions. The city was nominally within the Ottoman Empire but was also a British protectorate when Ismail Gaspirali, a Crimean Muslim, went there to organize a discussion on the social and cultural problems of a newly imagined entity, the Muslim world. Gaspirali was a prominent journalist who advocated for improved treatment of Muslims in the Russian Empire. He had few contacts among Egyptian intellectuals, but the Hungarian British Orientalist Arminius Vambery had translated his work, lending a certain esteem, and a Reuters story soon alerted Cairo of his plans. Upon reading this news, Rashid Rida, Cairo's leading pan-Islamist, contacted different hotels in the city to find out where Gaspirali was staying. The two would become close collaborators.

Thanks to the embrace of Rida and his circle, three hundred people attended Gaspirali's gathering to discuss the destiny of the Muslim world. But the proceedings avoided many of the topics one might associate with pan-Islamic discourse. Rather than nationalism and anti-imperialism, the congress focused on the causes of Muslim decline in economic, educational, and social life and strategies for Muslim revival.[1]

That Muslim subjects of the British and Russian empires were leading a pan-Islamic gathering in a British protectorate speaks to the peculiar configuration of the pan-Islamic geopolitical imagination in this transitional moment, when the fate of Muslims seemed more unified than ever, yet the reality of empire was unmistakable. What is more, even as Ottoman sultan Abdulhamid II endorsed pan-Islamic thinking and connection, he did not respond to a petition from Gaspirali seeking moral support and approval of the congress. Abdulhamid was concerned that such a gathering would further provoke racialized Islamophobia—the so-called Muslim peril—in Europe and refused to promote anything that could be construed as a Muslim challenge to the rule of European empires. Gaspirali might have followed similar reasoning to the opposite conclusion when he decided to hold his conference in the Ottoman Empire's second city, effectively ruled by Britain, empire of one hundred million Muslims. Pan-Islamists of the early twentieth century could celebrate the caliphate without forsaking British rule, leaving the other European empires at ease.[2]

The caliph's refusal must have stung Gaspirali. As spiritual leader of an increasingly interconnected global Muslim community, the Ottoman ruler was a prestigious figure in the lives of millions. And as the symbolic leader of Muslim imperial modernism, the caliph affirmed that Muslim tradition was compatible with progress and that Muslims deserved to be treated with dignity. Thus the caliphate became an important focus of not only spiritual but also political attention within the global Muslim intelligentsia, and Istanbul served as a hub for the exchange of information, ideas, discontents, and aspirations. For a brief period from the 1880s to the 1920s, the meaning of "caliphate" became globally synchronized and refashioned, and it is this meaning—a polity representing all Muslims—whose legacy would mark the entire twentieth century.

Religious ties to the Muslim subjects of European monarchs were important to the Ottoman elite too, but mainly as a bargaining chip in an effort to restore the alliance with Britain and maintain relations with other empires. The caliph wanted his spiritual sovereignty to be the basis of a peaceful and stable imperial world order, not a clash of civilizations.[3] Similarly, the Muslim subjects of Christian-ruled empires used the idea of pan-Islamic solidarity in their negotiating strategies. Muslims did not generally reject the legitimacy of Christian rule. Their main goals were to gain more rights as imperial subjects or citizens and to criticize white Christian racism, not necessarily to secede.

By this point, racism, which had long been a significant source of discontent, revealed in both colonial administration and the treatment of the Ottoman Empire on the world stage. But the political and intellectual condition of high imperialism worsened the situation. Christian nationalism had weakened the Ottomans, while Europeans preaching liberty and civilization took control of more and more Muslim-majority territory. Meanwhile, relatively new disciplines such as sociology and geopolitics joined biology in producing increasingly rigid theories of racial hierarchy. Orientalists—students of "Oriental" languages, literature, and culture—and historians provided background and ammunition for racial theories but generally were more nuanced and appreciative, albeit patronizing, toward the Muslim civilization and religion they studied. "Scientific" racism associated with Charles Darwin, Herbert Spencer, and Gustave Le Bon proved more influential among the intelligentsia and the public, solidifying an overt discourse of Muslim inferiority and further reinforcing the ideas on essential Muslim difference found in the works of Orientalists such as Thomas Arnold, Alfred Le Chatelier, Louis Massignon, and Ignaz Goldziher.[4]

It was this new racism that pan-Islamists contested, but their strategy backfired. The more articulate and vocal Muslim mod-

ernists became, the more suspicious colonial elites and metropolitan populations grew. By emphasizing spiritual ties to the
Ottoman caliph and comparing the lives of Ottoman Christians
to those of Muslims under European rule, Muslim reformers fostered European paranoia about the clash of Islam and the West.

Encounters with European ideas and colonialism were not
the only forces shaping modern Muslim thought and, in turn,
the new racialized narrative of empire. To contest European
claims of Muslim inferiority, Muslim intellectuals tried to re-
define the history, civilization, and achievements of Muslim
peoples, producing a rich body of ideas and global discourses in
which Europeans engaged. Muslim modernists thickened the
racial discourse by proudly talking back to an imagined European imperial center. Gradually there developed a sophisticated
body of writing on the essential civility, rationality, and unity of
Islam and Muslims. In critical engagement with European Orientalist and geopolitical arguments, Muslim intellectuals essentialized Islam and Muslim identity on their own terms.

Islam as Civilization and World Religion

The last quarter of the nineteenth century witnessed an extraor-
dinary level of interconnectivity among Muslim publics strewn
across Eurasia and Africa. Muslim intellectual and political
elites used these connections to talk to each about the shared
predicament of racism.

European empires, especially the British Empire, built most
of the infrastructure that made this possible. Eurasia and the Indian Ocean were suddenly linked via steamships, telegraph
lines, and trains. More Muslims began traveling long distances
and received up-to-the-minute news via telegraph. The Muslim
press boomed after the 1860s; journals were published cheaply
and distributed widely. After the Istanbul-based Arabic journal

al-Jawaib in the 1860s, the most successful pan-Islamic journal was *al-Urwat al-Wuthqa* (discussed in Chapter 2), published in Paris in 1884.[5] Despite the complex imperial positions of its publishers, *al-Urwat al-Wuthqa* argued that Muslims had an obligation to defend the imagined Muslim world from foreign rule and work for its revival. The journal made its case by means of powerful rhetoric. Underlying the notion of unity *(wahdet)* was a metaphor in which each mosque and *madrasa* formed a link in a global chain that bound the Muslim scholars and resisted intrusion by outsiders. The journal also emphasized *ijtihad*—reasoning in profound commitment to Islamic law, theology, and text—in a modernist and anti-imperialist context.[6]

The most influential journal of the pan-Islamic era was *al-Manar,* edited by Rida and published in Cairo from 1898 to 1935. Rida lived through the traumatic transformation of the international order from the 1890s to the 1930s, and the journal reflected these ambiguities borne along shifting sands. Its positions ranged from pan-Islamism and Ottomanism to Arab nationalism and pan-Arabism. Whatever its position of the moment, though, *al-Manar*'s global subscribership demonstrated that the Muslim world was much larger than the Ottoman. The journal's largest funding source was Indian Muslims. This reflected a larger pattern: relative wealth and position in the British Commonwealth made Indian Muslims especially influential.[7]

The power of Muslim journalism was augmented by the boom in book publishing. The period from the 1860s to the 1920s was one of the most prolific and productive in Muslim thought across every discipline. Books and other writings in Arabic, Ottoman Turkish, Persian, and Urdu were rapidly translated from one language to another. Because the Muslims writing these books were dealing with the same set of concerns—Orientalism, social Darwinism, Eurocentric narratives of history, racialization—

key concepts migrated across major intellectual circles from Southeast Asia to North Africa. Although pan-Islamic writers were closely attuned to practical challenges in the lives of Muslims and the geopolitics of late empire, they produced an enduring discourse. The six major themes they developed still shape much of transnational Muslim thought.

First was the idea of an Islamic civilization. Hostile Europeans argued for the essential inferiority of Islam vis-à-vis the West, prompting a Muslim modernist literature that defended Islam's civilized nature by reinterpreting the history of Muslim societies in a way that made them more palatable to modern Europe.[8] This history started with Muhammad but centered on the scientific and philosophical achievements of the late Abbasid period. Arguably, modern European civilization would never have gotten off the ground without the work of Abassid-era thinkers, turn-of-the-century pan-Islamists argued. This, they believed, proved the innately progressive orientation of Muslims.

Ernest Renan's 1883 lecture "Islam and Science" exemplifies the racist European narrative Muslim modernists hoped to undermine. Renan viewed Muslim civilization as rigidly separate and inferior. The scientific achievements of the late Abbasid period came about, he argued, in spite of Islam. The fanaticism of Islam, and its Semitic roots, were sure to bring down the Muslim world.[9] Hundreds of Muslim intellectuals responded to Renan and other influential Europeans, such as Gladstone, making similar remarks.[10] Syed Ameer Ali presented Muhammad as not only a prophet but also the initiator of a civilization. Islamic civilization, on the reformist reading, inherited the legacy of Greece, merged it with rational and humanistic Islamic values, and, during the Muslim golden age, contributed to the emergence of the modern West. This Euro-Islamocentric view of world history implied that service to the rise of the modern West was a criterion of civilizational worthiness and dignity, a standard whose achievement made Muslims racial equals.[11]

Even reputedly irreligious and positivist intellectuals felt compelled to write apologia defending Islam against Orientalist and social Darwinist positions.[12] Because racism toward Muslims was a bias against a civilization, not skin color, racist arguments had to be countered within their own Orientalist and social Darwinist framework. The only way to contest them, it seemed, was to rethink the Muslim history, theology, and science whose supposed inferiority substantiated European racist discourse.

Thus the Muslim modernist project at this stage could not escape engagement with dominant European social science theories, and Muslim intellectuals carefully debated the details of scientific racism.[13] They produced a variety of interpretations and appropriations, mostly eschewing distinctions among Arabs, Turks, Indians, and Persians. In the debate on social Darwinism, Muslim intellectuals generally conceded that Muslims were underdeveloped and backward, but they denied that this was a permanent condition. Intellectual elites believed they could intervene with a call for reawakening and thereby "end the decline."[14] The Muslim modernist critique of decline was harsh and directed blame inward. It argued that Sufism and contemporary vernacular Muslim practices were the cause of the decline, and therefore the purity of early Islam was the solution.[15] This desire to revive pristine values was easily wed to intellectuals' interest in establishing European rationalism and work ethic, a set of commitments shaped by Darwinian concerns about the survival of the Muslim race in a competitive and insecure international political arena.

In these arguments, the decline of the Muslim world implied the existence of the Muslim world, and not just contemporaneously. If the Muslim world was declining, then it must have existed before. Thus the earliest Islamic text and history were yoked to an idea, the Muslim world, that would not have made sense in their own time. This new, global narrative, a product of nineteenth-century geopolitics and fresh scientific and political theories, was projected centuries into the past.

The second major product of pan-Islamic writers and their networks was a novel conception of Islam as a universal religion that could dispute the claims of both Christian missionaries and secular Orientalists. Religion was a racial marker of the Muslim world and the inferiority of Islamic tradition a justification for discrimination against Muslim subjects within and across European empires. Muslim modernists therefore sought to elevate the status of Islam to a universal position comparable to those of Christianity and the Enlightenment. The idea that "real" Muslims are enlightened and tolerant gradually became the standard fare of Muslim modernism.

This project tried to define Islam for all peoples, in all places, at all times and in such a way that the religion would champion rationality, modern civilization, and progress—just what European racists believed most lacking in Islam. It was a reactive posture. For instance, it is impossible to understand Muhammad Abduh's rethinking of Islam without considering his response to French foreign minister Gabriel Hanotaux's claim that Islam was backward, despotic, and intolerant.[16] Likewise, Sayed Ahmad Khan and Syed Ameer Ali's English writings on Islam as a rational religion make little sense except in response to missionaries and Orientalists such as William Muir. *Al-Manar* devoted many column inches to the reformulation of Islam as a world religion, especially in polemics directed at evangelism, Christian missionaries, and European Orientalism.

Islam was not the only religion that underwent such transformation. In this era, Judaism, Hinduism, and Buddhism too became abstracted from their actual practice and reconfigured on par with universal Christianity. The shift was particularly wrenching for Buddhism and Hinduism, which suddenly found themselves endowed with a standard set of classical texts and doctrines.

One can see the roots of Islam as a world religion in the anti-Muslim polemics of Christian missionaries, such as Pfander. Recall Kairanwi's case that the Quran was the literal and uncorrupted word of God, from which Christian writings diverged.[17] Eventually, in 1920, Indian Muslims established their own missionary movement, Tablighi Jemaat, to respond to Christians by copying their evangelical methods. The new Ahmadiyya Muslim sect in India was similarly formed to refute missionary Christianity as well as Hindu and Sikh missionaries and revivalists such as Arya Samaj. The Ahmadiyya movement used evangelism, construed as nonviolent *jihad*, to disseminate a version of Islam they considered genuine and universal.[18]

But the reinvention of Islam as a world religion did more than respond to Orientalism and racism. Muslim reformers embraced the notion of a united global faith to lessen their fear of actual diversity, which seemed to be a source of division and weakness. The cross-border mobility of Muslims alerted reformers to the immense pluralism of Muslim practices and beliefs. Reformers had different ideas, though, because they viewed consensus as a source of strength under the new imperial conditions. By the 1890s, shared talking points about Islam emerged. Reformers defined Islam as the most internally consistent, rational, systematic religion on earth. This Islam had less space for miracles and saints and was prouder of its civilization and philosophy. Reformers depicted this universal Islam as more united than Christianity, with its sects and schisms.[19]

The Spirit of Islam, an 1891 book by the Shia pan-Islamist Syed Ameer Ali, exemplifies this reformist impulse to craft a universal Islam in harmony with the Enlightenment and other world religions.[20] The book compares Islam with the universal religions of Christianity, Judaism, and Buddhism—but not Hinduism, the major competitor in Ali's home country of India. The notion that Islam had "a spirit" was something new, a departure from the claims of earlier scholars, who rarely presented their opinions as truth "according to Islam." Abduh's *Theology of Unity* (1897) is another representative publication.[21]

The word "Islam" appears rarely in premodern titles, but after the nineteenth century, it is everywhere. Most of these books were either translations of works by non-Muslim Europeans or were written by Muslims in response to European writings. Book or chapter titles such as "Women according to Islam" or "*Jihad* according to Islam" responded polemically to European anti-Muslim writings and also put forward a rationalized, systematic, and modernist religious project.[22]

A third important aspect of the pan-Islamic narrative, alongside Islamic civilization and world religion, interpreted recent Muslim history as a product of Western humiliation. Islam had to be redeemed in order to live up to its glorious past. For example, Indian Muslim writers living under the British Empire made emotional references to the decline and humiliation of the Muslim world and Islam, either due to the disintegration of Muslim empires or the loss of civilizational unity at the hands of European interlopers.[23]

The narrative of decline often merged with nostalgia. Muhammad Iqbal, an influential Indian Muslim poet and politician, lamented the end of Arab rule in Sicily and the condition of the Cordoba Mosque, which was converted to a Catholic church after the expulsion of Andalusian Muslims. Iqbal's writings often speak of *ummah,* but it is clear that this term is synonymous with modern geopolitical Islamic civilization. Past moments of humiliation and redemption are cited partly to inspire the remaking of the Muslim world. As is often true of nostalgia, the notion of a golden age giving way to humiliation was always faulty. Muslim education, literacy, and publishing flourished under imperial globalization. Muslim merchants in the Indian Ocean experienced a golden age of their own under British rule in the late nineteenth century.[24] Yet the arc of glory, humiliation, and redemption offered a potent political image.

The fourth major theme of pan-Islamic discourse was a new historical consciousness positing eternal conflict between Islam and the Christian West. This too was mistaken. Medieval Muslim historians did write about the Crusades, but a Muslim world–Christian West conflict was never foremost in their accounts. More Muslims in history live in close proximity to Buddhists and Hindus than to Christians. By the early twentieth century, however, Muslim history was being rethought primarily in relation to a Christian European center, from the perspective of the Mediterranean and Eastern European borderland experiences. This was in part a response to European historical narratives, which emphasized military encounters with Muslims as constitutive of European identity. In these circumstances, civilizational conflict was the principal lens through which global history was understood.

Why did both European elites and educated Muslims embrace this narrative of civilizations at war, even when their own imperial experience showed its falsehood? As noted earlier, European narratives that spoke of liberating Ottoman Christian populations from oppressive Muslim rule were formative factors in creating this duality. Russian and Habsburg propaganda also emphasized a historical vision of a clash between Islam and Christendom. And as the new imperialism took shape, European colonial officers attributed claims for Muslim rights, and the slightest expression of Muslim discontent, to Muslims' innate rejection of Western Christian empires. Colonial observers and imperial strategists believed that Muslims were prone to violent rebellion against Western empires thanks to age-old theological disagreements. Initially, Muslim reformers rejected the validity of the eternal-conflict narrative. But eventually they too tied modern imperialism to historical narratives of Christian attacks on Muslims. During the Balkan Wars of 1912–1913, the Ottoman press often depicted modern European imperialism, due to its racism and Islamophobia, as a kind of Crusade.

It was in this context that Muslim reformers initiated a historical romanticism that continues to reverberate. For example, Salahuddin al-Ayyubi, who staved off Crusaders at Jerusalem, was resurrected as a hero and redeemer of the Muslim world. In the 1870s, Namık Kemal wrote a play in which Salahuddin appeared as a noble and patriotic Muslim hero who repelled a Western Christian attack on the Muslim world. The implication was that if Muslims had defeated the Crusaders under Salahuddin, they could defeat the modern crusade of imperialism as well. Ottoman rule in Eastern Europe was glorified in similar terms, as an instance of civilizational greatness, despite the fact that the Ottomans cherished membership in the concert of European empires and strove to avoid making enemies of Eastern European Christians under their control. The false narrative of enduring conflict also revived interest in Muslim Spain. Averroes and other Andalusian Muslim philosophers were examples of Islam's contribution to Western civilization, while the Reconquista was another instance of Muslim humiliation by the West.

It is important to emphasize that all of the clash-of-civilization theories stemmed from literature on international affairs produced and read in European and American universities and reproduced in the Western media. Thus it is not surprising that the major pan-Islamic and pan-Asian texts on Islam–West or white–yellow race conflict were produced by Muslim and Asian

thinkers trained in Europe or the United States. Halil Halid's
The Crescent versus the Cross (1907) derives from a master's thesis
written at Cambridge University.[25] Kodera Kenkichi's one-
thousand-page *Treatise on Pan-Asianism* (1916) is based on his
PhD work at Columbian University (now George Washington
University).[26] Pan-Islamic and pan-Asian thinkers were attentive
to the work of Lothrop Stoddard, a white supremacist with a PhD
from Harvard, precisely because Stoddard wrote on international affairs through categories of civilizational and racial conflict.[27] The Arabic translation of Stoddard's 1921 book *The New
World of Islam* contains long dissenting commentaries by leading
pan-Islamist Shakib Arslan on issues of detail, but Arslan agrees
with the basic framework of interpreting international affairs as
a conflict between the Muslim world and the West.[28]

The fifth major aspect of pan-Islamic thought was growing
awareness of the sheer extent of Muslim-majority territory and
the large populations within it. By the turn of the century, it was
common to see maps showing the Muslim world as a continuous
geographic space from Southeast Asia to North Africa. Christian missionaries were the first to develop a map showing
Muslim-majority areas and indicating the Christian populations
in these lands.[29] In fact, evangelical missionaries had a great
deal to do with establishing the imagined unified Muslim world,
having created a successful journal with the title *The Muslim
World* in 1911 at Hartford Seminary.[30] Between the 1880s and
the 1930s, several journals with that title were published in
English, German, French, Italian, Japanese, Arabic, Ottoman
Turkish, and Malay.

On the eve of World War I, it was often asserted that the world
contained 250 million Muslims. Counting the number of Muslims reinforced European racism by emphasizing the size of the
perceived danger to Western hegemony. If, according to the European racist imaginary, Jews were the internal threat, the giant

Muslim world was the external menace. The image of the great mass of Muslim populations between China and Europe provoked a fearful discourse of Muslim peril. And just as European Jews were both feared for their supposedly globe-straddling power and loathed as inferior beings, Muslims were both threatening and debased. Some Europeans indulged geopolitical fantasies of a white empire mobilizing these at once fierce and apparently docile Muhammadan masses against their rivals.[31]

Whether tabulations of Muslim population were accurate matters little; the numbers had political meaning for both Muslims and Christian colonizers. Muslims living under the rule of European empires boasted of the global Muslim population as evidence of potential power deserving of respect. Membership in such a large bloc was also empowering in the moment and further emphasized global ties. Muslims in India, for example, could think of themselves not as a religious minority among a larger group of Hindus but as a religious majority in the broader Indian Ocean zone. Beyond the Indian context, the large global Muslim population lent confidence to the humiliated: if they worked together, Muslims could negotiate with European imperial powers to gain dignity and autonomy. As al-Afghani wrote, "If you [turned] into flies, your buzzing would deafen the ears of Great Britain. . . . And if God changed each one of you into a turtle, that would cross the sea and surround Great Britain, you could drag its islands to the depths of water and return back to your India being liberated."[32]

The last major theme of pan-Islamism was anticolonial internationalism, embracing non-Muslim societies in Asia and Africa as well as other cosmopolitan and inclusive ideologies. One could be a committed anarchist, positivist, or socialist but still be a Muslim. And the shared experiences of colonialism, Orientalism, and scientific racism brought the Muslim and non-Muslim intellectuals of Asia together around the notion of an Asian-

Eastern identity. Muslims approved of Japanese modernization and Chinese nationalism.[33] According to medieval Muslim categorizations of peoples, Muslims were supposed to favor People of the Book, such as Christian colonial officers, over those, such as Shinto Japanese, outside the monotheistic Abrahamic tradition. But pan-Islamic intellectuals such as Mustafa Kamil had greater sympathy for Japan than for Britain.[34] In turn, many non-Muslim Asians from Sun Yat-sen to Gandhi appreciated pan-Islamism, which they did not think of as a conservative religious movement. Muslim internationalism extended to Hindus and Buddhists as well. Pan-Africanists such as Edward Blyden and Marcus Garvey saw pan-Islamism as an ally.

Cooperation between theosophists in Europe and the United States and pan-Islamic organizations was another sign of Muslim internationalism. Driven by his interests in Buddhism and Theosophy, the American writer and diplomat Alexander Russell Webb looked eastward and eventually converted to Islam and became a pan-Islamist.[35] In 1907 the magazine *Theosophist* published a positive account of the opening of a London pan-Islamic society.[36] Theosophists' Asiaphile anti-Enlightenment critiques empowered the claims of Indian nationalists.[37]

It is also important to keep in mind that Europe was not a place of unyielding racism, and Muslims could find intellectual allies in metropolitan life. Racist arguments about Muslims were supplemented by discourses of Muslim revival. Sometimes these were patronizing, as in French fantasies depicting noble North African Berbers as former Christians abandoned in the middle of Semitic Muslim Arabs. Yet at the same time, between 1906 and 1914 the French Empire hosted scholars writing for *Revue du monde musulman* (Review of the Muslim world) who believed in a kind of "Muslim spring," noting approvingly the constitutional revolutions, active presses, modernist reforms, and mobility of Muslim populations across the world. During

World War I, the French Army included about two hundred thousand Algerians. Counting civilians working for the empire, Algerian support for the French war effort was even greater. There were large numbers of Hindus and Muslims in the British military fighting against the Ottoman military that was recruiting Armenians and Greeks.. Rigid racial distinctions coexisted with the experiences of millions of people who lived in proximity and cooperation.

Metropoles such as Paris and London also provided a space where African, Asian, and Latin American intellectuals could meet and exchange ideas and criticism about race, exclusion, and colonialism. There were roots of a kind of Third World internationalism in these exchanges.[38] In London, for example, Pan-Africanist Marcus Garvey met Pan-Islamist Dusé Mohamed Ali and worked for his magazine. After World War I, Ali visited Garvey in the United States and contributed to his Universal Negro Improvement Association.

The choice of European and American locations also symbolized the continuing importance of an abstract notion of the universal West decoupled from its imperialism. All the major intellectuals in Asia and Africa had to be well informed about European thought and paid close attention to anti-imperial and antiracist trends in the metropoles. Subaltern, European, and American intellectuals critical of imperialism and white racism influenced each other. For example, Auguste Comte's positivism was popular among both Brazilian elites and Muslim intellectuals of the Ottoman Empire. The liberal Ottoman Committee of Union and Progress owed Comte a large intellectual debt. Socialism and anti-Enlightenment German romanticism also attracted anti-imperial intellectuals in colonized territories.

Finally, a small number of energetic European and American converts to Islam, Buddhism, and Hinduism offered moral support to anticolonial, pan-Islamic, and pan-Asian projects.

Conversion of white intellectuals and the presence of active mosques in Paris, London, and Liverpool were important to Muslim intellectuals. These proved that Islam really was a universal religion that could be embraced by anybody; it was not limited to colored people in the colonies.

A Pan-Islamic Vision for a British-Ottoman Alliance

Today pan-Islamism registers as a form of anti-imperialism. But it was not ever thus. Around the turn of the twentieth century, South Asian Muslims and Ottoman elites used the idea of the Muslim world to promote a Ottoman-British alliance. Sultan Abdulhamid II and some British top brass joined them.

The pursuit of a Ottoman-British alliance reflected a variety of interests and realities. In the 1880s and 1890s, the British ruled about half of the world's Muslims, and some British elites hoped that friendship with the Ottomans would ensure these subjects' loyalty. The Ottomans, acutely aware of their vulnerability after the Russian defeat, needed the British Empire as a strong ally and therefore argued that the size of Britain's Muslim population made it a natural, perhaps necessary friend of the caliphate. Muslim subjects of the British Empire hoped that better relations with the Ottomans would undermine metropolitan white supremacy and imperial racism.

Britain played such a dominant role in Muslim lives that, in 1894, Mirza Ghulam Ahmad, founder of the Ahmadiyya movement, implied that Queen Victoria was Muslim at heart. The queen was much admired by some Muslims, who also celebrated her Indian Muslim assistant, Munshi Abdul Kareem. Queen Victoria learned Urdu from Abdul Kareem, who had a prayer space in Buckingham Palace and was allowed to cook halal meals in the palace kitchen. This relationship was well publicized among British Muslims, for whom Queen Victoria symbolized the ideals of an inclusive empire, despite being head of the Anglican Church and a devout Christian.

Yet the British Empire was also Islamophobic and evangelical. Many British officers saw Muslims, heirs of the 1857 Indian Rebellion, as the queen's least loyal subjects. Metropole media demonized Muslims as fanatics, alienating Muslims in England and throughout the empire.[39] Amid wars against the Sudanese Mahdi, Somali rebels, and South Asian frontier tribes, the British fantasized about mad mullahs and dark-skinned jihadists. The queen's family and government officials distrusted Abdul Kareem, whom they suspected of sharing sensitive information with Muslim friends in London.[40] For their part, Indian Hindus suspected that Abdul Kareem prejudiced the queen against them. After the queen died, King Edward immediately removed him from the palace.

Pan-Islamic intellectuals such as Abduh, Rida, and Syed Ameer Ali wrote positively about Queen Victoria and even Anglo-Saxon achievements in empire-building and science, but they vehemently criticized Christian missionaries and racist abuse. For example, the same Muslims who, on Britain's behalf, fought the Sudanese rebels were disturbed by the mutilation of corpses of fallen Muslim foes—including Mahdi's, which was dug up and thrown in the Nile. Adding further insult, British Christians saw the empire as a vehicle of liberation and protection for Christians living under the rule of Muslim monarchs, especially the Ottoman sultan, whom they identified as a despot. Christian subjects saw the empire's global power as a divine reward for their faith, a gesture that alienated Muslim subjects from "the greatest Muhammedan power."

Further complicating imperial legitimacy were the complex geopolitics of the empire's relationship with the Ottomans. Gladstone's hostile remarks about Muslims and Turks, and

European exclusion of the Ottoman Empire in discourses on
the Eastern question, reflected both a popular and vulgar
European sentiment about "infidel Muslims" and a more re-
fined European Orientalist discourse on Muslim inferiority.[41]
Gladstone argued that he was championing human rights—
specifically those of Christian minorities in Bulgaria—while
Ottoman rulers were concerned mainly with imperial sovereignty. But for Muslim subjects, the issue was not that simple,
especially given the Russian massacre and expulsion of southeastern European and Caucasian Muslims in 1877–1878, a fact
that British liberals rarely acknowledged. Indian Muslims insisted that if the British could legitimately rule them, then the
Ottomans could legitimately rule Balkan Christians. After all,
as Indian Muslim intellectuals consistently emphasized, since
the Tanzimat reforms of 1839, Ottoman Christian subjects had
enjoyed more rights and privileges than Muslim subjects of
the British and French empires. The Ottoman government appointed Christian ministers and ambassadors, while the British
reserved all high positions for white Christians—even Abdul
Kareem, the apparent exception, did not have an official title.[42]
To British Muslim subjects, it was clear that Europe's anti-
Ottoman discourses, which extended from Gladstone to longtime Foreign Secretary Sir Edward Grey and beyond, reflected
not just Christian liberalism but bias against Muslims.

Pan-Islamic intellectuals might have fostered rebellion in response, but instead they tried to transform the British Empire
into a Muslim-friendly realm. Some of the staunchest imperial
loyalists, including Syed Ameer Ali and Agha Khan, also championed pan-Islamism and pro-Ottoman policies. For their part,
pioneers of pan-Islamic thought such as Abduh and Rida praised
British achievements. Many pan-Islamists thought the best vehicle for improving the Crown's treatment of Muslims would be
British rapprochement with the Ottomans.

What drew far-flung Muslims to the Ottoman Empire was the caliph's status as a modern monarch. As khan, sultan, and caliph, the Ottoman ruler represented cosmopolitan and tolerant governance practices. The example of a modern Muslim monarch might buttress Muslim demands for rights within the British Empire. Indian Muslims hoped the caliph protector would speak out for educational improvements, political dignity, and an end to British insistence on the inferiority of nonwhites.[43]

Indian Muslims were not alone in promoting a British-Ottoman alliance. Some British officers harkened back to the bonds of an earlier era, when British and Ottomans fought side by side against the Russians in Crimea. The alliance had frayed only recently, in the 1870s, and might be resurrected. They hoped that its renewal would assure Muslim loyalty to the queen and head off Russian threats to British interests in Afghanistan and Central Asia. Pan-Islamism and British Russophobia seemed made for each other.

The Ottomans themselves advocated for alliance on the basis of pan-Islamism: caliph and Crown complemented each other in their spiritual and temporal rule over the world's Muslims. The caliph-sultan offered to encourage Muslim loyalty to the British Empire, as long as the British supported Ottoman geopolitical interests and rule over diverse populations, including Christians, in Anatolia and the Balkans.

To achieve such an alliance required a fundamental revision of the political meaning of the Muslim world. The British had to see Muslim unity as the basis for imperial strategy rather than a source of conflict among civilizations. Arguing this position for the Ottoman Empire was a British convert to Islam, Abdullah William Quilliam. In his role as shaikh ul-Islam, the chief Muslim religious authority, of the British Islands, Quilliam acted as a spokesperson of the caliph. He published influential books and essays making the case that the biggest Muslim empire in the world, the British, ought to have a solid partnership with the Ottoman Empire.[44]

Born William Henry Quilliam in Liverpool in 1856, Quilliam grew up as a member of the Wesleyan Church and later joined the Unitarians. A temperance and antiracist activist, he opposed slavery and sought to overcome Christian sectarian divisions and harmonize the faith with science. In 1887 he converted to Islam and initiated Muslim missionary activity in that city. At this point, the British Empire had had direct control over India for three decades, but in spite of its strong connection to the empire via active ports and the presence of a cosmopolitan elite, Liverpool was not a welcoming place for Muslims. The small community of converts, led by Quilliam, was frequently harassed. Quilliam's mosque was vandalized several times, especially when it hosted interracial marriage ceremonies.

After converting to Islam, Quilliam published a weekly magazine, *Crescent,* and a monthly journal called *The Islamic World.* Both had large readerships, especially among Muslims in India and in Anglophone countries such as South Africa, Australia, New Zealand, and the United States. Various Muslim monarchs supported Quilliam's activities. In the process, he developed a reputation speaking for Islam as a world religion and became known as a representative of the Muslim world within and beyond the British Empire.

It was an 1890 letter to the London *Times,* coauthored by Quilliam, that attracted Sultan Abdulhamid's attention. Quilliam and his Indian Muslim assistant, Rafiuddin Ahmed, wrote to protest the opening in London of the play *Mohamet,* written by Sir Thomas Henry Hall Caine, which they feared would be insulting to Muslims. Their critique was strongly loyalist, as befit both Quilliam and Ahmed, who later became a good friend of Abdul Kareem. In the letter, Quilliam and Ahmed argued that it was improper for a London theater to host a performance offensive to the queen's subjects. They also leaked information about the play to Indian Muslim journals, which led to protests in India and prompted the Indian and foreign offices to request, successfully, the play's cancellation.

Soon after, Sultan Abdulhamid wrote to Quilliam to commend his efforts in dispelling negative views of Muslims in Britain. In April 1891 Quilliam and his son Robert went to Istanbul, where they stayed in Yıldız Palace as the sultan's guests and received various gifts and honors. From this moment onward, Quilliam's Muslim faith and identity were politically linked to the geopolitics of the Ottoman caliphate. The "civility" of the Ottoman Empire and its caliph-sultan became key components of Quilliam's pan-Islamist vision.[45]

In 1894 the sultan asked Quilliam to deliver on his behalf a Majidiyya medal to Mohammed Shitta Bey, a Nigerian Muslim who had built a large mosque in Lagos. In this capacity, the sultan appointed Quilliam shaikh ul-Islam of the British Isles. Queen Victoria confirmed the title. Quilliam was often invited to high-level civic occasions, and he welcomed Ottoman visitors to their consulate in Liverpool. He took advantage of London's and Liverpool's status as hubs in global imperial networks to connect with Muslim communities in Africa and Asia.

Quilliam's profile as a modernist Muslim in an important and multicultural city of the empire illustrates that, despite prejudice against Muslims, his community could find a respectable place. Friday prayers at the Liverpool mosque were impressively diverse along lines of race, ethnicity, and class, mixing poor sailors and orphans with upper-class Muslims and middle-class converts. Quilliam had cordial ties to Jewish communities as well as theosophists. He was also successful in articulating a vision of Islamic civilization equal to that of the West. His formulation of Islam as a world religion was in harmony with principles of reason and science. Indeed, he viewed Islam as a more rational alternative to Christianity, which condoned racism in the United States and sectarianism in England.

Along with other educated Muslims in the British metropole and Muslims living under British imperial rule, Quilliam was convinced that the anti-Ottoman geopolitical arguments of Eastern Question discourse were driven in part by the Islamophobic sentiments of Christian and Anglo-Saxon supremacists. When anti-Muslim crowds came to protest the mosque in Liverpool in 1897, they chanted, all at once, slogans such as "Remember Armenia," "Down with the Turks," and "To hell with the Muhammedans," indicating a collapsing of geopolitical and religious spheres.[46] What most disturbed Quilliam was that the overwhelming majority of British Muslims were loyal to the Crown, yet British public opinion, stoked by the likes of Gladstone, was dominated by threatening visions of Muslim disloyalty and barbarism.

But it was the British imperial armies that acted barbarically against Muslims. Quilliam spoke for Muslim public opinion within the British Empire and beyond when he offered sharp critiques of British imperial disrespect for Muslim dignity, violation of Muslim rights, and Christian missionary behavior. Although Quilliam supported British wars against Muslim groups in Sudan, Somalia, and India's northwest frontier, he tried to present a more balanced account of them than was to be had in most newspapers, to make sure they would not become an instrument for humiliating Muslims and supporting Islamophobia. Quilliam also addressed the issue of Ottoman Christian subjects, whose supposed oppression was a major source of British anti-Muslim sentiment. He pointed out that the same Christians speaking out on behalf of Bulgarians did not feel any sympathy for Irish Catholics living under siege in the next neighborhood.

This was something of an irony, given the position of Ottoman defenders on Armenian rights. During the pro-Armenian Christian agitation in Europe and the United States in the late 1890s, both Quilliam and Webb, as well as Indian Muslim intellectuals, rushed to the Ottomans' side. Quilliam noted that the Ottoman Empire contained many provinces similar to Ireland and that Britain should appreciate the Ottoman right to control Armenian separatists, just as it demanded a right to control its internal minorities.[47] He also wondered how white British Christians could support Armenians yet ignore the lynching of blacks in the United States. Such a position illustrates how confusing the concept of minority protection was. Was it acceptable for the British to suppress Irish rebels as long as they condoned Ottoman suppression of Armenian rebels? Quilliam opposed racism, yet he, along with the Ottoman elite and their other Muslim defenders, was more concerned about global Christian solidarity undermining Ottoman sovereignty than about the safety of the Armenian minority.

Perhaps this contradiction was the price of dual loyalty. Quilliam valued his British status but also supported the Ottoman caliph spiritually *and* geopolitically. Thus he worked hard to promote a British-Ottoman alliance. He viewed joint governance of British Muslims by the caliph and the Crown as a moral and pragmatic necessity. Beyond Quilliam's writings, the majority of the pan-Islamist literature emanating from India in the early twentieth century envisioned an Ottoman-British alliance rather than Muslim revolt against the Crown. For instance, during the Italian invasion of Libya in 1911 and the Balkan Wars of 1912–1913, pan-Islamic thinkers primarily argued that the British Empire was morally obligated to support the Ottomans since the British themselves were the world's greatest rulers of Muslims.

Some in Britain questioned an Ottoman alliance on strategic grounds, without succumbing to racism. At times they even argued in pan-Islamic terms. In the late 1870s and early 1880s, Wilfrid Blunt and others, doubtful about the viability of the

Ottoman state, recommended the formation of an Arab caliphate under British protection.[48] Blunt's ideas mixed a reading
of early Muslim theories of caliphate—especially their stipula-
tions that caliphs descend from Prophet Muhammad's Qureshi
tribal lineage—with pragmatic calculations of empire. With a
large Arab kingdom-caliphate under its umbrella, the British
would rule half the globe.

Among Muslims, the pro-Ottoman pan-Islamist camp won
this argument decisively. By World War I, British Muslim subjects, whether Indian or Arab, had no doubt of the legitimacy of
the Ottoman caliphate.[49] Blunt himself adjusted his ideas to the
reality of Ottoman appeal and remained sympathetic to the notion of an Ottoman-British alliance for the purpose of governing
the world's Muslims. Blunt's promotion of joint British-Ottoman
custody over the Muslim world influenced his friend Winston
Churchill, who went on to oppose war against the Ottomans, although he also led the Gallipoli Campaign in World War I.

British Muslim subjects continued to encourage stronger rapprochement between the Ottoman and British empires until
World War I, which the Ottomans entered on the German side.
At that point, in an effort to avoid insulting a caliphate dear to
millions of their subjects, British colonial authorities crafted a
new narrative depicting the Ottoman caliph as a victim of the
Young Turk government. They insisted that the war against the
Ottomans was a political act, not a religious act. The British
hoped the fragile arrangement of dual loyalties would hold.[50]
Until the moment of the anti-imperialist turn in pan-Islamism
on the eve of World War I, however, most of the Indian Muslim
admirers of the Ottoman caliphate did not want a war between
the empires of the caliph and the queen. There were many elite
Ottomans, including Abdulhamid, also utilizing the idea of the
Muslim world as a justification for imperial peace and Ottoman-
British rapprochement.

Contradictions in the Imperial Politics of a Muslim-World Identity

What was distinctive and unprecedented in the early twentieth-century Muslim-world identity was its political investment not only in the ideal of a global caliphate but also in the Ottoman Empire as the voice of an imagined Muslim collectivity. As Muslim populations grew more closely connected, the Ottomans nearly created a cultural order akin to that of the pre-nineteenth-century Confucian world.

The Ottoman policy of linking Muslim organizations, rulers, and subjects to Istanbul via spiritual sovereignty was an important part of this effort, greatly facilitated by the transit and communication networks of empires. In this the Ottoman government took cues from Russian, French, and British interventions in the political affairs of Ottoman Christian subjects. By instrumentalizing the prestige of the caliphate, the Ottomans flipped the equation, subtly observing the political affairs of Muslims beyond their borders while insisting on the purely religious nature of the caliphate's sovereignty.

The Omani-Zanzibari Al-Basaid Dynasty's relationship with the Ottoman caliph illustrates this shift in geopolitical thinking about Muslim identity. Under Sultan Bargash bin Said, Zanzibar enjoyed a strong bond with Istanbul. When Bargash was preparing to perform the pilgrimage to Mecca in 1877, Ottoman sultan Abdulaziz granted him a special imperial title, Majidiyya. The Zanzibari ruling dynasty hosted many Ottoman merchants and followed reformist Muslim thought in Istanbul, Cairo, and India. The strength of these ties peaked during the reign of Zanzibari sultan Ali (r. 1902–1911), who introduced the Ottoman-style fez and coat as the official dress, even when Zanzibar was under a British protectorate. In their exchanges, Ottoman and Zanzibari elites criticized Christian European colonial rule in

Africa and emphasized the need for Muslim solidarity in international affairs, though they did not advocate an end to the British Empire in the Indian Ocean. The Zanzibari reading public also followed news of the Ottoman Empire and joined various Ottoman causes, such as a boycott of Italian goods upon Italy's 1911 invasion of Libya.[51]

Other Muslim societies, with little by way of pre-nineteenth-century connections to the Ottoman Empire, established modern links just as they were coming under European Christian rule. Moroccan intellectuals, for example, developed an interest in Ottoman reforms and pan-Islamic solidarity, even though Moroccans and their clerics remained loyal to the Moroccan sultan.[52] Afghanistan's ties to Istanbul peaked in the early twentieth century, after a humble start in 1878. One key figure in the relationship was the Afghan aristocrat Mahmud Terzi. While exiled to Damascus between 1897 and 1909, Terzi established close links with the Ottoman elite. Upon his return to Kabul he rose to become the country's reformist prime minister as well as father-in-law of the future king Amanullah Khan (r. 1919–1929). Ottoman legal experts, engineers, and military offices trained generations of Afghan elites and contributed to the formation of the 1923 Afghan Constitution.[53]

Sultan Abu Bakar of Johor, in the Malay Peninsula, too, looked to Istanbul. He visited twice, first in 1870, on his way back from a trip to London, and again in 1893, after a pilgrimage to Mecca. Abu Bakar was received by the Ottoman sultan, honored with medals, and, during each visit, given a palace-trained concubine from the harem.[54]

It was also not unusual for Southeast Asian Muslim leaders to seek Ottoman support for rebellions against Dutch rule, as in the Banten Uprising in 1888, the Pahang War in 1891–1895, and uprisings in Jambi and Riau (1904–1905). Yet even in peaceful times and among Muslims loyal to the Dutch, connections to the

Ottoman lands became more important as Muslim-world identity took root. In addition to expressing their respect for the spiritual sovereignty of a caliph, Indonesian Muslims began to see Ottoman consulates as caliphate representatives. They invoked the Ottoman sultan in Friday prayers and sent students to study in Istanbul's modern schools.

On the eve of World War I, Russian Muslims constituted the third largest group of pilgrims to Mecca, and they often stopped in Istanbul along the way.[55] Russian Muslims, too, sent their children to Istanbul for education. The Russian consulate there tended to object when Russian Muslims—such as Gaspirali, the Crimean who spearheaded the 1907 pan-Islamic conference in Cairo—tried to attend Istanbul's military academies, but they could not control their subjects' mobility.

The new Muslim-world identity also fostered closer ties between Persia and the Ottoman Empire, which had long been rivals. Iranian constitutionalists advocated alliance with the Ottomans, and the Iranian public developed pan-Islamic ideals that bridged Shia-Sunni boundaries, which had previously been a source of division from the Ottomans.[56] Persian shahs were warmly received by Istanbul's elite in 1889 and 1900. During Mozaffar ad-Din Shah's month-long visit in 1900, he was given the title "most special guest of the caliph" and accorded the highest level of imperial protocol.[57] Iraqi Shia, too, were overwhelmingly loyal to the Ottoman Empire, contributing to other Sunni-Shia connections forged partly in contacts between Ottoman and Persian merchants and intellectuals.

The legacy of these late nineteenth-century links to the Ottoman Empire is easy to see in the appropriation of an Ottoman emblem: the crescent. The crescent appeared on the Ottoman flag and other symbols of the empire, such as medals bestowed by the sultan, but it has never had theological significance. After 1878, however, the Ottomans began supporting the Red

Crescent as an alternative to the Red Cross, thereby imbuing the crescent with a significance akin to that of Christianity's principal symbol. Today the crescent is a symbol of Muslim identity, adorning the flags of more than ten postcolonial Muslim-majority countries.[58]

As Muslim networks and identity became more globalized via pan-Islamic thought and the new caliphate-centered politics, European paranoia and Islamophobia mounted. For instance, when the Dutch government granted Japanese citizens legal equality in 1899, it continued to deny equality to most Arabs in its territories. Arabs with Ottoman passports were granted equal status, but the majority of Arabs in the Dutch Indies were of Hadramite Yemeni descent and lacked Ottoman papers. When Hadramite Arabs adopted the Ottoman fez and requested Ottoman intervention on their behalf, the Dutch objected. When one Indonesian prince wore a fez during his visit to Istanbul, Dutch authorities questioned his loyalty to the Dutch Empire. Even the sultan of Siak's (Sumatra) brief stop in Istanbul, en route to the Netherlands and Germany, caused alarm in Dutch colonial circles. In 1906, Christiaan Snouck Hurgronje, a Dutch Orientalist and colonial officer, responded to Prince Sosronegoro of Kutai's (Borneo) visit to Istanbul with a broadside about pan-Islamic peril. In 1898 Dutch authorities asked Istanbul to recall the consular officer Mehmed Kamil Bey on suspicion of pan-Islamic activities, such as his marriage to the widow of the sultan of Johor. When Kamil Bey was considered for the Ottoman consular post in Singapore, the Dutch government successfully petitioned the British to reject his appointment.

Sultan Abdulhamid himself assured the Dutch envoy in Istanbul of his respect for Queen Wilhelmina and instructed Indonesian Muslims to be loyal to her. But Dutch authorities were not mollified. They considered Indonesian Muslims' travels to Istanbul more dangerous than travel to Cairo or Mecca, even when Indonesians went to the Ottoman capital to attend schools offering Westernized, Tanzimat-style education in French.[59]

Yet Western empires did not always oppose global Muslim networks and identity. Sometimes they even encouraged pan-Islamic sentiment and recognized Ottoman centrality by seeking Istanbul's aid in pacifying colonial Muslim populations. For instance, when American colonial officers in the Philippines faced armed Muslim resistance in 1898, they consulted Istanbul. In response, Sultan Abdulhamid sent a message to Philippine Muslim leaders instructing them to refrain from rebellion as long as American rule respected their religion. President William McKinley was much impressed and praised Ambassador Oscar Straus, the U.S. envoy to the Ottomans, for winning the caliph's support.[60] Similarly, British imperial officers in South Africa invited Ottoman religious scholars to resolve intra-Muslim controversies and teach in their domains. For instance, Abubakr Efendi, Sultan Abdulhamid's religious envoy to South Africa, proved highly influential, leading the South African Muslim community and gaining its trust.[61] One of his sons was later appointed an Ottoman consular officer to Singapore, strengthening Ottoman-British ties. And Kaiser Wilhelm of Germany asked Sultan Abdulhamid to advise Chinese Muslims to stay out of the Boxer Rebellion.

The Ottomans might have rebuffed these requests, just as they had in the past largely avoided the affairs of Muslims in other imperial domains. But the Ottomans wanted to take advantage of their soft power over foreign Muslims in order to counter discrimination against the empire in international law and strengthen their relationship with European empires. International law was a favorite subject of Abdulhamid-era Ottoman lawyers and intellectuals, who supported specialized education in the discipline and saw international law as a means to protect the empire even as its military strength was dwindling.[62] The

Ottoman government established the Office of Legal Counsel, staffed by experts on international law, to defend the empire's interest with recourse of norms and rules of existing Eurocentric international law.

Ottoman lawyers were especially interested in defending notions of imperial sovereignty against capitulations and unequal treaties, which the British and Russians used as an excuse to intervene in the affairs of Ottoman Christians.[63] Dating back to the sixteenth century, the capitulations granted European empires extraterritoriality—consular jurisdiction over their nationals in the Ottoman Empire. These grants of privileged treatment and legal pluralism were unilaterally bestowed by the Ottomans and thus a sign of the empire's power at the time.

But during the nineteenth century, when the Ottoman government tried to eliminate these privileges, European powers collectively insisted on their continuation by force. More important, the European powers reinterpreted the capitulations as international contracts extended to Christian Ottoman citizens under European protection. This placed non-Muslim Ottomans outside Ottoman jurisdiction, violating Ottoman sovereignty. Not only would Armenian or Greek Ottomans carrying a British or French passport or protected by their embassies be exempt from Ottoman courts, but they also benefited from lower taxes offered to European merchants under rules of extraterritoriality. This model was later applied in China and other territories, creating a global pattern of unequal treaties.

The British and Russian empires also began to use extraterritoriality to intervene on behalf of their Muslim subjects visiting Ottoman domains for pilgrimage and trade. Even in Mecca, when Indian or Russian Muslims became involved in legal disputes, they could request the aid of British or Russian consulates in Jeddah against the Ottoman authorities. Pan-Islamists celebrated the huge number of pilgrims going to Ottoman-ruled Mecca as a sign of increasing global Muslim connectivity, but these Muslim pilgrims carried documents and travel documents identifying their European imperial ties, and when it suited their interest, they could utilize European consulates' help against Ottoman authorities. The Ottoman government found this intercession of Christian empires on the legal rights of their Muslim subjects in the sacred Muslim city of Mecca especially troubling.

The Ottoman caliph's claim to spiritual sovereignty over British and Russian Muslims was partly a mirror image of European empires' claims on behalf of the rights of Ottoman Christians. If Christian monarchs could assert rights over the caliph's Christian subjects, the caliph could assert his spiritual authority over Muslim subjects of other monarchs. Thus the Ottomans would show European empires that fair application of international law was to every ruler's benefit. Pan-Islamists imagined an imperial world order in which the Ottoman caliph represented Muslim dignity and Muslim rights against discrimination by European colonial elites.

◆ ◆ ◆

Sultan Abdulhamid's promotion of Ottoman spiritual sovereignty over the *ummah*, alongside British temporal sovereignty, solidified the imagination of a geopolitical Muslim world in the age of high imperialism. This version of pan-Islamism was no *jihad* against the European empires. On the contrary, it aimed to guarantee Ottoman sovereignty by leveraging foreign Muslims' dual loyalty to empire—particularly the Crown—and caliph.

Yet this geopolitical argument for pan-Islamism produced unintended consequences. It aggravated Islamophobia and paranoia about Muslim revolts. Even if Abdulhamid's goal was entrenchment of imperial peace, the increasing spiritual respect he enjoyed from British, Russian, French, and Dutch Muslims made European colonial officers nervous. And their fears of Muslim peril could now be attributed to the caliphate. The Ottomans took the potential for alienation seriously; it is on the basis of this concern that they refused to openly endorse the 1907 Muslim congress in Cairo. The sultan built his connections to Muslims all over the world, but he did not want the European powers, especially Britain, to see pan-Islamism as an anti-imperial project. For the caliph and his Indian Muslim supporters in particular, pan-Islamism had to avoid appearing anti-imperialist, and in fact could be a force creating inter-imperial peace. This is what really distinguished pan-Islamic Muslim-world identity from black race, Buddhist world, or Asian identity: the existence of the Ottoman caliphate and its need to assert a rationale for the Ottoman-British alliance against the Russian threat. Pan-Islamism at the time of Sultan Abdulhamid and Queen Victoria did incorporate a subaltern appeal for better treatment of the colonial oppressed, but that appeal, often made while considering the interests of the Ottoman Empire itself, did not require an end to empires or visions of endless conflict between Islam and the West. The Ottomans still sought good relations between empires, and they used pan-Islamic ideology to pursue that harmony, not a clash of civilizations.

The Battle of
Geopolitical Illusions

(1908–1924)

On November 14, 1914, the chief Ottoman Muslim cleric announced two *fatwa* asking the Muslim world to revolt against Christian imperial rulers. The first declared a holy war against colonizers attacking the religion and lands of Islam and enslaving Muslims. The second singled out the Russian, French, and British empires, as well as their supporters, for their assault on the caliphate. Muslims ruled by these empires were obligated to join the *jihad*, which was supported by the Germans as well.

At the time of this *jihad* declaration, Sultan Abdulhamid II was no longer caliph. He had been replaced by his brother, Sultan Mehmet Reşad, in 1909, a year after the constitutionalist Young Turk Revolution. According to memoirs by his daughter and his physician, Abdulhamid, the father of pan-Islamism in the age of high imperialism, was uncomfortable with *jihad* against the British. He blamed the British for their anti-Ottoman positions, but he also regretted that the two empires ended up on opposite sides of the Great War.[1] Given his efforts to foster imperial order and an Ottoman-British alliance on the basis of pan-Islamism, it must have been dispiriting to see the caliphate's spiritual sovereignty over British Muslims deployed for anti-imperial *jihad*.

Ironically, when Young Turk leaders came to power after the 1908 revolution, they too wished to maintain the caliphate's position as a promoter of the imperial world order. The Young Turks also pursued Ottoman-British rapprochement until the summer of 1914. Leaders of the revolution did not want to discard imperial reforms based on European models; rather, they believed that Abdulhamid's autocratic rule was damaging the Ottoman Empire's reputation in a Europe to which they sought close ties. With a constitution and a parliament, they could revive the inclusive universalism of the Ottoman system, win the loyalty of Armenian and Greek citizens, and shift European public opinion in a pro-Ottoman direction.

But the strategic situation of World War I—not any surge in pan-Islamic sentiment or worsening oppression of Muslims under European empires—dramatically changed Young Turk priorities, leading to the eventual declaration of *jihad*. Germany's key decision makers understood the Ottomans' strategic needs and hoped to take advantage of the supposedly anti-Western sentiment of the Muslim world. Thus they supported the holy war for the benefit of their own war effort.

When the British and Ottoman empires found themselves enemies in World War I, both sides suffered the consequences of their Muslim-world delusions. Successful *jihad* required from Muslims deeper anticolonial commitments than they actually possessed. The pro-*jihad* camp also failed to grasp pan-Islamism's symbiotic relationship with the British Empire. For their part, Entente powers led by the British tried to separate the Ottoman caliphate from Arab and Indian Muslims, underestimating the global entanglements of their Muslim subjects as well as the religious and political significance of pan-Islamic identity.

When the Ottomans lost in World War I, the British enlarged their control of Muslim societies by taking over the Ottoman territories of Palestine and Iraq. But even in defeat, Ottoman leaders could turn to pan-Islamic sentiment. The period from 1918 to 1924 witnessed the peak of pan-Islamic mobilization in the name of saving and empowering the Muslim world. Indian Muslims under British rule strongly supported the Khilafat movement, which aided the Turkish War of Independence and peace talks between Ankara and London in 1923.

Yet this moment of pan-Islamic triumph revealed further the crumbling foundations of an imagined global Muslim solidarity that had been erected in the eras of Queen Victoria and Sultan Abdulhamid, leading to a traumatic turning point: the abolition of the caliphate in 1924.

Roots of the Final British-Ottoman Estrangement

As we have seen, the Ottoman and British empires were already at odds in the late nineteenth century, both strategically and ideologically, as anti-Ottoman ideas came to dominate European public opinion. In the early twentieth century, Ottoman-British competition in Africa and Arabia produced still more tension.

The Ottomans sought to extend their influence south of Libya but were blocked by British and French expansion in Central Africa.[2] The British created protectorates around Hijaz, the region of Ottoman Arabia containing Mecca and Medina, thereby undermining the Ottoman claim to the caliphate, which was founded on custodianship of the holy cities. For example, in 1901 the British tried to block the anchoring of an Ottoman frigate at a Kuwaiti harbor. The Ottomans insisted on, and received, formal recognition of sovereignty in the area, but the diplomatic damage was done.

Two events in 1906 exacerbated distrust between the two empires. One, the Dinshaway Incident, involved the unfair punishment of Egyptian villagers who were wrongly blamed for the death of a British soldier. His comrades had shot a number of pigeons owned by residents of the small town of Dinshaway, provoking local ire. British soldiers fired into a crowd, wounding the wife of a cleric and inciting the villagers further. One soldier attempted to escape to the nearest British camp but died of heatstroke along the way. British officers and Egyptian colonial collaborators held several Egyptians responsible and sentenced them harshly. One man was hanged.

The Egyptian public believed the punishments unwarranted, and the events came to symbolize unjust and humiliating colonialism and therefore energized Egyptian nationalists. At that moment of crisis, the British hoped and expected that the Ottoman caliph would intervene and mollify the outraged. Egypt was still under the nominal rule of the Ottoman Empire, and the Ottoman caliph was highly respected. But Abdulhamid refused to get involved. After all, a seemingly minor incident had grown into a major nationalist cause, shattering British confidence. Ottoman elites realized the power of public opinion just as surely as the British did.

Another large source of discord that year was the Taba Crisis, a border-drawing dispute in the Sinai. Egyptian nationalists supported Ottoman claims, showing their allegiance to the caliphate in spite of a quarter-century under the British protectorate, leading to further distrust. In response, Sir Edward Grey took to the House of Lords to decry rising Muslim fanaticism in Egypt. Other parliamentarians blamed the Ottomans for inciting pan-Islamic hatred of the British Empire.[3]

Sultan Abdulhamid strove to smooth over relations with the British, but British fears of rising pan-Islamism only deepened alongside mounting anti-Abdulhamid and anti-Ottoman public opinion in London. Some of Abdulhamid's opponents in exile tried to benefit. For instance, in an article for the London *Times*, the exiled Ottoman prince Sebahattin argued that, if Ottoman liberals under his leadership were in power, both England and France would be free of the dangerous political pan-Islamism cultivated by Sultan Abdulhamid. A liberal sultan, Sebahattin contended, could only promote cultural pan-Islamism, which would be in harmony with British and French imperial interests.

In reality, this is exactly what Abdulhamid had been doing since the 1880s—bolstering his credentials as a spiritual leader in order to gain sufficient leverage among British Muslims to win over their colonial masters—but Sebahattin was drawing on widespread anti-Ottoman sentiment in European colonial metropoles, where Abdulhamid II was seen as incapable of good governance within the imperial system. Upon the publication of Prince Sebahattin's article, an Islamophobic priest, Malcolm MacColl, sent a letter to the newspaper suggesting that the British government reject the Ottoman sultan's claim to the leadership of the Muslim world. An Arab from the Qureshi tribe should be caliph, he argued, and Muslims placed under British governance.[4] Several Indian Muslim intellectuals immediately tried to defend the validity of Abdulhamid's caliphate against MacColl's Islamophobic writings. But others, such as the influential pan-Islamist Muhammad Barakatullah, blamed Abdulhamid for wasting the loyalty of the world's three hundred million Muslims. Like the Young Turk opponents of Abdulhamid II, Barakatullah believed that a constitutional

and parliamentary regime would eliminate European grievances toward the Ottoman Empire and bolster its leadership of
the Muslim world. This strain of opposition to Abdulhamid II
was not inspired by anti-caliphate ideas. On the contrary, constitutionalist opposition to the sultan was equally invested in
the caliphate and the idea of the Muslim world.[5]

The writings of Yusuf Akçura, a Russian-Muslim intellectual
close to the Young Turks, are emblematic of the disapproval
facing Abdulhamid among Muslim intellectuals who believed
that the Ottoman caliph was not paying sufficient attention to
the Muslim world. Akçura's 1904 *Three Methods of Grand Politics*
argued that pan-Islamism could be a challenge to the British
Empire's status as the greatest "Muhammadan" power, although for many pan-Islamists, including Sultan Abdulhamid,
there was no contradiction between Muslim solidarity and
British imperial interests. In any case, Akçura didn't recom-
mend challenging the British. Instead, he argued that the Ottomans could regain British support through a revival of British
Russophobia. His method involved a pan-Turkic version of pan-
Islamism that would only threaten the Russian Empire and
thus sustain Ottoman-British cooperation.[6] The caliph could
use his spiritual sovereignty to support Muslim anti-imperialism
in Russian Central Asia while maintaining a pro-imperial tone
in British India. Though both men sought a British alliance,
Akçura's suggestion diverged from Abdulhamid's policies. Abdulhamid used the caliphate to support the imperial system at
large, thereby creating conditions for an imperial alliance of
London, Istanbul, and Moscow. Akçura's approach to currying
British favor would have risked the principles of imperial peace
and universalism on which alliance was based.

The transition from Abdulhamid's pan-Islamism to the more
confrontational variety of the Young Turks is evident in Ali
Fehmi Muhammed's *El-Hilafetül Islamiyye ve'l Camiatul Os-*

maniyye (Islamic caliphate and Ottoman community). First serialized in journals in 1910–1911, after the Young Turk takeover, Ali Fehmi's book emphasizes pan-Islamism as a cultural-social movement, not the anti-Western political conspiracy of British Islamophobic imagination. But Ali Fehmi also prioritizes loyalty to the Ottoman sultan over loyalty to European empires, arguing that Muslims, no matter their location and their masters, must first protect the caliphate and follow its leadership. Otherwise, Ali Fehmi warned, Muslims would be divided and become an easy target for further European colonization and humiliation.[7]

When the Young Turks came to power in 1908, they radicalized Abdulhamid's cautious pan-Islamism with new elements of anti-imperialism in the vein proposed by these writers. Familiar with the white man's civilizing ideology, as well as dominant theories of geopolitics, the Young Turks began to see the Ottoman Empire a member not of the club of empires but of the victimized East and Muslim world. Given the Japanese victory over Russia in 1905, it seemed to the Young Turks that the racial basis of the Eurocentric world order was already delegitimized. They believed the Ottoman Empire could do for the Muslim world what Japan did for the "yellow race": lead communities awakening to their subaltern identity by pursuing the self-strengthening reforms of constitutionalism, parliamentary democracy, and military restructuring. Muslim intellectuals all over the world also hoped for a resurrection of Muslim power after the Young Turk Revolution of 1908. The revolutionaries themselves expected to turn the Ottoman Empire into the "Japan of the Near East."[8]

And yet, despite their anti-imperialism, the Young Turk government understood that they ruled an empire. They were concerned about rebellion among Greek and Armenian citizens. They soon realized that their new policies of constitutional government and internal unity would not prevent secessionist movements unless the Ottomans received European support. They had to convince the British and other European empires that Ottoman constitutional sovereignty over Christians was worth preserving. Thus they initially reverted to Abdulhamid's strategic game, using the illusion of the Muslim world and the caliph's spiritual sovereignty over it to geopolitical advantage. They supported an alliance with the British while strengthening ties to the German Empire as leverage, in part to inspire greater solicitousness from London.

But events would eventually make alliance with the British impossible, and the Ottomans turned decisively toward Germany and Austria-Hungary. It was under these circumstances that Ottoman elites tried to reinterpret their perceived leadership over Muslims in a newly anti-imperialist direction, transforming the political significance of the idea of the Muslim world.

One of these events was Italy's unexpected and unlawful invasion of the Muslim-majority Ottoman province of Libya in 1911. The Ottoman navy responded weakly, and soon local Arab forces, led by Ottoman military officers, were engaged in guerrilla warfare. The invasion prompted a massive, global pan-Islamic boycott of Italian products and aid to the Libyan resistance. Every Muslim magazine and journal in India extensively covered the Italian actions and Muslim resistance. Muslims believed that the British Empire should respond by upholding international law, which vindicated the Ottomans. And, beyond the dictates of law, Muslims expected the British to support Ottoman claims because Britain ruled almost half of the world's Muslims and must have appreciated the symbolic significance of the invasion in the minds of its subjects. Yet the British government offered little beyond verbal condemnation of the invasion. Even the Hindu press was astounded. On

October 7, 1911, an article in the English-language paper *Punjabee,* published by Hindu Indians, wondered "why Great Britain, the strongest and most influential power, has not protested against Italian aggression." The article argued that "Great Britain should interfere and prevent the downright injury to the Muhammedan State of Turkey" because "there are over a hundred million Muhammadans under British sway and their good will and loyalty ought to have some effect in determining the foreign policy of Great Britain."[9]

The Balkan Wars of 1912–1913 would cause even greater agitation in the name of saving the Muslim world and further its metamorphosis into an anti-imperial ideology. These wars were to some extent successors to the Italian invasion of Libya. Ottoman military weakness as demonstrated in that war and the big imperial powers' tacit approval of further European colonization of Muslim lands encouraged small Balkan states to ally under Serbian leadership against Ottoman rule and Muslim presence in Europe more generally. The fighting was bitter. Balkan Muslims were massacred and forced from their homes. Eventually, the Balkan coalition was victorious, and the Ottomans had to cede almost all of their European territories.[10]

Despite the assurances of the European powers that they would not accept any changes in the status quo as a result of this war, Balkan winnings were internationally recognized at the London Conference of 1913.[11] European sympathy for the massacres, and the inability of the European state system and international law to prevent them, supported the general perception among Ottomans that a new Crusade was under way. Young Turk governments continued to uphold the earlier pro-British Abdulhamid policy of leveraging pan-Islamic networks and public opinion as a bulwark against Russian aggression, but dissent was on the rise. After all, the policy wasn't providing any benefits. In addition to losing territories they had controlled for more than five hundred years, the Ottomans had to deal with a wave of Muslim immigrants escaping Greek, Serbian, Montenegrin, and Bulgarian armies bent on atrocities and ethnic cleansing.

Foreign Muslim solidarity mounted as a result of the Balkan Wars. The Red Crescent Society received massive financial donations from India, Central Asia, North Africa, and Southeast Asia, and Indian Muslim physicians volunteered for service. Later this emotional, humanitarian, and economic mobilization on the part of Muslims in Asia and Africa would prove fateful, as it convinced the Germans that there was a Muslim world worthy of alliance. Indeed, by the eve of World War I, the densely interwoven Muslim press, along with emotional links to the Ottoman caliphate, sustained a stronger sense of global Muslim identity than the previous millennium had ever known. When the British allied with Russia against Germany, a pro-German and anti-British interpretation of pan-Islamism, with the Muslim world under the Ottoman caliph's leadership, became a viable option.

The Muslim World in
Ottoman Geopolitical Strategy

It is tempting to look back at the Ottoman challenge to the Allied European empires in World War I as a sincere *jihad* on behalf of an imagined Muslim world. But this misdiagnoses the situation. The Ottoman position in the war was not an inevitable result of the clash between civilizations or world religious, nor was it a necessary response to Western colonial hegemony.

In reality, the path from imperial cooperation to confrontation took many detours. Contingent events, interpreted through illusory geopolitical lenses, led into the fall of 1914, when the Ottomans cast their lot with the Germans. Ottoman territorial losses in the Balkan and Libyan wars, coupled with Armenian nationalism in eastern Anatolia, led to a crisis of Ottoman legitimacy and sovereignty. The writings of several influential Young Turks can help us grasp the nuances of the politics that informed Ottoman decision making on the eve of World War I.

The person who best represents the changing arguments and influence of pan-Islamic thinking in the Ottoman Empire from 1908 to 1914 is Şehbenderzade Ahmed Hilmi.[12] A Sufi with a keen interest in other mystical traditions, as well as an opponent of Abdulhamid II's regime, Hilmi lived in Egypt and Fizan (southern Libya) as an exile.[13] Upon returning to Istanbul after the 1908 Revolution, he published the journal *Ittihad-i Islam* (Islamic unity), which argued that Muslim political solidarity was both a moral duty and a source of leverage for the Ottoman Empire within the global balance of power. He sought the sort of international Muslim cooperation that would allow the Ottoman Empire to serve as a viable economic and military power for the Muslim world.

Hilmi knew well that the idea of a single, united Muslim empire was a utopian fantasy and never advocated such a thing. As his 1911 book *The Muslim World in the Twentieth Century and Europe* demonstrated, he was a realist.[14] He even supported, alongside Muslim unity, Ottoman participation in the European alliance system. Perhaps Hilmi's greatest innovation came in his conclusion that the Ottomans would have to choose one of the two alliance systems in Europe. Like any good realist, he preferred that the Ottomans ally with the British-led Entente powers. But he understood that the Ottomans would be forced to partner with the German-led Axis unless the British Empire changed its hostile policies.[15] European claims to civilize the world were bankrupt, Hilmi argued. So was their fear of an awakening in the Muslim world, in Asia, and among the colored races.[16] Either Britain, France, and other powers would have to discard these ideas, or the Ottomans would make their way with Germany. Hilmi appealed to the nationalist sentiments of Anatolian Muslims. For example, in *How the Turkish Spirit Is Formed* (1913), he urged Muslim Turks to revive their national consciousness and thereby recover the dignity and power of the Ottoman state. Hilmi was not an ethnic nationalist, however. In his generation, the nationalism of Turkish-speaking Muslims complemented a pan-Islamic Ottoman foreign policy. Yet the fact that he talked about Anatolia as a homeland of Turkish Muslims without mentioning the sizable Armenian and Greek populations living there already indicated a paradigm shift, from a cosmopolitan empire to a Muslim empire. He envisioned both the mobilization of Anatolian Muslims and solidarity with foreign Muslims. This would pressure European empires to support Ottoman sovereignty while rescuing Ottomans from their isolation.[17]

Another influential Ottoman pan-Islamist voice was Celal Nuri. Nuri offered the most sophisticated realist formulation of pan-Islamism in the post–Balkan War period. In a 1913 book also called *Ittihad-i Islam* (Islamic unity), Nuri criticized the Eurocentric world order in moral terms and offered realpolitik suggestions for Ottoman pan-Islamism.[18] Nuri was deeply anxious about the increasingly insecure international order and discussed the division of Iran into Russian and English spheres of influence, Morocco's incorporation as a French protectorate, the Italian invasion of Libya, the Balkan expulsion of Muslims, and the European powers' support for the Balkan coalition. To these woes he added the polarization of Europe reflected in the alliance among Britain, Russia, and France, which he feared could lead to a great confrontation between the forces of pan-Germanism and pan-Slavism. Finally, he noted the awakening of the Far East as evidenced by the rise of Japan and the establishment of a republican regime in China. He thus constructed a framework of confrontation between an "Awakening East" and an "Imperialist West."[19]

This interpretation of international affairs through the prism of conflict between an emerging East and imperialist West seeking to provoke independent Eastern nations such as Ottoman Turkey led him to important questions: Was the gap between East and West eternal and unbridgeable, or could there be rapprochement?[20] What would be the role of Muslims in this new phase of the relationship between East and West? What should Muslims do to liberate themselves from oppression and gain their rightful place in the civilized world? Whenever Nuri spoke of Muslims and the Muslim world, he had in mind not a community of believers but rather a racial and civilizational category comparable to the "black race" and the "yellow race."

Nuri was committed to pan-Islamism as a viable approach to international relations and criticized those who associated it with religious obscurantism and utopianism.[21] Anyone who thought in such overcautious ways would never understand what Islamic unity meant, he argued, for three reasons. First, in a racialized world, the Ottomans already shared the destiny of other Muslims. Both colonized Muslims and independent, Muslim-ruled countries were subject to the same mistreatment by white Christians. Thus they had to understand the reality of other Muslim societies, even if they could not help them. Whatever policies were chosen, the Ottomans should know everything about conditions in the Muslim world in order to decide whether pan-Islamic projects were worth pursuing. Second, Nuri rejected the exclusively religious approach to pan-Islamism associated with Abdulhamid II's regime and with the conservative reaction against constitutionalism and modernity. Pan-Islamism confronted problems of backwardness and unfreedom and thus should be a political phenomenon, not a religious one. Third, Nuri insisted that the destiny of the Muslim world could not be separated from Ottoman efforts to gain full equality in international relations.[22] In its pursuit of equality, the Ottoman Empire should continue to Westernize and modernize, to improve the lives of Ottomans and eliminate excuses for outside interference. For example, he argued that the court system should be improved to such high levels that even enemies of the Ottomans could find no defects in it and use it as an excuse for unequal treaties. Muslim solidarity could strengthen the Ottomans to the point where they did not have to rely on untrustworthy outside powers. Which is to say, for Nuri, Muslim unity was necessary to achieve progress modeled on the European design.[23]

The secularism of Nuri's pan-Islamism is most obvious in his vision of solidarity with non-Muslim nationalists in China, India, and Japan. Opposition to Western hegemony would bring them together.[24] He noted that had the Japanese not reformed and self-strengthened, China too would be divided and colonized—a second India.[25] Japanese modernization had not only halted Asian decline but also had heralded the age of Asian awakening. Nuri was therefore disappointed by the Sino-Japanese conflict. If only Japan would improve its policy toward China and win over Chinese nationalists, the future of the Asian awakening would be much brighter. Instead of fighting with each other, China and Japan should cooperate, he argued, in accordance with the "second principle of Darwin," so that both could survive against outside threats.[26]

Nuri presented a highly detailed account of the state of various Muslim nationalities—including Arabs, Turks, Iranians, Afghans, Indians, and other Southeast Asians—to provide his readers a more concrete account of political developments in the imagined Muslim world. He emphasized ties that already bound

Muslims: the caliphate; pilgrimage; and transnational Muslim educational institutions, curricula, and literature.[27] These constituted the minimal requirement for Muslim unity.

However, for Nuri, the essential unity of the Muslims still derived from their common need to respond to European Orientalism, racism, and imperialism. Thus he wrote extensively on European colonial policies and negative Western images of Muslims in order to outline strategies to oppose them. He lamented that if the British Empire had given to all colonies the same rights and autonomy it afforded Australia, Canada, and South Africa, the empire would have been respected by all people under its rule as the champion of real civilization and would itself have benefited economically and politically.[28] In his critique of the predominant practices of international relations, Nuri made frequent references to *hukuku düvel,* the rights of nations, and to international law.

In short, Nuri was not concerned about the possibility that pan-Islamism would lead to conflict with the British. If it did, so be it. Muslims and other colonized people needed to be free, and an alliance based on mutual interest would further that goal. The Ottoman Muslim elite was much taken with these arguments.

Another good example of the Ottoman elite's shift toward explicitly political and anti-Western pan-Islam can be seen in the policy papers of Naci Ismail Pelister, a prolific Young Turk leader who used the pen name Habil Adem. A philosopher and journalist working for the Ottoman intelligence apparatus, Adem was an articulate advocate of realist pan-Islamist policy. His *After the (Balkan) Wars: The Policy on the Caliphate and Turkism* (1915) was sponsored by the Ottoman government and published in Arabic translation, the better to spread its message.[29]

Similar to Nuri, Adem offered a pragmatic policy option for the Ottoman Empire by combining pan-Islamism with Ottoman grand strategy. Recalling Ottoman defeat in the Balkan Wars, Adem emphasized the sadness felt in the hearts of Muslims as far away as India, Egypt, Afghanistan, Tunisia, Algeria, Morocco, and Libya. As a solution to Ottoman isolation in international affairs, he suggested departing from earlier attempts to preserve cosmopolitan empire and focusing instead on the Ottomans' Muslim and Asian credentials. This meant finally abandoning the pursuit of alliance with the British as well as a foreign policy based on diplomacy rather than military power. A keen observer of European imperial rivalries, he predicted that, in light of its competition with Russia, Germany would support a new Ottoman pan-Islamic policy. Adem expected a negative response from the British, who worried about connections between the caliphate and Indian Muslims. Yet he refused to separate the institution of the caliphate from Turkey's foreign policy. He was aware of British attempts to create an Egypt-based caliphate and provoke anti-Ottoman sentiments in Syria with the goal of uniting Arabs inside the British Empire, but he was confident that Arab Muslims would realize the faultiness of a plan for Arab unity under the British.

In Adem's view, there was no contradiction between pan-Islamic internationalism under Ottoman leadership and the nationalist awakenings of Muslim countries such as Egypt and Iran. Transnational solidarity would strengthen nationalist struggles against colonial regimes. Even if Arabs gained independence without the protection of the caliphate, the Ottomans would benefit as long as the British didn't assert protectorates over the newly freed states. The revival of the caliphate would give Indian Muslims dignity, glory, and fame and would strengthen their determination against British colonialism. Under conditions of global Muslim solidarity, Afghanistan could be an industrial center in Asia. Adem praised Russian Muslims for combining faith and modernity and counted their economic and political power as a potential benefit to the Ottomans, should they implement a pan-Islamic policy.[30]

Fundamentally, Adem proposed a modernist and secular interpretation of the caliphate as a means to increase Ottoman international power. The appeal of this idea lay in its apparent necessity: the British-led imperial alliance in Europe was crushing the Ottomans. In other words, the Ottoman relationship with the rest of the imagined Muslim world was secondary and derivative. The primarily Ottoman relationship was with the Western powers. Pan-Islamism, on this reading, was not in any sense a religious obligation or an internationalist value but rather a demand of realpolitik.

A War for the Muslim World

The complex politics of Muslim identity and imperial rivalry led to various misguided strategies on the part of imperial leaders of the Great War. Ottoman elites redefined pan-Islamism and Muslim-world identity as anti-British, anti-Russian, and anti-imperial, even though, as late as the first months of 1914, these same Ottoman leaders had interpreted the caliphate's spiritual sovereignty in India as a basis for British-Ottoman alliance. Convinced that the war effort would benefit from the power of anti-imperialism and what they perceived as Muslim's primordial hatred of the Christian West, Ottoman and German officials proclaimed Muslim liberation from European rule one of their aims. Kaiser Wilhelm wanted to provoke "the whole Mohammedan World" into a "wild revolt," and Chief of the General Staff Helmuth von Moltke imagined an "awakening of the fanaticism of Islam." Even before the Ottomans entered the war, the scholar and diplomat Max von Oppenheim drafted the "Memorandum on Revolutionizing the Islamic Territories of Our Enemies" in hopes of turning Islam into "one of our most important weapons."[31] This mistaken conviction that Muslims would rise up against colonial masters was also the basis of British, French, Russian, and Dutch Islamophobia. Yet in spite of their fears of insurrection, the Allied powers promised colonized Muslims self-empowerment if they remained loyal to their monarchs and kept their distance from the Ottoman caliphs.

Some Muslims did respond sympathetically to the *jihad* declaration. But only in areas that Ottoman and German agents could reach with their armies and financial aid, such as Libya and Afghanistan, did they find military allies. Even the 1915 mutiny in Singapore was no Ottoman-instigated holy war. Though partly driven by Muslim soldiers influenced by the caliph's call for *jihad*, the revolt's origins had more to do with racism toward Indian soldiers than with Muslim sensibilities.[32]

What the Germans and Ottomans discovered was that the British had not simply given Muslims the steamships and telegraph lines that connected them—leaving them open to Ottoman influence—but in fact had provided leadership worthy of their loyalty. Many Muslims mobilized for the British, French, and Russian armies. Prominent Indian pan-Islamists even supported expanded British rule over Muslims in East Africa and the Middle East.

Viceroy Charles Hardinge was aware of Indian Muslim sympathies toward the caliphate and promised Indian Muslim leaders that, in the event of a war with the Ottomans, the British Empire would prove its Muslim Great Power status by ensuring the holy cities were left untouched. Hardinge and other British leaders emphasized the political nature of the war, insisting on its irrelevance with respect to Indian Muslims' religious duties. Indian Muslims did not want to choose between king and caliph, and when the war started, leading Indian pan-Islamists wrote letters to the sultan and Grand Vizier Talaat Pasha urging neutrality. When the Ottoman Empire entered the conflict and declared holy war, the British had already prepared counter*jihad* propaganda proclaiming, "There may be no misunderstanding on the part of his Majesty's most loyal Moslem subjects in this war, in which no question of a religious character is involved. . . . Holy Places will be immune from attack or molestation by the British naval and military Forces. . . . At the request of his Majesty's Government, the Governments of France and Russia have given . . . similar assurances."[33] British propaganda further argued that the Ottoman government was under the control of infidel Germans and that the British would honor the institution of the caliphate as well as pilgrimage routes.[34]

Allied empires challenged the *jihad* proclamation by convincing their Muslim subjects to produce loyalist and anti-Ottoman opinions and tracts. Many pro-British Muslims joined colonial officers in distinguishing between religious and political aspects of the Ottoman caliphate. They assured Muslims that the Allies were fighting a secular, nationalist Ottoman government under German control, not the caliph. Soon Muslim notables from all the colonized lands were expressing their loyalty to the British, Russian, French and Dutch empires. Put in such terms, there was no contradiction between fidelity to European empires and the Ottoman caliph.

In short, Ottoman-German war propaganda badly misdiagnosed the relationship between European empires and global Muslim public opinion. The conviction that Indian, Nigerian, Indonesian, or Algerian Muslims would rebel against Christian rulers reflected a simplistic sense of pan-Islamic identity in the imperial world. Fomenting insurrection was a pragmatic, if cynical, effort on the part of the Ottomans, who seem to have forgotten that they themselves had once argued for and taken advantage of separation between the spiritual and political authority of the caliphate.

This battle for the soul and agency of the illusionary Muslim world provoked further propaganda, concerning the legitimacy of the caliphate. Books such as Hamdi Paşa's *İslam Dünyası ve İngiliz Misyoneri: İngiliz Misyoneri Nasıl Yetiştiriliyor?* (The Muslim world and the British missionary: How do they train British missionaries?), Hindli Abdülmecid's *İngiltere ve Alem-i Islam* (England and the Muslim world), and Şehbenderzade Ahmed Hilmi's *Senusiler ve Sultan Abdulhamid* (Sanusi order of Africa and Sultan Abdulhamid II) argued for the Ottoman caliphate's leadership of Muslims living under British rule and beyond.[35] Meanwhile, Allied propaganda focused on scholarly refutations of the Ottoman claim to the caliphate. The Allied case took its cues from Sunni political texts of the first three centuries after the death of Muhammad, which stated that a caliph must be from the Qureshi tribe of Arabia. In making their argument, the Allies relied on Orientalist writers such as the Russian Vasili V. Barthold, whose "Caliph and the Sultan," appearing in the journal *Mir Islama* (Muslim world), was the first influential and comprehensive article to challenge the legitimacy of the Ottoman claim to the caliphate.[36] Italian Carlo Alfonso Nallino made related arguments in his *Uppunti Sulla Natural del Califfato in Genere e sul Presunto Califfato Ottomano,* a 1917 report for the Italian Foreign Ministry later translated into both English and French.[37] George Samne, an Arab Christian, joined in with his French *Le Khalifet et le Panislamisme.*[38] Arnold J. Toynbee kept the discussion going in 1920, after the war had ended, with "The Question of the Caliphate."[39] Even Americans such as A. T. Olmstead joined the fray, publishing *The New Arab Kingdom and the Fate of the Muslim World* in 1919.[40]

In reality, the Qureshi rule had long since been disregarded. For centuries, Muslim scholars accepted Ottoman and Mughal claims to the caliphate. This Allied propaganda convinced few

Muslims of the invalidity of the Ottoman caliphate, though it created a convenient template for use in other contexts.

What many Muslims did do in response to the propaganda war was reiterate their loyalty to empire—with conditions. Indian Muslims proposed a new imperial contract: they would serve the king and sacrifice their lives for the British Empire in return for London's recognition of Muslim religious rights and sensibilities, which included respect for the very same caliph the British were trying to undermine. Muslim soldiers also insisted on the continuation of Muslim, preferably Ottoman, rule over the holy cities. The colonial government acceded to these demands, and Indian Muslims held up their end of the bargain. After the war, Indian Muslims would repeatedly rely on this contract when criticizing British policies toward the Muslim world. Similarly, at the end of the war, French Muslims who fought alongside imperial forces drew upon their own sacrifices to condemn French Islamophobia.[41]

On both sides, the pan-Islamic propaganda of World War I contradicted the realities and aims of the warring empires. The Ottoman Empire was still recruiting its non-Muslim citizens, such as Armenians, Greeks, and Jews. In Gallipoli, multiethnic, religiously diverse Ottoman soldiers defeated the multiethnic, religiously diverse British Navy. Russian soldiers hailed from a large variety of ethnicities and followed many religions, although the army preferred not to order Muslim soldiers into battle against the Ottomans for fear of disloyalty.

These empires were not unaware of their own diversity. Indeed, Russian and Ottoman elites hoped they could overcome domestic fissures through wartime mobilization. However, the opposite happened: internal strife, combined with the trauma of war, shattered the Russian and Ottoman empires.[42]

The Ottoman ethnic cleansing of Anatolian Armenians in 1915 followed from no eternal religious hostility between Christians and Muslims. Rather, it came about as a long-term result of southeastern Europe's population politics—with Christian nationalist armies massacring Muslims and driving them out of Bulgaria, Romania, Greece, and elsewhere—as well as contingent events and decisions early in the war. Once the Armenians were subjected to mass murder and expulsion, Ottoman Greek citizens could not imagine their future in an empire ruled by Muslims. Both the call for *jihad* in the name of the Muslim world and the plan to minimize the Christian population of Anatolia were intended to save the empire. Instead, they brought about the end of the Ottoman Empire as it had existed for centuries.

While the Ottomans alienated internal minorities and abandoned earlier cosmopolitan imperial norms en route to defeat, the British betrayed their promises to large Muslim populations on the path to victory. When General Edmund Allenby entered the Old City of Jerusalem in December 1917, British journalists wrote of Crusader victory. Prime Minister David Lloyd George described the capture of Jerusalem as "a Christmas present for the British people," even though the British people—and military—included large numbers of Muslim and Hindu soldiers.[43] The Balfour Declaration, issued that same year, contradicted British promises that Palestine would be part of the future Arab kingdom. For Muslim supporters of the British war effort, the Balfour Declaration meant that the British Empire was choosing the interests of the imagined Jewish world over those of the equally imagined Muslim world by reserving Muslim-majority Palestine, and the holy city of Jerusalem, for Zionist political projects.

The British also broke their pledge to Sherif Hussein, king of Hejaz and leader of the British-allied Arab revolt against the Ottomans in Arabia. The British had promised Hussein that, after the war, he would rule a major Arab kingdom across the Middle East. But the Balfour Declaration and Sykes-Picot

Agreement scuttled that. This was no small breach of covenant. Hussein's rebellion had been a great achievement for British anti-*jihad* policies. It was the first instance of a Muslim revolt against a Muslim monarch since the rebellion of Muhammad Mahdi in Sudan during the 1880s. More important, Hussein's forces severed the Ottomans' physical connection to the holy cities of Mecca and Medina, eliminating a key dimension of the Ottoman claim to the caliphate: the sultan's sovereign rule over holy cities in Hejaz. When T. E. Lawrence and Sherif Hussein's son Faisal famously sabotaged the Hejaz Railway, which connected Medina to Damascus, they were, in a way, illustrating the power of British-controlled Indian Ocean networks and steamships over Ottoman-German-controlled railways. Ottoman railways had been financed largely by Indian Muslims under British rule, thus the Hejaz Railway connecting Damascus and Jerusalem with Medina was a symbol of global Muslim modernity, pan-Islamism, and British-Ottoman imperial harmony. The destruction of an Ottoman-owned, Indian Muslim–financed railway by British-supported Arab rebels was a critical blow to the caliphate, hollowing it from within. Yet the British failed to repay Hussein for engineering this massive victory.

Observing these dramatic events from afar, the begum (queen) of the Indian princely state of Bhopal noted that Mecca was still ruled by a Muslim, and it would be acceptable for Muslims if an Arab dynasty took over the caliphate.[44] Nothing like this happened. When the British effectively took Mecca, Medina, and Jerusalem out of Ottoman control, they also cut transit links between Medina and Jerusalem and refused the formation of an alternative Arab caliphate.

On the surface, the Allies, especially the British, emerged triumphant in the battle over the destiny of the Muslim world. But it was a misleading and costly victory. Indian Muslims began to see wartime and postwar British imperial policies as a betrayal of their contract. The British Empire won the war but lost the loyalty of its Muslim subjects.

Beyond Lenin and Wilson: The Pan-Islamic Moment of 1918–1924

Historians tend to think of the period following World War I as the beginning of the end of empire, when colonized peoples made strong turns toward, on the one hand, anti-imperial internationalism and, on the other, nationalism. In the East, Vladimir Lenin preached self-determination on the path to world proletarian revolution and the eventual merger of nations under a unitary socialist state. In the West, Woodrow Wilson promoted nationalist self-determination: independent nation-states interacting on a footing of legal equality.

Colonized Muslims—as well as leaders of Ottoman Turkey, Afghanistan, and Egypt—did try to use both Wilsonian and Bolshevik critiques of the existing world order to press claims for their rights on the international stage. But neither approach could fully articulate Muslim discontent about racialized empire. Some Indian Muslims joined Bolshevik movements, but from 1919 to 1924, Indian Muslim interest in Bolshevism was overshadowed by the Khilafat movement, a pan-Islamist effort to preserve the Ottoman caliphate. The flaws in Wilson's scheme were clear in his neglect of political issues important to Muslims and in his support for a defective League of Nations that perpetuated both imperialism and racial governance associated with it. In theory, the League was intended to maintain parity among independent states, but in effect it served a novel British and French strategy of imperial governance. New principles of self-determination demanded subtler justifications of colonialism in Arab, African, and Asian lands, and the League provided one with its Mandate system, an idea attributed to the South African statesmen Jan Smuts.[45] But Arab nationalists in former Ottoman territories understood that this was a new name for old colonialism. From their perspective, the Mandate system simply maintained the standard discriminatory discourses and practices against Muslims. It was an extension of the scramble for Africa to the Muslim-majority Near East.

Arab populations and other Muslim elites did try to use the Wilsonian idiom to articulate their demands, but they did so cannily and without erasing commitments to pan-Islamism. In fact, disillusionment with grand promises of liberation—whether Wilsonian self-determination or Bolshevik internationalism—buttressed the appeal of global Muslim solidarity in the post–World War I period.

One source of that disillusionment was Allied treatment of the Ottomans in peacetime. Wilsonianism initially seemed like an acceptable political vision for the Ottoman Muslim elite after the defeat of World War I, as they hoped for a Muslim-majority sovereign state in the rump of the empire. Leading intellectuals of the era formed a Wilsonian Principles Society in Istanbul, and the official Ottoman delegation at the Paris Peace Conference in 1919 argued for a Muslim-majority sovereign nation in post-Ottoman Turkey on the basis of Wilsonian values. But the August 1920 Sèvres Treaty, which created peace between victorious Allied powers and the Ottoman Empire, rejected that possibility. Instead, remaining Ottoman lands were divided into various Greek, Armenian, Italian, French, British, Kurdish, and Turkish zones.

The failure of Wilsonianism at Sèvres was particularly galling because the British not only rejected but actively undermined Turkish demands for sovereignty over the remaining Ottoman territories under Istanbul's control. Even before Sèvres, Greek armies had invaded western Anatolia in an attempt to secure

Ottoman territories promised to them by British prime minister Lloyd George. This triggered organized Ottoman Muslim resistance under the leadership of the nationalist Mustafa Kemal Atatürk. Turkish Muslim nationalists realized that Ottoman Turkey would be punished for being on the losing side in World War I, and neither Wilson nor victorious Allied leaders cared much about demands for a Muslim homeland in Turkey, which contradicted Armenian and Greek demands. Nationalists would have to fight Greek, French, and British forces to prevent the division of Turkey while formulating the legitimacy of a sovereign Muslim-majority state.

Atatürk and his friends immediately revived older tropes of Abdulhamid-era pan-Islamism by asking Indian Muslims to make financial contributions to their cause while pressuring the British government to withdraw support from the Greek Army invading Anatolia and recognize Turkish nationalist demands. Thus postwar Muslim-Turkish leaders sought aid from the Muslim world within the victorious British Empire without mentioning the word *jihad*.

With a Wilsonian deal for the Ottoman Empire rejected at Sèvres, and the future of the caliphate shrouded in ambiguity due to the British invasion of Istanbul, the moment was ripe for India's pan-Islamic Khilafat movement. These Indian Muslims sought to restore the Ottoman caliphate within the ambivalent postwar imperial system. Theirs was not the pan-Islamism of wartime Turkey, whose declaration of *jihad* was a matter of strategy, intended to turn Muslims globally against their British masters. This pan-Islamism reflected genuine anxiety about the destiny of the Muslim world and the Muslim race, which could no longer be represented by an independent empire ruled by a caliph. There was also deeply rooted support in India for the Ottoman caliph. He no longer ruled over Mecca, Medina, and Jerusalem, yet he was even more popular in British India in 1920 than in 1914.[46]

The Khilafat movement emphasized the implicit contract of World War I Muslim loyalty—namely that the victorious British Empire must honor Muslim sacrifices for their cause by respecting Muslim religious sensibilities and demands, as well as the holy sites. But after the war, the Allies occupied both Jerusalem and Istanbul. Greek armies, backed by Britain, were fighting Turks. Muslims all over the world detected betrayal, but Indian Muslims proved especially vocal and organized in protest.[47] They funded the Turkish nationalists' fight and sent a delegation to Paris to remind Wilson that his original Fourteen Points speech had promised independence and self-determination for "the Turkish portion of the present Ottoman Empire." It seemed that Wilson and his delegation forgot this part of the fourteen points, and it was the Indian Muslim delegation that was trying to remind them of this promise. There were, however, conflicting interpretations of what the Turkish portion included and of how to resolve Greek, Armenian, and Kurdish demands for self-determination conflicting with Turkey's. Both the American public and President Wilson wanted to see an Armenian state established in post-Ottoman Anatolia and to punish the "terrible Turks."[48]

Beyond offering material and moral support for Turkish sovereignty and independence, the Khilafat movement symbolized a desire for a collective deal on behalf of the imagined Muslim world. The goals were racial equality, justice, dignity, and empowerment for Muslims—within the imperial order. Postwar Muslim political demands were formulated in a hybrid language encompassing pan-Islamism, internationalism, Wilsonianism, and imperial civility.[49] For instance, during debates surrounding the convening of the Paris Peace Conference and formation of the League of Nations, influential Khilafat supporter Syed Ameer Ali focused on the neglect and subjugation of colonized Muslims. Drawing on earlier pan-Islamist arguments, he emphasized the past glories of Muslim civilization and the rationality of Islam to assert that Muslims were not inferior to white Christians. The Khilafat movement wished for Turkish sovereignty, but the goal wasn't nationalist success everywhere. It was the political and spiritual rebirth of the Ottoman Empire, with its unique position as champion of Muslim civilization.[50] Lothrop Stoddard, the white supremacist scholar of Muslim societies, thus noted a revival of Muslim world unity, not nationalist fragmentation, after World War I.[51]

South Asian financial aid was essential to the Muslim nationalist government in Ankara. So was moral support. Witnessing the Indian Muslim outpouring on behalf of an independent, sovereign Turkey fighting a Greek army backed by British imperialists, the Soviets endorsed the Turkish War of Independence on behalf of the oppressed Muslims of the world. At the Baku Congress of the Eastern Peoples in 1920, Soviet representatives encouraged colonized Muslims everywhere to revolt and win their emancipation from imperialists.[52]

This seeming alliance of Bolshevism and pan-Islamism paralyzed the British, who feared that the movement in India, supported by Hindu nationalists like Gandhi, would turn violent and upend the empire in South Asia. Worried British officers asked the nationalist government in Ankara and the caliph in Istanbul to encourage South Asian Muslim loyalty to the British Empire if they wanted to negotiate a deal with London.[53] But the pressure of Indian Muslim mobilization continued to mount as Turkish nationalists won battles over the Greeks and signed treaties with the Soviets and French. In 1923, with the Turks on their way to military victory and recognition by the Great Powers and pan-Islamic mobilization in South India frightening colonial officials, the British agreed to revise the terms of the Sèvres Treaty. The result was the Lausanne Treaty, ensuring Ankara's full sovereignty over remaining Ottoman territories in return for renunciation of all rights, claims, and privileges in former Ottoman territories in Iraq, Syria, Egypt, and Sudan.[54] The implicit bargain was that Turkey could be a Westphalian sovereign nation so long as the Ottoman Empire was relegated to the past. The new Turkey would have no transnational or imperial position.

Nationalist Turkey's diplomatic success might be construed as also the Muslim world's success. Indian Muslims had played a significant and direct role in bringing the British to the table at Lausanne. Fear of a worldwide Muslim turn to Bolshevism was also a factor. But at the same time, Turkey agreed to give up the temporal, imperial power that had mated sultan with caliph, lending geopolitical heft to Ottoman leadership of the imagined Muslim world. So while the body of the imaginary Muslim world came to Turkey's aid, Turkey seemed ready to cut off the head.

Abolishing the Caliphate

The stripping of the caliphate's worldly position was not forced on Turkey. In fact, on November 1, 1922, before the Lausanne Treaty, the Ankara government abolished the Ottoman Dynasty, thereby depriving the caliph of his titles as sultan and khan.[55] Sultan Vahdettin, the last Ottoman monarch, remained caliph for seventeen days before leaving the country. After that, Turkey's Parliament became the first representative council to elect a caliph, choosing Vahdettin's cousin Abdulmecid. This new instance of the caliphate was akin to a Muslim papacy, located in Istanbul, and it continued to enjoy immense prestige and respect among Muslims, including Shias and Ismailis, in Africa, Asia, and Central Asia.

But Turkey's leaders had to consider the downside too. The caliphate in Istanbul claimed spiritual authority over several hundred million Muslims, a majority of them under foreign colonial rule. The caliphate no longer had physical jurisdiction over any Muslim holy sites. Turkey itself held sovereignty over only eight million people in Anatolia. As Atatürk later noted, it was unreasonable that eight million Turkish Muslims should host an internationally significant caliphate capable of interfering in the affairs of British colonial domains home to more about one hundred million Muslims.[56]

Realpolitik weighed heavily against maintaining even the formally spiritual caliphate. Some Turkish leaders argued, from religious and secular perspectives, that the new caliphate still offered leverage in Turkey's relations with the great powers. It could be a diplomatic blessing empowering the new sovereign state rather than a liability. But meddling in the affairs of imperial subjects might also impose severe burdens on Ankara's foreign policy just as the terms of Lausanne demonstrated that Turkey was expected to stay out of imperial politics.

The caliph was also a potential danger because Europeans perceived him as the leader of the Muslim geopolitical threat at the heart of their racist imaginings. Leaving the caliph behind would be an opportunity to secure sovereignty against the aggression of discriminatory European powers. The diplomat and writer Valentine Chirol, one of Britain's leading Anglo-Saxon supremacists and Islamophobes, explained the rationale: "The new Turkish State is a Republic, and has proclaimed itself a lay republic, which is the very negation of Islam. . . . The attitude of other Powers toward it will be determined no longer, as in recent years, by the weight of Mahomedan sentiment, real or artificial, mobilized in its favour."[57] André Servier, whose 1923 *Islam and the Psychology of the Musulman* formulated one of the most systematic accounts of French imperial racism against

Muslims, likewise argued that the French should treat Republican Turkey differently because "in the Musulman world the Arab is an element of disorder, the Turk is an element of stability."[58] Many Turkish republican leaders thought that the new state's legitimacy would be harmed if Turkey were viewed as the leader of the Muslim world. They preferred a firm embrace of Western civilization—impossible with the caliph in Istanbul.

Alongside concerns about the trouble a globe-straddling caliph might cause, Turkey's republican leadership didn't see a great deal of good emerging from it. For one thing, in the postwar milieu, there was little point in maintaining an institution whose role was to promote cosmopolitan governance. Recall that the caliphate had been a vehicle for asserting Ottoman equality with competing empires. All were universal institutions, governing diverse societies. But the Ottoman Empire was over, and nationalist fervor had effectively brought an end to cosmopolitanism. The Balkan Wars and ethnic cleansing of Anatolian Armenians demonstrated as much. Lausanne resulted in additional homogeneity, as Atatürk's diplomats negotiated a population exchange with President Eleftherios Venizelos of Greece. Greek Muslims would immigrate to Turkey, while Anatolian Greek Christians would be resettled in Greece. The plan further entrenched Christian-Muslim identity conflicts, but this was a side effect. The population transfer was arranged by secular Turks such as Atatürk, who was born in the Greek-ruled city of Thessaloniki, and the secular Greek head of state, Venizelos, from cosmopolitan, formerly Ottoman, Crete, with the blessing of a Swedish Nobel Peace Prize winner, Fridtjof Nansen. The plan had no theological basis and was intended, in the realpolitik terms that had once inspired the caliphate, simply to ensure the geopolitical stability Turkey needed in order to build its new state.

The realism of the new Turkish Muslim elite owed something to the lessons of Abdulhamid, who had promoted the caliphate's spiritual sovereignty in order to gain British support against the Russian Empire. But by the time of the Lausanne Treaty, the Soviets were in Turkey's corner. In the absence of a Russian imperial threat to Turkey, a British alliance was largely irrelevant. Thus special ties between Indian Muslims and the caliphate offered few gains. The golden age of pan-Islamism based on an Ottoman-British alliance had, in any case, been irreparably damaged by the World War I declaration of *jihad* and by the Arab revolt. It was not clear that a caliphate could support strengthened British-Turkish ties, even in theory. Thus another past benefit of the caliphate was no more.

Turkish leaders had any number of strategic reasons to believe the caliphate's time had come. On March 3, 1924, Turkish parliamentary deliberations on the caliphate came to a close. After centuries in Istanbul, the institution was abolished by majority vote and the last caliph exiled to France. Muslims outside Turkey protested the decision but accepted its legitimacy. They did not try to invite the exiled caliph to their country or follow him as a caliph in exile. Later conferences aimed at instituting a caliphate, discussed in Chapter 5, tried to establish a new lineage, distinct from the Ottoman caliphate.

Abolition of the caliphate brought to an end a half century of global Muslim political thought tied to the model of Ottoman modernism. The caliphate may not have had the same meaning throughout history, but between 1880 and the 1920s, it clearly had become a repository for Muslim demands under empire. Imperial globalization had established across Muslim societies intellectual and political networks that transmitted progressive ideas such as legal modernism, constitutionalism, abolition of slavery, and increased rights for women. The endorsement of these ideas by the caliph-sultan empowered reformist Muslim elites in Afghanistan, Persia, and Egypt. But the idea of a Muslim world could have emerged even without Ottoman leadership or a caliph in Istanbul. The construction of the Muslim world was a product of Muslim subjecthood under empire and a means to criticize European racism. Pan-Islamism responded to Orientalism and social Darwinism, asserting that Muslims were also civilized and deserved dignified treatment. The caliphate and the Ottoman Empire simply served as hubs for the larger network expressing these claims. The Ottoman Empire did not attempt to represent the world's Muslims because it could fairly do so but because it was strategically wise, given imperial entanglements. Thus the same pan-Islamic nerve system continued to operate after the caliphate, but without the influence of imperial cosmopolitanism and great power leadership.

After abolition of the caliphate, the Republic of Turkey played a key role in the political imagination of other Muslim societies, illustrating the persistence of pan-Islamic ideas and politics. More than Lenin and Wilson, it was Atatürk and his reforms that shaped the political imagination of Muslim societies. Indonesian Muslim elites followed the developments in Turkey closely, and Sukarno advocated a secular Muslim nation modeled on Atatürk's. King Amanullah of Afghanistan also looked up to Atatürk and the Turkish model as an inspiration for reform.[59] Turkey itself gestured toward its imperial past and Muslim identity. For example, in 1930, when France wanted to celebrate the centennial of the invasion of Algeria, the Turkish Foreign Ministry barred its representatives from participating.

Pan-Islamism and Islamic nationalism survived the caliphate in part because they addressed continuing problems. The majority of the world's Muslims still lived under racialized

European empires, and rights claims in the name of the broad racial and civilizational Muslim world were still being suppressed.[60] Thus geopolitical struggles over the future of the Muslim world would continue during the interwar period. But they would not be unchanged. New political circumstance erased the earlier imperial context from memory. Pan-Islamism would take many different paths through the interwar years and into World War II. In this period, it often served, still, as a tool in geopolitical conflict, albeit on fresh terms.

Yet simmering always underneath the strategic machinations would be the enduring source of pan-Islamism's appeal: the struggle for the dignity of Muslim populations suffering colonial oppression. The British may have hoped their Muslim problem was solved by the collapse of the Ottoman Empire and the abolition of its caliphate, but during the interwar period they would come to realize that the caliph was but a messenger and symbol of an imagined unity. Racialized Muslim subjects remained the real heart and animating force of pan-Islamism.

Muslim Politics
of the Interwar Period
(1924–1945)

On August 18, 1944, Abdurreşid Ibrahim, a leading pan-Islamic intellectual and activist, was buried in the Muslim section of the Tama Reien Cemetery, just outside Tokyo. It was a humble ceremony.

Ibrahim had been many places. He was born in Imperial Russia and educated in the prestigious Muslim cities of Mecca, Medina, and Istanbul. He traveled widely in China, Central Asia, and farther in the East, writing about the lives of Muslims under colonial rule. During World War I, he responded to the call for *jihad* and fought for the Ottoman cause as a propagandist. In 1933, he moved to Tokyo, where he became a leader of the local Tatar Muslim community.

It may seem odd. Why was an influential pan-Islamist living in World War II–era Tokyo? The two decades after the abolition of the Ottoman caliphate in 1924 were full of uncertainty and the complex repositioning of world powers—and people. Muslim intellectuals of the interwar period, such as Ibrahim, found themselves involved in a truly global debate on the idea of the Muslim world, whose meanings and purposes were constantly altered by geography, politics, local history, and apparent strategic necessity. Ibrahim's activities during the period speak to this variety and flux. He was one of a number of pan-Islamists who, convinced of the failure of nationalism, empire, and various internationalist models to improve the conditions of Muslims, worked in the Axis fold.

In the early years of the Turkish Republic, a time of cooperation and friendship with the Soviet Union, there was little room in either country for pan-Islamic activism. Both were busy with secular, modernizing programs, and the Soviets sought to transform and refashion the lives of non-Russian minorities, frustrating the alternative political visions of pan-Islamists such as Ibrahim. After the failure of his struggles for Muslims' rights in the days after the Russian Revolution, Ibrahim emigrated to a small Turkish village, where he might have spent the last of his years with nothing much to do. Yet the pan-Islamic ideas to which he had long dedicated himself would find a new life in Japan. His patron was the Japanese Empire itself, which invited him in 1933 to support its challenge to the Eurocentric imperial world order.

While Ibrahim worked in Japan, one of his former collaborators in the Ottoman pan-Islamist campaign, Shakib Arslan, was in Europe trying to convince the other Axis powers, Italy and Germany, to help liberate the Muslim world from European colonial hegemony. Similarly, the former *mufti* of British Mandate Jerusalem, Amin al-Husseini, sought German sponsorship for his vision of a self-governing Palestine. The Germans and Japanese appreciated the power of a propaganda narrative centered on the oppression of Muslims. So did the Allies.

Throughout World War II, Britain, the Soviet Union, and the United States responded to Axis appeals with action and propaganda of their own. Joseph Stalin gave new freedoms to Muslims in the Soviet Union. Just a few years after the opening of the Tokyo Mosque in 1938, King George VI, with encouragement from Winston Churchill, donated valuable London real estate to the Muslim community for the construction of the Regent's Park Mosque.

The broad contours are strikingly like those of World War I, with the Germans actively courting Muslims and the Allies reacting. Yet it would be misleading to imagine precise continuity between the two wars. As before, the Germans and their allies did hope to empower themselves and weaken their enemies by wooing the Muslim subjects of Western empires, and the Allies responded with their own overtures. But much had changed in the intervening years. The deal at Lausanne between the British Empire and Turkey revealed the illusion of Muslim-world unity, even if the Axis preferred not to see it. After the abolition of the caliphate, Muslim societies explored many political options, governed by no pattern. Some Muslims remained loyal to their colonial masters and put their hopes in progress within the imperial systems. Others, more nationalist in spirit, supported self-strengthening and modernization, seeking redemption from perceived underdevelopment, disempowerment, and decline. Turkey, Iran, and Afghanistan pursued authoritarian modernization. Soviet Muslims embraced secular anti-imperialism. Saudis and Yemenis tried their hands at a Salafist monarchy.

The interwar period provided a short-lived opportunity to reframe the international politics of Muslim societies. Rather than a story of clashing civilizations, the narrative might have shifted permanently toward justice within the global order, whether Muslims were colonial subjects or free to rule their own states. The idea of the Muslim world could have faded away as diverse Muslim societies worked toward diverse ends.

But as the efforts of Ibrahim, Arslan, and Husseini during World War II attest, this is not what happened. Pan-Islamic thought survived the multiplicity of the interwar years, returning in much the same shape it took at its peak during and immediately after World War I. Racialized concepts of Muslim decline, along with geopolitical discourse on the collective destiny of Muslims in relation to Western Christian empires, continued to circulate and would eventually drive the strategic thinking of the Great Powers once more.

What revived the illusion of the Muslim world was not only the persistence of shallow imperial notions of Muslim unity but also subaltern appeals to Muslim internationalism. Imperial, liberal, and socialist internationalism had failed to respond to the demands of various Muslims for equality, dignity, and political empowerment. When interwar European powers rejected Muslim demands for rights and self-determination, only some activists sought alliances with the Axis powers, which shared their geopolitical fantasy. These activists tended to be older and relatively weak; Ibrahim and Arslan relied on pan-Islamism to cover up their lack of grassroots support. In reality, the majority of Muslim combatants in World War II fought for Britain, the Soviet Union, and France. But the Allies took pan-Islamist claims seriously, hence their concessions in response to Axis propaganda. Once again, the Great Powers and self-appointed representatives of colonized Muslims worked in parallel, each advancing racialized illusions of a unified Muslim world.

A Body with No Head? The Caliphate Unclaimed

The pan-Islamic triumph at Lausanne, where Indian support enabled Turkish diplomatic victories, proved short-lived, undone when the new Turkish state traded away the caliphate for territorial sovereignty. Thereafter attempts to reconstitute the caliphate in the absence of the Ottoman Empire were fruitless. The political interests of interwar Muslim societies were simply too diverse to enable consensus or even robust coalition when it came to the installation of a new caliph.

On March 5, 1924, just two days after the Turkish National Assembly's decision to abolish the caliphate, Sherif Hussein of Mecca proclaimed his status as the new caliph. But he received little support among Muslim populations outside of Mecca and Medina. Given Hussein's collaboration with the British against the Ottomans, South and Southeast Asian Muslims, strong supporters of the former caliphate, were especially ill disposed. Others joined in. On March 10, Egyptian religious scholars announced their opinion that a congress in Cairo must discuss the future of the caliphate. The deposed caliph, Abdulmecid Efendi, also supported the idea of a congress and even suggested that a new caliph be democratically elected by representatives of Muslim societies all over the world.[1] Egypt's King Fuad sponsored such a congress in Cairo in May 1926, where he hoped to be made caliph. But his political leadership was also tainted due to his status as a monarch under British protection, and the congress participants did not even discuss King Fuad's caliphate ambitions.

Hussein was planning his own caliphate congress in Mecca, coinciding with the pilgrimage season of 1925, when the city was captured by Abdulaziz Ibn Saud, sultan of Najd and future king of Saudi Arabia. The Saudi-Wahhabi movement was not interested in the idea of a caliphate, which for them symbolized their former enemy, the Ottoman Empire. After all, it was the military forces of the Ottoman caliph that suppressed the earlier Saudi state, and the caliph sultans in Istanbul represented the cosmopolitan Muslim culture that Wahhabi ideology denounced as a deviation from the true principles of Islam. The major concern of the Saudi Muslim congress, held in 1926, was administration of the pilgrimage under the new government, not the caliphate. Even though Ibn Saud and future Saudi monarchs were not interested in being caliph, their names were occasionally discussed for this position. Yet they were even less likely than Hussein to receive widespread transnational Muslim support for caliphate claims due to Wahhabism's anti-Shia and anti-Sufi biases.

Candidates for the caliphate lacked qualities essential to the role. None could claim to represent the opinion of Muslims globally. And none led a great Muslim empire, which had been essential to the popularity of the Ottoman caliphate.[2] In the 1920s, dynastic rulership still mattered. The failure to institute a new caliphate illustrates how important the titles of khan and sultan—and the royal lineage they implied—were in buttressing the legitimacy of Ottoman caliphate claims.

Some Muslim thinkers, such as the Egyptian Ali Abd al-Raziq, sought to justify the new, caliphate-free circumstance. In 1925, he published a tract arguing for the religious contingency of the caliphate. He tried to convince his readers that the practice of caliphate that developed after the death of the Prophet Muhammad in 622 was not a religious obligation for Muslims, as it was not prescribed in the Quran. For him, that institution was based on the practical decisions of early Muslim communities, and contemporary Muslims could create another political system of their choosing. During the 1924 Turkish debates on the future of the caliphate, Seyyid Bey, a member of the Turkish Parliament with a background in Islamic law, made his own religious case against the necessity of the caliphate. This was by no means a majority position, however. Al-Azhar University, which hosted the Cairo caliphate congress in 1926 and was considered to be the center of religious authority in Egypt, condemned Raziq's book, demanded that it be banned, and declared his opinion invalid.[3] In his autobiography, Muslim Brotherhood founder Hasan al-Banna spoke for many when he worried about the future of Muslims in the absence of the caliphate and hoped for its reestablishment.

Yet the truest obstacles to the establishment of a new caliphate were not disagreement among leaders, intellectuals, or Muslim publics over the religious necessity and appropriate occupant of the role. One of the more significant barriers was lack of *political* necessity. Whatever its religious value, the caliphate had lost the strategic importance it enjoyed from the 1880s to 1914 in the context of Ottoman-British relations. Both before and after World War I, it was the British king, not any Muslim monarch, who ruled over the majority of Muslim societies. Loyalty to a caliph in Istanbul afforded Muslims ruled by Christians some leverage over their colonial masters. The globalization of the caliphate in the late Ottoman era was never a result of theological imperatives but rather an instrumental change enabling struggles for rights within European empires. It was a contingent feature of a Eurocentric imperial world in which the Ottomans were still a force to be reckoned with. With the Ottoman Empire disintegrated, and the new Turkish Republic in the good graces of both big Western imperial powers and the Soviet Union, the political utility of the caliphate was dramatically reduced.

Another major political impediment to renewal of the caliphate was the new Saudi state's control of Mecca and Medina. For almost a century, the British had blamed Muslim rebellions in their dominions on Wahhabi influence, yet British officers in Egypt and India arrived at an understanding with the Saudi state and discarded their former collaborator, the Hashemite kingdom of Sherif Hussein. Thus the new Saudi ruler of the holy cities was entrenched, and the vision of a great Arab kingdom and caliphate under Hashemite leadership was abandoned.[4] Saudi control of Mecca and Medina was traumatic for South

Asian and African Muslims, threatening the many Sufi orders, charities, and *madrasas* in Mecca and Medina funded by Muslims from afar. Wahhabis also restricted Muslim practices, breaking down distant connections to the holy lands, where previously pilgrims could perform diverse observances, such as visitations to the shrines of early Muslims. All the shrines and tombs of early Muslims, except Muhammad's, were demolished by the new Saudi government. More important, protection of Mecca and Medina was essential to caliphate claims, yet the Saudi dynasty was not interested in the title. Indian Muslim leaders imagined the creation of a Meccan republic as an alternative, but without British support this vision could never be realized.[5]

But while the head of the Muslim world had disappeared, unlikely to return, the body—the global Muslim network—remained, carrying on the legacy of the 1873–1924 period. Anti-imperial visions combined nationalism with pan-Islamic yearning, sometimes, still, yearning for the caliphate. For example, in 1928, Malaysians concerned about British foresting policies in the Terengganu region raised the Ottoman flag in protest.[6] Indonesians experienced deepening nationalism but never lost ties to Indian Ocean Muslims, Arabia, and Egypt.[7] The end of the Ottoman Empire, coupled with the model of the new Turkish nation-state, encouraged nationalist versions of globalized Muslim identity, and soon Muslim publics gave up on the idea of reinstituting the caliphate. Yet ideas about Muslim solidarity continued to be crucial in attracting transnational sympathies to Moroccan Muslims' military struggles against Spain and France between 1921 and 1926. The anticolonial revolt of the Rif Republic in northwestern Morocco mobilized pan-Islamic and pan-Arab networks.[8] Indian Muslims tried to send funds to rebels and proposed solidarity with them during the 1926 Muslim world congress in Mecca. Similarly, when Chinese and Uighur Muslims of East Turkestan established the short-lived East Turkestan Muslim Republic in 1933, they sought support from the imaginary Muslim world by sending emissaries and letters to assorted Muslim countries and organizations.

Interwar Visions of the Muslim World

One of the most influential pan-Islamic ideas to emerge from the collapse of the caliphate was commitment to Arab leadership of the imagined Muslim world. This combined a vision for the Muslim world with ethnic nationalism. While the Ottoman caliphate was still viable, the key organizers of pan-Islamic projects operated along an axis from South Asia to Istanbul. After the caliphate, pan-Islamists such as Rashid Rida began looking to the Arab Middle East as the new heart of the pan-Islamic network.[9]

As editor of the influential *al-Manar* journal in Cairo, the Lebanese Egyptian Rida was a central figure of pan-Islamic networks. During his travels in South Asia before World War I, Rida was hosted by *al-Manar* readers in almost every city he visited. He had also been a champion of the Ottoman caliphate, only wishing that the Ottoman administration in Istanbul would open itself to the participation of more Arab subjects. In his critique of the Young Turk rule from 1908 to 1914, he sought decentralization of the empire but without challenging the legitimacy of the Ottoman caliph. Until World War I, he continued to promote ways to maintain the caliph in Istanbul, even as he promoted autonomy for imperial territories.[10]

When the Ottoman Empire was defeated in the war, Rida had to look elsewhere for pan-Islamic leadership. First he embraced the Arab nationalist cause of Hashemite prince Faisal. He hoped that Prince Faisal's new Syrian Arab state would lead to a greater Arab unity and would prevent further British and

French colonization of post-Ottoman Arab lands. This hope was dashed, however, by the secret Sykes-Picot Agreement of 1916, which, as Rida came to discover, meant that the prince was not in fact in charge. He was ousted from Damascus, and his Arab state proved short-lived, as Sykes-Picot promised Syria to the French. After 1926 Rida turned to the leadership of the Saudi king. He thought that if Faisal—by this point serving as Iraq's king under British patronage—Yemen's Imam Yahya, and other Arab rulers cooperated with the Saudis, they might forge unity among Arab Muslims. But these monarchs could not agree on alliance, frustrating Rida's vision of Arab unity as the core of a future pan-Islamic international solidarity. In the early 1930s, beset by failure, he lamented that even the arrogance of Turkish nationalists would have been better than the humiliation of living under the rule of Christian imperialism.

Formerly an ardent Ottomanist, Shakib Arslan similarly tried to create an Arab federation in the post-Ottoman Middle East by cementing alliance among the kings of Iraq, Saudi Arabia, and Yemen.[11] This was an impossible task given the rivalries between the Sherifid and Saudi dynasties over leadership in Arabia, but Arslan tried to mediate and kept the idea alive for some time by writing about it in the journal he published. He also took financial support from the Egyptian khedive Abbas Hilmi II, who hoped that Arslan would use his extensive pan-Islamic network to endorse the khedive as king of Syria once the French Mandate ended. Had Arslan's impractical dreams been realized, he would have brought together an Arab-ruled coalition extending from North Africa to the Indian Ocean, though it was not clear which Arab king he really favored for the leadership of this imagined Arab-Muslim zone.

Iraq's British-installed King Faisal had different ideas, though he too envisioned an Arab kingdom. The difference is that he had made peace with the era's imperialism. He hoped that a new

Arab state would emerge from the ashes of war—under the umbrella of a British imperial world order.

That these attempts at crafting Muslim unity focused on Arab kingdoms and took no input from South Asian Muslims illustrates a key contradiction of interwar pan-Islamism. A new caliph or Muslim-world leader would, more sensibly, have been found in British India, where the Muslim population was wealthier and more numerous. Nizam of Hyderabad was arguably a more appropriate candidate. He ruled a territory as large as France and was one of the world's wealthiest monarchs. A patron of many prominent Muslim intellectuals, Nizam financed Muslim charities from Mecca and Jerusalem to England. His capital hosted a vibrant university and international journals. At least one prominent pan-Islamist of the twentieth century, Abul Ala Maududi, put his hopes in Nizam and worked in his service in the 1930s. But British control over India meant that Nizam, with only a limited sovereignty over his state of Hyderabad, would never be taken seriously as a claimant to the caliphate. He arranged the marriage of his son with the daughter of the deposed Ottoman caliph in the early 1930s, but still he lacked full sovereignty and never received much consideration as a possible caliph.

Alongside assorted Arab-centered nationalist visions, Muslims promoted modernizing projects oriented toward the West. Iran, one of the sovereign Muslim-majority states, was a founding member of the League of Nations. Albania was the second Muslim-majority country to join the League, claiming that the unique and liberal Bektashi Sufi order to which most Albanian Muslims belonged was compatible with European civilization. In the early 1930s the Afghani and Iranian rulers visited Ankara to consult with Mustafa Kemal and observe the radical nationalist reforms under way in Turkey. Although pan-Islamists became disillusioned with Kemalist policies that disconnected

Turkey from the rest of Muslim-majority societies—such as replacing the Ottoman Turkish alphabet with the Latin script—Turkish sovereignty nonetheless was a model for many other Muslim nationalists.

For instance, in 1923 Muhammad Reza, the general who deposed the Persian Qajar dynasty, entertained the idea of creating an Iranian republic, as in Turkey. However, after the abolition of the caliphate, segments of the Iranian population, especially clergy, worried about the secularizing impact of the Turkish model. They preferred to crown Muhammad Reza as shah and monarch of Persia rather than risk a secular republic.[12] Also in 1923, Afghanistan's reformist and pan-Islamic King Amanullah Khan oversaw the creation of his country's first constitution, empowered by pro-Turkish and pro-caliphate public opinion. This Afghan constitution was inspired by Ottoman legal modernism as well as Indian Muslim modernism; Ottoman and Indian intellectuals helped draft the document. Again, though, news of the caliphate's abolition undermined the legitimacy of reform, and the constitution was revised several times for fear of secularism and Westernization. Amanullah Khan maintained his links with Atatürk, but the Afghan public was disillusioned by perceived Turkish nationalist betrayal of the caliphate. Mid-1930s Muslim public opinion in India was more sanguine. Atatürk, Amanullah Khan, Reza Shah, and the king of Saudi Arabia were all considered "great Muslim dictators" and sources of pride.[13] Even where Turkish reforms were not popular, they reinforced Muslim-world thinking by spurring debates on the appropriateness of Kemalist methods for the empowerment of Muslims across the globe.[14]

All of the diverse nationalist and self-strengthening movements of the interwar era were connected to discourses of Islamic civilization, especially in their challenge to Eurocentric notions of civilization and race. Indeed, belief in the existence of a Muslim world in need of saving, uplifting, and liberating grew stronger during the interwar period. Thus even among the reformist elites of Turkey, Iran, Albania, and Saudi Arabia, the historical memory of an unreliable, sinister imperialist West survived along with Muslim-world identity. These notions were reproduced and transmitted in national school curricula, often in complex tension and affinity with nation-state-centered historical narratives. Given the diversity of anticolonial histories, it should come as no surprise that civilizational conceptions of the Muslim world supported a range of responses to Darwinian discourses of Muslim inferiority and Orientalist discourses of Muslim backwardness.

One of these responses—popular among some radical nationalist movements, such as Kemalism—was antitraditionalism, which saw in old-line Muslim practices the source of Islamic civilization's backwardness. For adherents of this view, a Westernizing project was the solution. Republican Turkey became a symbol of such self-strengthening Westernization. In addition to radical secular reforms at home, Turkey distanced itself culturally from the rest of the imagined Muslim world in an effort to escape geopolitical Islamophobia. Writings on Islamic civilization and Islam as a world religion were essential to this process, allowing Turkish leaders to justify the idea that Islamic civilization was distinctive but backward and had to be discarded and replaced with something in the superior Western mold. Turkish Westernization did not challenge the notions of the Western and Muslim worlds; rather, it claimed that Turkey could leave the Muslim world for the West by revising its government, legal institutions, and culture. Turkey starkly illustrates the fact that the idea of the Muslim world did not disappear amid nationalism.[15]

The strengthening of nationalist claims among Muslims after World War I was critically influenced by the civilizational discourse inherent in Europe's own increasingly fervent nationalism and racism. Western publics and some elites were so chauvinistic about their civilization and religion that they embarrassed pro-imperial leaders. A good example can be seen in the 1930s Eucharistic Congress of Catholic Clergy held in the Tunisian city of Carthage. The congress was partly hosted by the city's Muslim elites, and the Muslim ruler of the French Protectorate of Tunis, Ahmad II (r. 1929–1942), was its honorary president. French colonial officers themselves were interested in integration, the age-old imperative of empire. Thus they were careful to observe a secular separation of church and state and avoided provoking Christian missionary zeal toward the Muslim majority. Yet the weeklong event saw multiple offensive anti-Muslim acts. Catholic youths in Crusader outfits marched in the streets to celebrate the centennial of the French invasion of Algeria. Catholic pamphlets in Arabic tried to convince Muslims to convert. A public sermon by papal legate Cardinal Alexis Lépicier described the darkening effects of Islam upon North African history and civilization. This inflammatory anti-Muslim rhetoric, along with celebration of the French Empire in North Africa as an extension of the Crusades, humiliated the Eucharistic Congress's Muslim patrons. For young intellectuals such as Habib Bourguiba, who would later rule Tunisia for some thirty years, this was a moment of nationalist awakening.[16]

During the interwar period, several themes solidified in Muslim-world thinking, sometimes in response to the kind of chauvinism on display in Tunis. One was the discourse of victimhood, discrimination, and betrayal by European empires. Certainly some colonized Muslims felt the sting of discrimination long before the interwar period, but victimhood was previously a less forceful position. For example, a sizable portion of Muslims in British-ruled India did not see themselves as victims of empire; they foresaw a future for Muslims within an imperial framework. But after the traumatic events of 1914–1924, the narrative of victimhood at the hands of Western empires became increasingly dominant among Muslims.

Meanwhile, Soviet reforms, like Turkish reforms, fostered another secular modernist strand in interwar Muslim thought and led to ideological divisions absent from pan-Islamism in the imperial age. Despite slogans about the incompatibility between Islam and communism, a significant group of Muslims believed Bolshevik visions of world order and Soviet reforms for Muslim citizens served general Muslim interests. There was clearly no single Muslim view of Bolshevism, and attitudes toward Muslim experience under Soviet rule were as varied as Muslim populations' attitudes toward other political issues. There were Muslim communists, for example, who especially noted the public visibility, unveiling, and educational advancements of Muslim women in the Soviet Union.

European empires responded to the crisis of their eroding legitimacy with multiple conciliatory gestures, which themselves reinforced a kind of Muslim-world thinking. During the 1930s, the British tried to add as many Muslim-majority countries as possible to the League of Nations, which represented British imperial internationalism against the alternative visions of Germany, the Soviet Union, and the Japanese Empire. The hope was to revive the kind of transnational Muslim cooperation that saw itself as a friend to empire. Thus, in the 1937–1938 term, the Indian Muslim Agha Khan III was president of the League's General Assembly.[17] Khan, who had formerly supported the Khilafat movement on behalf of Indian Muslims despite his unquestioned loyalty to the British Empire, did not see a contradiction in his loyalty to empire, leadership in the League, and championing of global Muslim identity and causes. Turkey and Iraq joined the League in 1932, followed by Afghanistan in 1934 and Egypt in 1937. Iraq's King Faisal and Egypt's

Khedive Farouq envisioned a future in which their countries would gain full sovereignty, and the League and British Empire seemed like mechanisms for making that happen.

After the abolition of the caliphate, Europeans and Americans continued to foster racial and geopolitical images of the Muslim world that influenced Muslim-world thinking within and outside of Muslim-majority societies. Texts such as Basil Matthews's *Young Islam on Trek: A Study in the Clash of Civilizations* insisted on the Islam-versus-West framework.[18] Matthews traveled in Muslim societies on behalf of the London Missionary Society and after 1924 worked at the Geneva headquarters of the World Alliance of Young Men's Christian Associations. In his book, Matthews draws an equivalency between religion and civilization. Noting rapid modernization in Muslim societies— full of combustion energy, steamships and railways, telegraph cables, telephones, wireless radio; enamored of Western cinema and novels—he asked, "If the civilization of Moslem lands breaks up, what will happen to the Faith of Islam?"[19]

Matthews also conflates religion and geopolitics: because Muslims fought on both sides during World War I, "the war divided the Moslem World."[20] He considered pan-Islamism the necessary political identity of every Muslim. He therefore saw nationalism as having a negative impact on the Muslim faith and tradition. Even though pan-Islamism and nationalism did not seem contradictory to Muslims espousing them, for European and American observers of Muslim societies, nationalism undermined essential Muslim unity. Matthews felt similarly about Western-inspired secularizing reforms, as in republican Turkey. "Islam really liberalized is simply a non-Christian Unitarianism," he wrote. "It ceases to be essential Islam."[21]

Similar convictions are found throughout interwar-era European and American writings, which packaged Islamic civilization, history, and faith tradition in the idea of the Muslim world. Thus Turkish secularism was a new experiment in the Muslim world, as was Soviet policy toward Muslims within the Soviet Union and beyond. Books such as Samuel Zwemer's *Across the World of Islam* (1925) and Hamilton Gibb's *Wither Islam? A Survey of Modern Movements in the Moslem World* (1932) tried to identify commonalities among Muslims in the middle of chaotic political developments. Charles Adams's *Islam and Modernism in Egypt: A Study of the Modern Reform Movement Inaugurated by Muhammad Abduh* (1933) likened the Muslim reformism to the Protestant Reformation within Christianity, and praised it. Thomas Arnold's *Legacy of Islam* (1937), and Gibb's *Modern Trends in Islam* (1945) closely intertwined Muslim faith, Islamic civilization, and the geopolitics of interwar-era Muslim societies.

Publications by Muslim authors also contributed to this canon. Abdullah Yusuf Ali's *The Message of Islam* (1940), Muhammad Iqbal's *The Reconstruction of Religious Thought in Islam* (1934), Muhammad Asad's *Islam at the Crossroads* (1934), Abul Ala Maududi's *Towards Understanding Islam: A Step towards the Study and Better Understanding of the Religion and Teachings of Islam* (1940), and Choudhary Rahmat Ali's *The Millat of Islam and the Menace of Indianism* (1941), along with Theosophist Annie Besant's *Beauties of Islam* (1932), all tried to articulate the unity of Muslim political ideas, aesthetics, and values, even as Muslim societies were exhibiting profound diversity in lifestyles and politics.

From Monarchy to "Islamic State"

Even though post-caliphate Muslim intellectuals tried to articulate a new political vision in harmony with racialized Muslim identity, we should not assume this vision was anything like the nation-state-based Islamism of later Cold War years. Much change and experimentation lay on the road between. Interwar Muslim political thought was eclectic, and it adapted to the age of nationalism gradually and nonlinearly, not giving up on the imperial era notions of Muslim kingship. The work of four interwar Muslim political thinkers considered key theorists of an Islamic state—Muhammad Asad, Hasan al-Banna, Abul Ala Maududi, and Shakib Arslan—illustrates just how far the politics of Muslim identity traveled and across what varied terrain.

Muhammad Asad was an Austrian Jewish journalist who converted to Islam in 1926 after he had spent several years living in Arab cities. After his conversion, Asad moved to Hejaz and Najd and soon became a close confident of King Saud. In European magazines Asad wrote approvingly about the emerging Saudi state. He believed King Saud would be an enlightened leader who found inspiration in both Muslim tradition and modern ideas. But Asad became disillusioned with the slow pace of reforms and traditionalism in the Saudi kingdom, and in 1932 he left Najd for British-ruled India. There he taught in different educational institutions and contributed to *Islamic Culture,* an international journal financed by Nizam of Hyderabad. In India, Asad developed a rapport with influential intellectuals such as the poet and scholar Muhammad Iqbal. In 1934 Asad published his first major text, *Islam at the Crossroads,* an anticolonial tract that categorically rejected Western imperialism and Orientalism as continuations of Crusader hostility.[22] He urged Muslims not to imitate the West but to restore their heritage. Asad had become convinced that revival was the precondition of Muslims' independence and agency.[23]

After World War II, Asad participated in the movement for the creation of Pakistan, which he thought could be an instrument of Muslim reform, the revival of the true spirit of the Muslim faith. He joined the Pakistani Foreign Service in 1949 and in 1952 became a diplomat to the United Nations. He eventually resigned from this position and dedicated the rest of his life to research and writing on modern Islamic thought. *The Message of the Quran*, his English translation with commentary, was partly subsidized by Saudi prince Faisal. This and his autobiography, *The Road to Mecca*, were highly successful, and Asad became a well-known transnational Muslim intellectual.[24]

What is crucial in this biography is Asad's shifting political commitments. Once convinced of the harmony between the Arabian monarchy and the Muslim faith tradition, he later pursued a more systematic notion of republican Muslim government, embodied in Pakistan. In 1957 Asad wrote *Principles of State and Government in Islam*, this time affirming accord between Islam and the modern nation-state.[25] Throughout his life, then, Asad struggled with the relationship between Islam and assorted political structures, from kingdoms to nation-states. That is, for this devoted and learned Muslim, text and tradition did not demand any one sort of politics. It was possible, depending on circumstance, to support a variety of political projects while retaining strong religious commitment.

While Asad explored the relationship between Islam and multiple state formations, Hasan al-Banna, an Egyptian who founded the Muslim Brotherhood in 1928, initially responded to the downfall of the Ottoman caliphate by promoting the empowerment of Egyptian monarchy as a first step for the liberation of Egypt and the rest of the Muslim world. Yet from its foundation as the Young Men's Muslim Association until al-Banna's assassination in 1948, the Muslim Brotherhood was less a project for Islamic government than an anticolonial nationalist organization that made recourse to pan-Islamic solidarity. Its biggest achievement was its philanthropic support for the Palestinian revolt in 1936. Al-Banna's main concern was to redeem Egyptian Muslim dignity. His followers were particularly enthusiastic about responding to Christian missionary activities.[26]

When al-Banna and the Brotherhood concerned themselves with governance, they preferred reformed Muslim monarchs. The Brotherhood sought to influence the monarchy rather than become involved in Egypt's complex parliamentary politics. Many in the Muslim Brotherhood saw Egypt's political parties and their parliamentary compromises as a corrupting influence on an idealized politics by wise and pious Muslim rulers.[27] Al-Banna himself was something of a pragmatist. He wanted to see a free Egypt led by more pious Muslims, but he didn't want to empower British imperialism by weakening existing Muslim rulers. Thus he still expected political leadership from the khedive, even as the dynasty's legitimacy was eroding.[28]

In South Asia, no one better represented the chaotic ambiguity of the post-caliphate Muslim political imagination than Abul Ala Maududi, founder of the Pakistani Muslim revivalist party Jamaat-e-Islami. Maududi was born in 1903 to a prominent family of Indian Muslims with roots in both the former Mughal imperial capital of Delhi and the princely state of Hyderabad. In his youth, Maududi was a fez-wearing modernist. As part of his language studies, he translated Qasim Amin's *al Mir'ah al jadidah* (Modern women) from Arabic into Urdu when he was just eleven years old. After World War I he wrote a laudatory biography of Gandhi, who supported the Khilafat movement. In 1921, he began working for the journal *Muslim*, a magazine of the Jamiati Ulama-i Hind (Society of Ulama of India), which backed the Ottoman caliphate and Khilafat.[29]

Maududi also published articles in the journal *al-Jamiat* defending Turkey against European criticism. Two pamphlets, *The State of Christians in Turkey* and *Tyrannies of the Greeks in Smyrna*, both written in 1922, responded to pro-Greek and anti-Turkish British propaganda by Arnold Toynbee and his ilk. Maududi also translated an Arabic book by Mustafa Kamil, titled *al-Masala al Sharqiyah* (The Eastern question), which tied European anti-Ottoman diplomacy to racialization of Muslims and Islamophobia.

At this point, Maududi was a pan-Islamist in the mode of Khilafat. A modernist, he believed that a strong Muslim dynasty, holding the title of the caliphate, in Istanbul was the best means by which to represent the interests of Muslims under colonial rule. But when the caliphate was abolished, Maududi rethought his political priorities. He began to blame both nationalism and Westernization for the collapse of the caliphate. Neither position was at odds with the Khilafat movement, but nor had antinationalism and anti-Westernization been Khilafat's major concerns. He also began to worry about the future of India's Muslims amid a Hindu-led nationalist movement, especially after Gandhi declared to Muslims, "We will win freedom with you or without you, or in spite of you." Maududi did not think democracy would be beneficial for Muslims and disagreed with Khilafatist-turned-nationalist leader Abul Kalam Azad's vision of Hindu and Muslim unity in a cosmopolitan South Asia.

As the years went by, Maududi developed an eclectic synthesis of Muslim political sensibilities. He maintained educational ties to modernist Aligarh and traditionalist Deoband schools as well as to Muslim modernists in Egypt. Maududi was disillusioned by the Arab revolt against the Ottoman Empire as well as the Ankara government's nationalism that abandoned transnational ties with the Muslims of South Asia. Upon the end of the Ottoman Dynasty he continued to place his hopes in another Muslim monarch. In fact, he spent more than a decade of the interwar period in Hyderabad, where Nizam ruled the most important and powerful Muslim monarchy in India. Maududi supported Nizam's self-strengthening policies and served Nizam's educational and cultural projects in various capacities, such as by writing textbooks.

Around 1938, Maududi stopped wearing the fez and began growing his beard, a choice that also symbolized the reorientation of his political vision. After losing hope in the viability of a Hyderabadi Muslim monarchy to uphold the rights and dignity of Indian Muslims, Maududi left for Punjab, where he joined a political party advocating a Muslim state based on principles of faith. It seems that, by the eve of World War II, Maududi had begun to believe the interests of Muslims were best served by a mass movement led by religious scholars, not necessarily by kings.

Shakib Arslan offered another ambivalent vision of interwar politics drawing on pan-Islamic ideas, but he was friendlier to Westernization than was Maududi. His book *Our Decline: Its Causes and Remedies* was written in the early 1930s upon the request of Rashid Rida in response to Shaykh Muhammad Bisyooni Umran of Indonesia, who sought to understand the strength of the Europeans and the Japanese, "the factors behind their glorious empires and sovereignty, their power and wealth," as compared to the perceived disadvantages of Muslim societies.[30] Arslan's long and careful response was first serialized in Rida's journal, then became a best-selling book. While showing multiple explanations, Arslan connected the varying experiences of Singaporean, Turkish, Chinese, Bosnian, and North African Muslims in a single narrative of the decline of the Muslim world.

Arslan kept the dream of creating a great Muslim kingdom or nation and tried to unify King Saud of Arabia and King Faisal of Iraq for that purpose. He kept in touch with Egypt's deposed Khedive Hilmi, a candidate to lead a potential free Syrian kingdom. At times Arslan depicted Yemen under the Mutawakkilite Dynasty as a safe and independent host for a new caliphate, beyond European colonial interference. With Muslim representation at the League of Nations weak, Arslan took it upon himself to represent the interests of colonized Muslims by submitting petitions on their behalf to the League's Mandate Commission. He also attended multiple international congresses, met leaders of the revisionist European Great Powers, especially Germany and Italy, and maintained a global pan-Islamic network through his Geneva-based journal, *La nation arabe*, which, despite its pan-Arabic name, was more pan-Islamic in content. For instance, the journal published on the problems and aspirations of non-Arab Muslim minorities in Europe, especially in the southwest.[31]

A comparison between interwar-era pan-Islamism and Cold War–era Islamism shows the ruptures between the two. Interwar pan-Islamists imagined a unified, subaltern racial group in need of solidarity and empowerment, while late Cold War Islamists distinguished among Sunni and Shia, good Muslims and bad. Arslan, for example, never concerned himself with reform of Muslim theology, a major issue for later Islamists. He was a member of the Druze, a minority sect, and nobody seemed to care. The Muslim solidarity of the interwar period continued to be more ecumenical than the solidarity of decades to come, such that Shias and other Muslims minorities could comfortably join Sunnis under the pan-Islamist tent.

Subaltern Muslim Internationalism

Between 1924 and the eruption of World War II, Muslims worldwide continued to demand rights and representation within empires. In particular, British imperial rule in Egypt, Palestine, and India inspired such demands and helped to solidify networks from the Middle East to South Asia. In the age of nationalism, the idea of the Muslim world remained crucial, because various imperial and subaltern actors still merged the politics of decolonization and imperial rivalry with

Muslim-world identity. It was in this context that the entangled questions of the future of Palestine and India became the core issues in Muslim-world discourse.

One of the key figures of interwar-era pan-Islamic politics under the British Empire was Haj Amin al-Husseini, who, as *mufti,* helped to establish Jerusalem as a focus of global Muslim activism. Husseini may be best remembered as the Palestinian leader who cooperated with the Germans against the British in order to liberate his homeland. Before World War II, however, he had carved out a place for himself as a Palestinian nationalist, pan-Islamist, *and* loyal subject of the British Mandate. Born in 1897 to a prominent Palestinian family in Jerusalem, Husseini served in the Ottoman Army as an officer during World War I. By 1918, when it had become obvious that the Ottoman Empire in Arabia was at its end, Husseini put his hopes in Britain's promised united Arab kingdom under the leadership of Sherif Hussein's son Faisal. But Husseini was soon left disillusioned by the betrayals of Sykes-Picot and the Balfour Declaration. That same year, he joined early Palestinian protests against British rule, leading to a warrant for his arrest. Still, it did not take long for the young Husseini to reconcile with the Mandate authority; the Zionist high commissioner of British-occupied Palestine, Herbert Samuel, appointed him *mufti* in 1921.[32]

In the first ten years of his tenure as *mufti,* Husseini used Mandate law and British notions of justice in efforts to articulate Palestinian objections to Zionism and to secure political autonomy and dignity. For instance, in March–April 1930, he joined the Palestinian Executive Committee's official visit to London to discuss the political conditions of Palestinian Arabs.[33] While operating through formal imperial channels, Husseini also sought to mobilize Muslims within and beyond the empire. He used money raised abroad, especially from British India, to renovate the Muslim holy sites in Jerusalem, increasing his prestige tremendously. In the process, he also elevated Jerusalem as a pan-Islamic hub, accessible from South Asia via air and steamship. His connections with Indian pan-Islamists, including the formerly pro-Ottoman Khilafatists, put him in a position to press London with claims on behalf of all the empire's Muslim subjects.

But, as had been true of colonized Muslim support for the Ottoman caliphate and various earlier pan-Islamic activities, such efforts were not necessarily intended to test the foundations of imperial rule. The goal was neither full decolonization nor rejection of the Mandate but rather retraction of the Balfour Declaration. In fact, Palestinian leaders and their Indian allies not only sought to work through British mechanisms but also pressed London through the League of Nations, a body designed to legitimize European empires and the post–World War I Mandate system in the Middle East amid growing calls for self-determination.[34]

Interwar Muslim support for the Palestinian cause was self-consciously borderless. The All-India Muslim League's main representative in Palestine-related activities, Chaudhry Khaliquzzaman, depicted Palestinian and Indian Muslims, and the Muslim world as a whole, in a struggle for the same goals of equality and self-determination. (After World War II, Khaliquzzaman would become the main organizer of the Karachi-based Muslim World Congresses.)[35] The Muslim League sent representatives to the World Inter-Parliamentary Congress of Arab and Muslim Countries for the Defense of Palestine. That the Muslim League, which was founded as an Indian Muslim civil rights organization, was involved in Palestinian concerns is telling. As the Muslim League made its presence felt internationally, it developed close ties with Arab leaders such as Husseini, the Yemeni royal family, the Egyptian government and Wafd Party, and the Muslim Brotherhood under al-Banna.[36]

Palestinian and Indian activists made frequent reference to the implied contract of World War I, in which Indian Muslims served Britain, and Britain, in return, was to respect the caliph in Istanbul and the Muslim holy cities. Activists argued that Jerusalem was one such holy city, and thus Britain betrayed the contract by agreeing to Zionist demands for a Jewish homeland in Palestine. In some respects, this was a last-ditch effort: with the caliphate gone and Mecca and Medina ruled by Saudis, the destiny of Palestinian Muslims had become one of the strongest symbol of British injustice against Muslims. The British largely dismissed this appeal, even though it arrived on the empire's own terms. British officers began talking more about American pressure to support Zionists, partly as an excuse for rejecting Muslim claims for justice and fairness within empire.[37]

Another possible strategy was a plea to the League of Nations, where India had a seat at the table. There were no Muslim great powers at the League that could articulate the rights of Palestinians. Thus Indian representatives seemed like the logical candidates to represent the Muslim world's discontent about the future of Palestine. But the League of Nations never considered the issue of rights of Palestinians in relation to Zionist projects and, in general, favored imperial interests over the demands of colonized populations.

Recognizing the failures of legal and rhetorical demands within the British Empire and League of Nations, Husseini mobilized the power of the imagined Muslim world at the grassroots. He called for a Muslim world congress to be convened in Jerusalem in December 1931, to augment the pressure on the British and the League. Plans for the conference were finalized during the funeral ceremony of Khilafat leader Muhammad Ali, who was buried in Jerusalem in January of that year. That the most important pan-Islamic leader of British India was buried in British-controlled Jerusalem rather than Mecca, his first wish, speaks to the state of Muslim internationalism during the interwar period: the Saudis, who had won their kingdom from other Muslims with British consent and were remaking basic Islamic pilgrimage rites in the Wahhabi image, were in no position to host a conference discussing the problems of the Muslim world. Husseini was. Reflecting his ability to unify conflicting Muslim publics, Husseini oversaw the burial of King Sherif Hussein in Jerusalem's Haram al-Sharif compound, just beside Muhammad Ali, that June. Thus the leader of the anti-Ottoman revolt was interred beside the leader of the pro–Ottoman caliphate movement. It was the sort of powerful image that made Jerusalem a fitting site for the Muslim World Congress in December.[38]

The 1931 congress was a source of widespread concern. Italians were upset by the congress's celebration of Omar Mukhtar, who became a martyr and symbol of Muslim resistance to European colonialism after leading the *jihad* against Italian rule in Libya. The British colonial government in India was similarly worried, given the key role Indian Muslims played in organizing the gathering. More important, the Turkish government was alarmed by the prospect of the last caliph's participation in the conference and by the possibility that a new caliph would be elected. Ankara rejected Husseini's invitation and urged other Muslim leaders to follow suit. Iran, Afghanistan, Albania, Egypt, and Iraq all joined Turkey in refusing official representation at the event. Turkey also made sure that its flag was absent from the halls, despite the flag's importance as a transnational Muslim symbol. (Likewise, in the late 1930s, the Turkish embassy in Tokyo prevented the use of Turkish flags at pan-Asian and pan-Islamic gatherings in Japan.) Turkey also successfully discouraged the exiled Mustafa Sabri Efendi, former Ottoman shaikh ul-Islam and opponent of the secular-nationalist government, from participating. Arslan would later blame Turkey for stymieing Soviet, Bulgarian, and Romanian representation as well and for greatly damaging the effectiveness of the congress.

Still, the very fact that Turkish officials were concerned about a pan-Islamic conference organized in British imperial domains illustrates the power of the event itself and the continuing synergies of the Muslim-world imperial network. The two locations discussed for the next meeting of the congress, Cairo and Delhi, were also under British imperial rule.

Despite the absence of representatives from independent Muslim countries and elsewhere, the 1931 congress welcomed influential figures. Abdurrahman Azzam, who would become the Arab League's first secretary general, was present until Mandate authorities removed him for openly condemning Italian policies in Libya as worse than Zionism.[39] The Levant and North Africa were well accounted for by Syrians Riyad al-Sulh and Shukri al-Quwwatli; Algeria's Said al-Jazairi, grandson of the anti-French resistance leader Abdelkader al-Jazairi; Abd al-Aziz al-Thaalibi of Tunisia; and Muhammad al-Makki al-Nasiri and Muhammad al-Kattani from Morocco. The Indian delegation included legendary poet Muhammad Iqbal alongside former Khilafat movement activists such as Shawkat Ali, Muhammad Ali's brother and an important nationalist leader in his own right. Well-known Russian Muslims in exile—such as Ayaz İshaki, Musa Carullah Bigi, and Said Şamil, grandson of Imam Shamil, who led Caucasian resistance against Russian expansion in the mid-nineteenth century—took part. Iran was unofficially represented by a former minister living in exile in Switzerland, Ziya al-Din Tabatabai. Another important participant was Shaikh Muhammad al-Husayn al-Kashif al-Ghita, a Shia cleric who fought for Ottoman *jihad* in World War I. While al-Ghita led the opening prayer, Sunni attendees prayed behind him, illustrating the nonsectarian quality of the era's pan-Islamism.

The congress produced a set of recommendations that included fund-raising for a Muslim university in Jerusalem to rival Hebrew University, forming a permanent executive committee, and creating strong cooperation among Muslim societies. But no one had the combination of will, wherewithal, and standing to direct the program laid out in Tabatabai's final report on behalf of the conference. Tabatabai's employer, former Egyptian khedive Abbas Hilmi, supported various pan-Islamic projects, but mainly he hoped to strengthen his claims within Egyptian dynastic politics, and his pragmatic links to Istanbul and Zionists raised suspicion among Palestinian nationalists and pan-Islamic activists. The king of Saudi Arabia could have financed the congress's proposals, but the Saudis still had their conflicts with Indian pan-Islamists. When Rashid Rida insistently recommended Saudi leadership, other delegates disagreed. Without the financial backing of an empire or powerful state, all of the congress's projects failed.

Even so, the British were alarmed. Orientalist observers such as Sir Hamilton Gibb considered the congress a turning point in Muslim politics, as this was the first time Muslim political leaders and intellectuals gathered to discuss the future of the Muslim world. Colonial officers were frightened by the specter of Muslim solidarity, despite the fact that this congress and its main organizer were not anti-British. It would be several years before Husseini turned against the Mandate authorities. Only after the brutal suppression of Palestinian uprisings in 1936 and Hussein's subsequent exile did the *mufti* turn to the Germans and begin using his influence for anti-British purposes. Throughout the 1931 congress, however, both Hussein and Shawkat Ali moderated anti-British rhetoric and recommended that participants focus on Zionism rather than rejecting the British Mandate in Palestine.

Before the Axis powers assumed sponsorship of pan-Islamic ideas and claimed custodianship of the Muslim world, there was one other major Muslim congress, in 1936. Organized in Geneva, the congress aimed to put pressure on the League of Nations while mobilizing European Muslims. The main organizer of the 1936 congress was Arslan, the former Ottoman partisan and Arab monarchist who had become the chief petitioner and representative on behalf of the Syrian and Palestinian people at the League's Mandate Commission. Per an agreement with Swiss authorities, the 1936 congress was to concern itself with religious matters alone. As a result, congress members refrained from condemning European colonial rule. The only political question discussed openly at the congress was again Zionism, on the grounds that Jerusalem's Muslim holy sites made the developing Jewish control of Palestinian territories a religious issue.

The 1936 congress featured a range of participants from across Europe, leading to starkly contrasting discussions of Muslim life under varying rule. Representatives from Yugoslavia, Poland, and Hungary praised their governments' policies enabling freedom of religion and minority rights. Meanwhile, Muslims from imperial metropoles spoke of their dismay over discriminatory policies in the colonies. Eastern Europe seemed to be more tolerant and racially enlightened than the empires.[40] This was an important factor underlying the geography of nationalist and pan-Islamic activity, which spiked in racialized Muslim-majority imperial domains and not in newly independent Eastern European nations such as Yugoslavia, where minority rights were well established.

The congress also tried to benefit from its proximity to the League of Nations by claiming to represent the interests and demands of Muslim populations in various League meetings and committees. By 1936, however, the League was already being overshadowed by the rise of the Axis powers. If their imperial loyalist and internationalist strategies failed, subaltern Muslims could receive support from Germany, Italy, and Japan instead.

Mobilizing Muslims in World War II

During World War II, the chaotic multidirectionality of interwar pan-Islamism gave way to a revived discourse of Muslim-world unity. Reinvestment in the claim that the Muslim world both existed and mattered geopolitically came from empires themselves, albeit a new set of them: the Third Reich, the Japanese Empire, and Italy under fascism, all of whom championed an alliance with the Muslim world against their rivals.[41] From the Axis perspective, this was an instrumental partnership, but they pursued it by means of pan-Islamic rhetoric and ideas having little to do with their strategic goals. In the absence of a caliph and Muslim great power, the Axis empires declared themselves representatives of Muslims' interests and proclaimed anti-imperialist *jihad* on their behalf. As during World War I, the British, French, Dutch, and Soviet empires felt they had to respond to Axis propaganda by promising Muslims more rights and autonomy—and, this time, even independence.

The Axis sought to mobilize the Muslim world in part because it was there for the mobilizing—that is, the various strains of subaltern pan-Islamism had failed to achieve their political goals through imperial justice, Bolshevik internationalism, and the League of Nations, creating opportunities for a new savior. Axis courtship of figures such as Husseini, Arslan, and Ibrahim—favored, respectively, by Germany, Italy, and Japan—was not especially deft, though. By World War II, these men no longer represented significant grassroots movements and were overshadowed by a new generation of nationalists or by state leaders. These men flirted with Italian, German, and Japanese sponsorship of Muslim unity because they had been marginalized; no Muslim-ruled state would listen to them and represent their demands.

Arslan's openness to Italy makes sense only from a position of weakness. Arslan developed a special rapport with the Italian government during the 1936 Muslim World Congress, which hosted an Italian delegation of observing Orientalist scholars. One of the delegates converted to Islam during the congress in order to participate as a representative, and Arslan agreed to let him go ahead. The decision to grant voting and speaking rights to an Italian was highly contradictory given Arslan's and others' anti-Italian activism in 1911–1912. More important, Italy's invasion of Ethiopia during the same year as the congress shattered its claims of friendliness toward the oppressed colored races of Asia and the Muslim world. Pan-Islamists already had a very negative perception of the Italian invasion of Ottoman Libya, which inspired the first modern Muslim boycott of a European empire. Arslan's compromise reflected his isolation in Geneva; he organized and presided, but with a decade of failure behind him, he had to look far and wide for friends.[42]

Thus, just two decades after the German-Ottoman *jihad*, the Axis invocation of Muslim-world solidarity resounded upon an even more divided bloc. In addition to political fragmentation across empires, nations, and kingdoms, there were new divisions over Muslim reformism. India was still playing its timeworn role as a mélange of imperial fealty, nationalist movements, and pan-Islamic agitation. But other forces had emerged to further complicate the politics of Muslim-majority societies. As we have seen, socialists promoted pro-Soviet policies of Muslim modernization. Kemalists argued for secular nationalism. Saudi Arabia was building a nation on the twin pillars of royal family and religious renewal.

The Axis powers responded to this complexity by retrenching. They essentially replayed their World War I game plan, adopting an old-fashioned and strongly Orientalist view befitting their conception of the Muslim world as a cohesive faith tradition, civilization, and geopolitical unit. The Nazis read and promoted the same Orientalist intellectuals whose policies had failed to secure unified Muslim allegiance in World War I. So convinced were the Germans and their allies of Muslim unity that they believed they could trumpet Muslim anti-imperialism even as Italy dominated Muslims in Africa. The Axis thought that convincing one meant convincing all, and so focused propaganda on British, Soviet, French, and Dutch hegemony while figuring that, with enough persuasion, Muslim opponents of these regimes would look the other way when confronted with the Axis's own imperial aims. Of course, Axis leaders were not alone in bundling disparate groups under the label of unified Islam. German and Italian elites shared with their British and French counterparts a European discourse on Islam and Muslims, also attributing to the Muslim world characteristics such as fanaticism and aggressiveness.

In spite of their inelegant and dated approach, the Axis did have long-term impact on the discourse of the Muslim world, particularly in relation to Jews. German policymakers categorized Arab Muslims as Aryan rather than Semitic and attributed to Islam an anti-Semitic essence. This contradicted centuries of Jewish-Muslim coexistence under the rule of multiple cosmopolitan empires, as well as the Semitic label once applied to both groups. German policymakers were aware of the disappointments caused by the Balfour Declaration and channeled that disappointment toward anti-Semitism. This was a new strategy, unfamiliar to pre-1930s pan-Islamists, who may have been upset by the Balfour Declaration but did not see Jews as a global enemy. Axis propaganda drove wedges deep into what had previously been manageable cracks between Muslims and Jews. Axis propaganda also asserted an essential enmity between Islam and communism, the better to persuade Soviet Muslims to turn against their leaders.

Axis outreach to Muslims would have failed entirely had there not been genuine Muslim grievances against their imperial masters. And indeed, the Axis found collaborators among nationalists and pan-Islamists seeking sponsors for Muslim emancipation projects. After all, interwar-era efforts to appeal to independent Muslim polities, efforts at transnational networking, congresses, and petitions to the League of Nations and Soviet Union all failed. The majority of Muslim societies were colonized; mistreatment and humiliation at the hands of colonial officers continued. And the few independent Muslim polities, such as Turkey, Iran, Afghanistan, and Saudi Arabia, were too weak or preoccupied with their own reforms to get financially or militarily involved in the destiny of an imagined Muslim world. It therefore seemed pragmatic for some subaltern activists to ally with Axis elites and find common ground in their Muslim-world illusions.

Among the Axis powers, Japan developed an Islam policy that best exemplifies the linking of geopolitics with ideas of Islam as a world religion and non-Western civilization as a foundation for alliance.[43] Japanese policymakers believed they would be uniquely successful in reaching Muslims because both Muslims and Japanese were Eastern civilizations and colored races. As the Greater Japan Islam League pamphlet on Muslim-world policy argued in 1939, "The majority of the Muslims live in Asia. They have the self-consciousness of being oppressed colored peoples, and they hold, very sincerely and fiercely, anti-Bolshevik and anti-Western ideas. Meanwhile, they keep very warm feelings toward our country as an Eastern nation and as the leader of Asia. Even concerning the present China Incident [the Japa-

nese Empire's war against China since 1931], the Muslims' attitude is different from the Western and Soviet position as they
hope to get the support of a strong Japan in order to revive their
homelands."[44]

Japanese advocates dismissed English, Russian, and French
policies toward Muslims. These would never stand in a Muslim
world understood in Japan as anticolonial, anti-Christian, and
anticommunist. Italian claims to be "friends of Muslims" were
also laughable, given the legacy of Ottoman-Italian wars and
Italian military expansion in North Africa.[45] According to Japanese elites, only Germany had any success in its policy toward
the Muslim world as they were former allies of the Ottoman
caliphate and they did not have any large Muslim colonies.
Meanwhile, Japan had no negative colonial history with the
Muslims, as officials noted routinely throughout World War II.[46]
In contrast to these white powers, Japanese leaders thought
they could go far in the Muslim world. In reality, though, Japan
had little prestige among Muslim leaders. The only evidence
the pamphlet writers could find for Japan's recognition in a
Muslim-majority society was a call for collaboration issued by
Prince Huseyin of Mutawakkilite Yemen, who attended the
1938 opening of the Tokyo Mosque.

Japan's embrace of the Muslim world reflected its appropriation of European scholarship, though the Japanese claimed, on
the basis of pan-Asianism, to have overcome negative Western
prejudices toward Muslims. In the first issue of the journal
Isuramu Bunka (Islamic culture), Japanese academics declared:

> In sincere estimation we, the Japanese nation as a branch of the
> Asiatic, hold Islam and the Musulman nations as a powerful
> religion in the East and the nations belonging to the East. But
> once very rare were the chances for us to get into direct con-
> tact with them. Unfortunately, as we happened to know the

Christian Civilization previous to the Islamic, even though the former is very much antagonistic to the latter, when the latter were not so well situated politically in the world in modern ages, our understanding on Islam has been too much crooked mostly because of the anti-propaganda on the part of the Christian nations. As it is, the time is now with us at last when we can hold our cordial hands forth to Muslim people. Friendship is ensured, and our door is open to the Islamic nations including Turkey, Persia, Afghanistan and Egypt. Traffic is now vivid between them and us: we may fully grasp a true idea of them through direct and non-prejudiced media.[47]

With wartime funding from the Japanese government, the Institute of Islamic Studies published a monthly journal, *Kaikyôken* (Muslim world). Two other periodicals on Muslim issues, *Kaikyô Sekai* (World of Islam) and *Kaikyô Jijyô* (Conditions of Muslims), were published by the Greater Japan Islam League and Foreign Ministry research section, respectively.[48]

The Japanese, like any who hoped to cultivate relations with the Muslim world, had to contend with the fact that it didn't exist. They could not embrace one Muslim figure or group and thereby embrace all. They could not accept the diversity of political agency and practices of millions of human beings who happen to be Muslim. They called Abdurreşid Ibrahim, an elderly pan-Islamist, to Tokyo long after his heyday. They also took enormous risks in seeking allies. In a daring 1933 experiment, for example, the Japanese government hosted a prince from the abolished Ottoman Dynasty, presumably to weigh in on Japan's Muslim policy in Central Asia in case of a conflict with the Soviet Union. The plan was soon abandoned, but it was reckless and unrealistic from the start. Tempted by their own Asianist theories, Japanese officials were willing to jeopardize diplomatic relations with the Turkish Republic in hopes of finding a fictitious global Muslim leader.

Japan was also led astray with respect to Muslims at home. Its anti-imperialist policy contravened the interests of Indian Muslim merchants, whose trade depended on good relations between the British and Japanese. Indeed, the first mosque in Japan, opened in Kobe in 1936, was a symbol of Muslim networks between Japan and British-ruled South Asia. Once Japan declared war on the British Empire in 1941, Indian Muslims had to depart the country, leaving their mosque to the care of Tatar Muslims who immigrated to Japan after the Bolshevik Revolution.[49]

Japanese plans to divide Chinese Muslims from Chinese nationalists also failed for lack of Muslim unity. In order to convince Muslims that their invasion of China was morally acceptable, the Japanese government sponsored a Japanese-Muslim pilgrimage. The government hoped that, by going to Mecca, the pilgrims would demonstrate the Japanese alliance with a putative Muslim-world cause. In response, the Chinese nationalist government organized a Chinese-Muslim hajj. Neither party had much impact because, in truth, the hajj has never been a useful opportunity to propagandize. At the very least, however, the presence of competing Japanese and Chinese Muslims in Mecca symbolizes the chaotic political conditions of the era's diverse Muslim societies and demonstrates that there was no Muslim world to manipulate.

Japan's alliance building wasn't wholly unsuccessful, but where the Japanese did manage to cultivate Muslim partners, it was not on the basis of a shared delusion of Muslim solidarity. For instance, when Japan invaded the Muslim-majority areas of Southeast Asia, it cooperated with local Muslim organizations and leaders. In Indonesia, nationalist leaders such as Sukarno

collaborated with Japanese forces in order to end Dutch colonialism. But these Muslim collaborators had their own agendas
and hoped to use Japan for their purposes. There were also some
Indian Muslims sympathetic to Japan, as well as Japanese who
supported the Indian National Army based in Singapore,
prompting British counterpropaganda toward Muslims. The
British claimed that Muslims were morally obligated to side
with them, Christian People of the Book, over supposedly idol-
worshipping Shinto Japanese. Needless to say, this counterpropaganda was also ineffective. Anti-imperialism among Muslims
had little to do with religion and much to with modern Muslim
political visions, leaving the bulk of Indian Muslims poorly disposed to the range of outside powers vying for their loyalty.[50]

Because the Axis was proactive in courting Muslims and the
Allies reactive, it is tempting to believe that there actually was
an Axis-Islam alliance. And yet conditions in Muslim societies during World War II demonstrate nothing so much as the
complexity and confusion of the era's international political
context, and it is impossible to honestly assert one narrative of
what Muslims did in the war. Thousands of Muslim soldiers
fought and died for British, French, and Soviet causes during
the war. Turkey was neutral. Reza Shah of Iran hoped to remain neutral and so refused various Allied demands for assistance and expulsion of German nationals but was deposed by
invading British and Russian forces collaborating with his son,
Mohammad Reza Pahlavi. The Axis powers produced much
rhetoric but won no significant Muslim support. Late in the war,
when Germany was certain to lose, some Third Reich leaders
admitted their propaganda was fruitless, as evidenced by their
failure to protest and condemn Italian and Vichy colonial inter-

ests in the Middle East and North Africa. Muslims themselves were as critical of German and Italian policies and actions as they were of Soviet, British, and French hegemony.[51]

Although Muslims were not convinced by Axis propaganda, the Allies were. Hence a number of too-little-too-late gestures, such as the British monarchy's support for the Regent's Park Mosque during the war. More important, the U.S. Office of Strategic Services worried about what it perceived as the success of Japanese policies among Southeast Asian Muslims and responded by urging the Allies to emphasize the role of the United Nations in any postwar vision. Return to empire appeared dangerous, for it would strengthen and legitimize Muslim nationalist claims, which suddenly seemed viable from a geostrategic perspective. In other words, whether or not they had anything to fear, the Allies decided they needed to compromise with major Muslim demands.

Once the war was over, the Allies realized just how shallow Axis propaganda had been. But it would have been too late for the Allies to reverse the new order of self-determination they were promoting, even if they had wanted to. Before the war ended, all existing Muslim states had declared war on the Axis powers and thereby joined the United Nations. These states were thus ensured sovereignty and parity in international diplomacy. As the imagined Muslim world revealed itself to be full of separate, internationally recognized, sovereign components, colonized Muslim societies saw their opportunity for independence.

The postwar order was to be something entirely different from every formation that came before—whether universal empire, autonomous dynasty, or semisovereign state within the imperial milieu. Under the auspices of the UN, eventually all peoples would be allowed their own nation-state, and each nation-state would be equal in rights and obligations. Years of pan-Islamic experimentation and revitalization had seemingly come to naught by the second half of the 1940s. For within just two decades of the Khilafat movement's attempted rescue of the imaginary caliphate head of the Muslim world in Istanbul, there appeared to be neither space nor need for such a figure.

6

Resurrecting
Muslim Internationalism
(1945–1988)

On August 21, 1969, a mentally ill Christian Zionist zealot, Denis Michael Rohan, set fire to the pulpit of the Al-Aqsa Mosque in Jerusalem. In response to the burning of Islam's third-most sacred site, King Faisal bin Abdulaziz bin Saud of Saudi Arabia called for a summit of leaders of Muslim-majority countries. Held that year on September 25 in the Moroccan capital of Rabat, the summit brought together Iran's shah, Turkey's foreign minister, Pakistan's prime minister, and many besides. It was the first ever gathering of representatives from independent countries in the name of Muslim-world solidarity. At the top of the agenda were Palestine and its Muslim holy sites.

Just a few years earlier, an event of the sort probably wouldn't have attracted such high-placed officials. During the 1965 Arab Summit, King Faisal had proposed a meeting of global Muslim leaders, but in the heyday of Egyptian president Gamal Abdel Nasser's secular nationalism, international Muslim solidarity was unattainable, and plans for the meeting never got off the ground. Events change minds, though, creating space for new politics. In this case, it was military defeat in 1967, when Nasser and his allies tried to liberate Palestine, along with the humiliation and sense of urgency brought about by the 1969 arson, that altered the political context. Secular nationalist Muslim leaders came to recognize common problems facing Muslim populations divided across national boundaries and accepted the Saudi king's invitation.

A Saudi monarch might not seem like the obvious person to lead the revival of pan-Islamism among the nearly fifty Muslim-majority states that emerged from colonial domination. When King Faisal's father, Abdulaziz bin Saud, declared himself king of Hejaz in 1926, his domains were among the world's poorest, with little by way of either money or exploitable natural resources. Even as the kingdom grew and gained wealth from the oil industry, Saudi cities lacked the cosmopolitan qualities of former Ottoman and Indian metropoles such as Istanbul and Delhi. Ruling over Mecca and Medina, sites of pilgrimage for all Muslims, gave Saudi rulers a chance to connect with their coreligionists across the globe, but they had no interest in the caliphate and did not get involved in any pan-Islamic projects. And Wahhabism, the puritanical strain of Islam practiced and enforced by the royal family, placed the Saudis at odds with most of the world's Muslims. Many obstacles stood between any Saudi leader and the possibility of global Muslim leadership.

Prince and later King Faisal changed the image of the Saudi kingdom among Muslim publics of the world. From his youth, he was more internationally engaged than King Abdulaziz's other sons. When the Saudi state in Najd conquered the Hejaz region in 1925, Faisal was given charge of Mecca and Medina,

placing him closer to the spiritual heart of Muslims. He participated in the Meccan Muslim Congress in 1926 and, after World
War II, embraced the Palestinian cause as a symbol of enduring
Muslim humiliation. After he became prime minister, beginning in 1958, Faisal remained active in foreign affairs by focusing
on bilateral ties between his kingdom and newly independent
Muslim-majority countries of Africa and Asia. At the same time,
Faisal helped to establish the Islamic University of Medina and
the Muslim World League, both significant mechanisms of
nongovernmental outreach to Muslim populations. Internationalism and pan-Islamic solidarity were clearly priorities for
Faisal even before he assumed the kingship of his country. After
his ascension to the throne in 1964, he actively contributed to
the emergence of a Muslim bloc at the UN General Assembly
with the participation of Muslim-majority African and Asian
countries.[1]

Throughout his reign, which ended with his assassination by
a nephew in 1975, Faisal's commitment to Muslim-world solidarity was inflected by the exigencies of the Cold War. Against
Nasser's visions of pan-Arab and Third World solidarity, Faisal
developed a Muslim network with Saudi Arabia at the center. As
prime minister and king, he joined a long line of modernizing
Muslim leaders by investing in economic development, media,
and education for women; promoting religious inclusion; and
abolishing slavery—moves that helped to establish Saudi global
prestige. Through institutions he built and inspired—such as
the Organization of the Islamic Conference, which emerged
from the 1969 summit—he oversaw the symbolic, and sometimes actual, transfer of social, intellectual, and cultural capital from South Asia and Egypt to the self-strengthening Saudi
kingdom.

In all these ways, Faisal was a kind of Abdulhamid II for
his time, reinventing a Muslim world solidarity in an age of

nation-states rather than empires. And like Abdulhamid II, he pursued his international goals pragmatically, without antagonizing and challenging the superpower of his time, operating through the global organizing institutions and principles available to him. For instance, he used the UN General Assembly to showcase the collective voting power of postcolonial Muslim-majority states. Attempts at leadership of this emerging bloc of countries in the postcolonial international order helped the staunchly anticommunist Faisal gain the trust and friendship of the United States, illustrating the strategic value of the idea of the Muslim world in the context of Cold War rivalries. Yet he also established institutions in Mecca and Medina that would link different Muslim civil society organizations, individuals, and publics to Saudi leadership in an imagined global Muslim community.

King Faisal's leadership in reviving Muslim-world solidarity came during a period of transition, between postwar decolonization and the late 1970s, when the Camp David Accords and the Iranian Revolution precipitated an anti-American turn in pan-Islamic movements and ideas, drawing heavily on the grievances of the late Cold War era. By studying the intellectual history of the idea of the Muslim world in the post–World War II period, we can answer these key questions: What happened to the idea of the Muslim world in the immediate aftermath of World War II? Was there a Muslim world in the era of popular secular nationalist Muslim leaders such as Egypt's Nasser, Indonesia's Sukarno, and Iran's Mohammad Mosaddegh? What factors led to the reactivation of earlier notions of Muslim-world solidarity in the mid-1970s?

Cold War pan-Islamism associated with King Faisal's name eventually helped revive earlier imperial-era tropes, including racialization of Muslims and the humiliations perceived by Muslim-majority publics even after the official end of colonialism. Early excitement over the successes of new Arab nations gave way to discontent, as it became clear that pan-Arabism could not secure Palestinian self-determination. The loss of Jerusalem in 1967 shattered confidence in the redemptive capacity of secular nationalism. The violence of decolonization and the Cold War—as seen in the CIA's 1953 coup in Iran, the Suez War in 1956, and the 1954–1963 Algerian War of Independence—reinforced Muslim dissatisfaction with the new international order.

Muslim-world solidarity was only one potential response to these ills. Socialism, pan-Africanism, pan-Arabism, Cold War alliances, and nonaligned movements offered competing tools for collective expression and bargaining. That Muslim-world solidarity emerged from this ideological ferment is largely a function of the contingent political struggles of the 1970s. One set of intellectual and geopolitical conditions fostered a climate of opinion receptive to King Faisal's pan-Islamic initiatives, and another redirected that pan-Islamism to more radical goals after the 1973 Arab-Israeli War. The tensions were inescapable after Camp David, where Egypt essentially abdicated possible leadership of the imagined Muslim world by agreeing to a separate peace with Israel and shutting out the Palestinians, whose cause had become essential to pan-Islamic thought.

Similar to how the anti-Russian pan-Islamism of the 1870s became radically refashioned into an anti-British *jihad* by the Young Turk government in World War I, the anti-communist pan-Islamism of the 1960s was redefined as a *jihad* against the American hegemony in the Muslim world by the followers of Iran's Ayatollah Khomeini. Thus the field was made ready for Iran's and Saudi Arabia's forceful and competing pan-Islamic campaigns of the 1980s—projects themselves responsive to world events such as the continuing struggle of Palestinians against Israeli occupation and the Soviet invasion of Afghanistan.

Leaders of both Iran and Saudi Arabia saw Muslim-world solidarity as their solution to both global and domestic governance crises, but emerging strife between Sunni and Shia heightened the rivalry between them. Iran's Ayatollah Khomeini radically reshaped tropes from both Abdulhamid's imperial and King Faisal's nation-state-oriented pan-Islamism by directly appealing to Muslim public opinion through the tool of mass media. Whatever its intentions, the pan-Islamism of the late Cold War ended up reviving racialized Western Islamophobia and, among Muslims and others, delusional narratives of the clash of civilizations.

Decolonizing the Muslim World

During World War II, the Axis failure to cultivate the allegiance of the Muslim world revealed the emptiness of the claim that Muslims formed a single global unit. But this perception of solidarity was difficult to escape for the ideas and practices maintaining it persisted.

A 1957 U.S. government report offers a straightforward illustration. Arguing for the necessity of studying Islam and paying attention to the Muslim world, the report focused on the size of the global Muslim population. Sixteen of the UN's eighty-one members that year had Muslim-majority populations, and dozens had Muslim populations larger than fifty thousand. The report concluded that the world's estimated 350 million Muslims could be an important U.S. ally in the Cold War.[2] In other words, even in the age of postcolonial nationalism, Muslim-majority lands were seen as a bloc whose potential power resulted from supposed uniformity across borders. Both Cold War superpowers and some of the new, independent Muslim-majority countries indulged in such fantasies.

In reality, postwar Muslim countries lacked any sense of political unity. In the formative era of pan-Islamism between the 1880s and 1920s, shared experiences of racism under empire created a sense of Muslim solidarity. But with European empires retreating after World War II, Muslim societies were actually less politically unified than before, partitioning into ever-smaller units of administration. There was also no Muslim great power to fill the vacuum left by the British and Ottoman empires. Hence some American observers described the postwar Muslim world as "divided" and "headless," as well as "stagnant" and "poor."[3] Even former pan-Islamists did not have a clear vision of Muslim unity after World War II. For example, Arab League secretary Azzam Pasha's 1946 book *The Eternal Message of Muhammad* discusses racial equality, the new world order, and Muslim universalism based on Islamic doctrine and the Prophet Muhammad's biography, but it contains no vision for a caliphate, united Muslim federation, or international pan-Islamic organization.[4]

The 1955 conference of newly independent Asian and African nations in Bandung, Indonesia, exemplifies the extent to which the geopolitical imagination of the Muslim world had been submerged. Fourteen of the thirty participating countries at Bandung had Muslim majorities.[5] Hajj Amin al-Husseini spoke for the Palestinians, and Indian Muslims were represented by the Indian delegation. But while the speeches at the conference drew on earlier pan-Islamic (as well as pan-Asian) critiques of the racialized imperial world order, and delegates emphasized the significance of their Muslim and Asian identity, the gathering's major theme was secular Third World internationalism. The geopolitical illusion of Muslim-world unity was replaced by a more realistic desire for cooperation among the newly independent countries.[6] At Bandung, redemptive nationalism coupled with modernization and recognition within the UN-centered international system offered a kind of end of history for the international political imagination of Muslims. The new Muslim-majority countries would not have been content with just international recognition, though. They also wanted to act on the global stage as their diverse interests demanded. Thus the early Cold War era saw much division among Muslim-majority states. What little solidarity was achieved—for instance, at the UN General Assembly in opposition to the partition of Palestine in November 1947—proved unsustainable. Of the thirteen UN voting members that opposed partition of Palestine (out of fifty-six total members at that time), ten of them were Muslim-majority countries. India also supported the Muslim bloc. But many voting members with large Muslim populations—the British Empire, China, Yugoslavia, Thailand, and Ethiopia—abstained.[7] And once the UN recognized Israel as a sovereign country, Turkey and Iran also recognized Israel and established diplomatic relations, while most Arab-majority countries refused to do so. Throughout the Cold War, some Muslim-majority countries allied with the United States, others with the Soviet Union. Significantly, throughout the 1950s, NATO member Turkey did not vote for any of the UN resolutions supporting Algeria's right to self-determination. Despite strong historic ties between Algeria and Turkey—and Algerians' admiration for Mustafa Kemal Atatürk, hailed as a Muslim nationalist hero—Turkey prioritized its relations with France, which, as Algeria's colonial master, opposed any nationalist movement there.[8]

Muslim-majority states continued to emerge and divide long after the war, finally reaching their maximal representation in the UN in the mid-1970s. None of these fifty-odd countries grasped the role of Muslim great power, although Pakistan tried after its independence in 1947. Pakistan could potentially inherit not only the caliphate's moral leadership of Muslims but also the British Empire's status as the largest Muslim population center. Thus Pakistan would be both the main body of the Muslim world and its head, in contrast to the early twentieth century, when Indian Muslims looked up to Istanbul as spiritual sovereign and London as political ruler. Pakistan's leaders also hoped to sway the financial, cultural, and political power of Muslims who remained under the Raj. In short, Pakistan would be the "Muslim Zion."[9]

If Pakistan was to lead the Muslim world, it needed to establish moral supremacy within a crowded field of postcolonial political projects. And in the run-up to independence, the future leaders of Pakistan did have some success in this regard, winning some pan-Islamists away from Indian Congress Party initiatives. The All-Indian Muslim League, the major proponent of a separate Pakistan, tried to prove its clout by undercutting the Congress Party's 1947 Asian Relations Conference in Delhi. The Congress Party of India sought pan-Asian support for independence from Britain and for Indian leadership over British-ruled Asia, overshadowing the Muslim League's appeals for a separate homeland. But while delegations from Malaya, Tibet, Soviet Central Asia, Burma, and Ceylon attended the conference, the Muslim League convinced Syria, Lebanon, and Yemen to turn down their invitations. The Arab League and Muslim Brotherhood in Egypt sent only observers. In a letter dated May 28, 1947, Brotherhood founder Hasan al-Banna assured the Muslim League's charismatic leader Muhammad Ali Jinnah that his representatives wanted only to connect with Indian Muslims, not to support the Congress Party. Reiterating his movement's support for the "sacred Pakistan movement," al-Banna wrote, "There is no power on earth, after today, which can cut those ties which the brotherhood of Islam has welded or could suppress the freedom and independence of the Mohammedan Nations, or could prevent the attaining of their just national claims."[10] Yet this correspondence between Jinnah and al-Banna in 1947, conducted in English, reflected as much the importance of the British imperial framework in facilitating their ties as the religious notions of *ummah*.

After independence, Pakistani leaders sought to gain pan-Islamic prestige by hosting several Muslim world congresses between 1949 and the late 1950s. These congresses also served as venues for Pakistan's rivalry with India's pan-Asian internationalism. Thanks to its large economy and population and its political appeals to the postcolonial world, India had naturally emerged as a leader in postwar Asia. Even Muslim leaders from Nasser to Sukarno expressed admiration for India's first prime minister, Jawaharlal Nehru. But Pakistani officials hoped that transnational Muslim leadership would generate leverage against India in disputes over Kashmir.[11] Pakistan-sponsored Muslim Congress organizers therefore presented the gatherings as continuous with the Muslim world congresses of 1926 in Mecca and 1931 in Jerusalem. About twenty representatives from different Muslim organizations attended the first conference in 1949, mainly to discuss trade and economic development among Muslim-majority countries.

Yet after several meetings, it became clear that foreign governments were not interested in Pakistani leadership of a Muslim-unity organization. Pakistan's government was discovering that their state was not a natural successor to British-ruled India. The power and appeal of the Muslim world in the late nineteenth century lay in the residence of so many Muslims within the British Empire. Imperial attention to internal agitation was the source of Indian Muslims' clout. But there was no imperial metropole listening to Pakistan and therefore no one to respond to and amplify its grievances and claims.

Pakistan was also a weaker, rump descendant of Muslim India. Today it can seem as though Pakistan was destined to part from India, but partition was not inevitable, certainly not predetermined by fundamental differences between Muslims and Hindus. Millions of Muslims stayed behind.[12] Muslim supporters of composite nationalism argued powerfully against partition. Some who stayed behind assumed prominent leadership positions in the Congress Party and, after independence, the Indian cabinet. Today India has one of the world's largest Muslim populations—almost 180 million people, more than either Pakistan or Bangladesh. Indian Muslims who objected to partition argued that a united Hindu-Muslim India would better serve the interests of the Muslim world by definitively defeating British and Western colonialism in Asia and Africa and thereby helping other colonized societies gain independence and dignity. This undercut Pakistani claims to Muslim-world leadership. Meanwhile, Pakistani independence also created the basis for India's identification with Hinduism. Had India remained united, it would have been home to about a third of the world's Muslims.[13] Instead, despite the continuing presence of large numbers of Muslims, India could now easily be identified as a Hindu nation, and the country became a rival to Pakistan. Depriving Pakistan of all of its Muslim population, the partition of India sapped Pakistan's capacity to inherit all the prestige of British India as the greatest Muslim empire and serve as head of the imagined global Muslim body.

Pakistan continued to host the secretariat of the Muslim World Congress throughout the Cold War, in spite of its ineffectiveness, which was already clear by the time of the Bandung Conference in 1955. But the secretariat soldiered on well into the strongest years of pan-Arabism. For instance, as late as 1964, the secretariat advocated a commonwealth of Muslim countries, declaring in one its pamphlets, "Islam is neither a tribal nor a

racial nor a national nor a regional religion. It is a world religion. Nay, it is more than a religion; it is a World Order."[14] Although some of this Pakistan-centered pan-Islamism would
contribute to and shape Saudi-led, anti-Nasser pan-Islamism,
Pakistani leaders eventually were forced to admit that appeals
to Muslim internationalism were of little use in their rivalry
with India. By the mid-1950s they had shifted toward an anti-
Soviet alliance with Britain and the United States in order to
ensure Pakistan's interests in conflicts against India, which
emerged as the leader of the nonaligned movement. In conflicts with India over Kashmir, Pakistan frequently courted
Muslim public opinion, but the war over East Pakistan's independence and the eventual separation of Bangladesh in 1971 finally killed off any prospect of Pakistani centrality in a global
Muslim polity or movement. If Pakistan itself was being parti-
tioned, how could it convince other countries of the importance of transnational solidarity?

The divergence of pan-Islamic and pan-Asian internationalism
in the partition of Pakistan and India should be understood
as a contingent but significant result of a rivalry that weakened
Muslims on both sides. Before, pan-Islamic and pan-Asian internationalism comfortably coexisted in British-ruled South
Asia. Among Indian and Indonesian Muslims, there was no contradiction between these forms of solidarity. The British feared
Muslim power in part because during both the 1857 Rebellion
and the 1919–1923 Khilafat movement, Muslims and Hindus
cooperated. Such unity made a postcolonial world, free from
Western racism and hegemony, seem realistic.[15] Yet after partition, countries such as Indonesia and Egypt had to balance
their good relationship with Nehru's India against Pakistan's
drive for pan-Islamic solidarity and sometimes choose one over
the other. In the early 1950s, Sukarno openly called Nehru his
mentor, shunting aside pan-Islamic internationalism. Nasser

threaded the needle, at once allying with India as a fellow Third World country while projecting enough pan-Islamic sentiment to maintain relations with Pakistan.

And while Pakistan found itself a lesser remnant of the imagined Muslim world within British-ruled South Asia, Muslims in newly independent India were now a much-weakened minority. The rapid disintegration of Muslim princely states drained their global power and prestige. It seems as if the Muslim monarchs in Hyderabad and Bhopal, who had promoted and financially supported pan-Islamic intellectual and cultural networks, passed the flag of leadership not to Pakistan, which had failed to install itself atop the imagined Muslim world, but to Arab-majority countries such as Egypt and Saudi Arabia.[16] As soon as the mid-1950s, it was clear that the illusion of Muslim unity, and the centrality of South Asian Muslims in that illusion, could not be sustained.

One reason Pakistan could aspire to global Muslim leadership in the first place was the lack of a credible alternative in the Middle East. The standing of the Egyptian khedival dynasty, which ruled the world's largest Arab population, was shattered by defeat in the Arab-Israeli War of 1948. The kings of Iraq, Jordan, and Saudi Arabia lacked the wherewithal and global legitimacy to lead the imagined Muslim world. Thus when defeat in 1948 prompted a pan-Arab and pan-Islamic search for regional unity as a solution to the problem of Palestinian refugees and statehood, there was no Arab leader to look up to.

After 1948, Jordan hosted several Muslim congresses and gatherings in Jerusalem, which it then controlled. The location of the events spoke to the symbolic centrality of Palestine within transnational Muslim public opinion as well as Jordan's interest in stewardship of the city, the better to justify its rule there rather than establish an independent Palestinian state. These gatherings attracted official and unofficial participation, including that of Shia clerics such as Ayatollah Talagani and Muslim Brotherhood–linked intellectuals such as Sayyed Qutb. But these Jordanian initiatives ultimately gained little traction. The Arab leadership vacuum began to fill only after the 1952 Egyptian Revolution. The new government in Cairo immediately expressed its support for Muslim congresses. Minister of state and future president Anwar Sadat went to Jerusalem in 1955 to solidify Egyptian commitment to the Palestinian cause. Egyptian-Saudi relations improved, as would become evident in Saudi Arabia's expulsion of British diplomats from the country upon the 1956 invasion of the Suez Canal by British, French, and Israeli forces. Egypt, Saudi Arabia, and Pakistan even considered creating a three-country pan-Islamic bloc.

But under Nasser's leadership, beginning in 1956, Egypt's foreign initiatives became more pan-Arab and nonaligned. The Egyptian-Saudi Islamic congress continued to function under the management of the Egyptian Foreign Service, but its major purpose was to attract international students to at Al-Azhar University in Cairo and to sponsor projects dealing with Jerusalem. Between 1956 and the 1967 Arab-Israeli War, pan-Arabism, postcolonial nationalism, and various Cold War geopolitical rivalries overshadowed the leftover memories of imperial-era pan-Islamism.

Prioritizing Arab nationalism and Third World solidarity above notions of religious identity–based international cooperation was valuable domestically for Egypt, given the large body of Christian Arabs in that country. It also elevated and extended Nasser's global popularity; in a 1970 speech at UCLA, Shirley Graham Du Bois, wife of pan-African intellectual W. E. B. Du Bois, could depict Nasser and Sadat as pan-African heroes championing the revival of the colored races. Egypt's Afro-Asiatic Third World internationalism could also encompass a notion of Muslim solidarity within this large bloc, though even at this early point, the Cold War had created sharp ideological divisions among Muslim-majority countries. In NATO-allied Turkey, for example, the press depicted Nasser as a gullible Arab leader manipulated by the cunning Soviet Empire.

When Nasser emerged during the 1956 Suez War as a charismatic leader able to win U.S., UN, and Soviet support against British, French, and Israeli forces, Egypt already overshadowed Pakistan as the most significant Muslim-majority country. This passing of Muslim leadership claims to Egypt ended a century-long period, from 1857 to 1956, when Indian Muslims were numerically, financially, and politically ascendant as well as the central figures in the global imagination of the Muslim race. When Malcolm X made his historic pilgrimage to Mecca in 1964, he also visited Egypt and met pro-Nasserite pan-Arab and pan-African intellectuals. If Malcolm X had to choose between Nasser and King Faisal, he would likely have chosen the former because Nasser was both a Muslim and an African, championing the awakening and independence of the "colored races."[17] Yet, Malcolm X would not think of visiting Istanbul, former seat of the Ottoman caliphate just four decades earlier, as by the mid-1960s it was the Arab lands from Algeria and Egypt to Saudi Arabia that mattered most in the global Muslim political imagination.

While Nasser and his ilk perceived their struggles and their political goals in the terms of secular universalist ideologies such as nationalism, socialism, pan-Africanism, Third-Worldism, and colored-race alliance, European publics and colonial elites could not let go of the old tropes of racism and paranoia. Despite the fact that the 1954–1963 Algerian War of Independence coincided with the peak of secular pan-Arabism, the French government tried to depict Algerian demands for self-determination as signs of fanatical pan-Islamic anti-Westernism. During the bloody counterinsurgency, France targeted Nasser's support for the Algerian cause, blaming him as the arch villain challenging its empire in North Africa. It was this French animosity to the pan-Arab leadership of Nasser's Egypt that led to French military support for Israel, including the building of an Israeli atomic bomb.

Against depictions of their national struggle as a form of religious fanaticism, Algerian leaders emphasized the shared global values their effort represented. However, Algerian nationalists, including socialists, were proud of their Muslim race, heritage, and identity. In their own words, their fighters were *mujahid* and their national struggle *jihad*. When Algeria won independence, it became a secular and socialist republic, embracing pan-Arab, Third World, and socialist internationalism. Algerians did not see a contradiction between Muslim identity and secular, socialist government.[18]

Algeria proved to be a potent symbol and source of influence. Its struggle for national sovereignty on the basis of multiple internationalist solidarity projects was so successful that populations from as far away as Brazil and China offered their support. Algeria's independence from a settler-colonial regime inspired a general pan-Arab conviction that Palestinians could also liberate their homeland with the aid of multiple internationalisms and global public opinion.[19]

Muslim decolonization and nationalist modernization projects upset the traditional terms of Western Orientalists and international relations scholars. These intellectuals, like their forbears for at least a century, tended to bundle all Muslims into a single geopolitical, racial, and religious group and to explain their politics primarily by reference to their shared religion. But by the early 1960s, it had come to seem even to this group as though Islam was unimportant in world politics dominated by secular nationalisms and internationalisms as well as the strategic exigencies of the Cold War. When the Duke University

Committee on International Relations held an interdisciplinary conference on Islam and international relations in 1963, in the aftermath of Algerian independence and at the peak of Cold War rivalries, the twenty-six participating scholars could not agree on what role Islam played in global politics. According to a book collecting papers from the symposium, "Most of the principal speakers maintained that Islam is actually of quite limited significance in shaping the attitudes and behavior of Muslim states in international relations today, but others differed sharply and few were prepared to dismiss its relevance altogether."[20]

One of the participants, the Palestinian American philosopher Fayez Sayegh, challenged the premise of a connection between Islam and international relations in a paper discussing neutrality during the Cold War. "With respect to 'neutralism,'" he wrote, "Islam has had little, if any, noticeable influence upon the reasoning, planning, decision-making, or expression of Muslim policy makers."[21] Papers on the appeal of communism among Muslims, the significance of religion in Arab nationalism, the role of Islam in Egyptian foreign policy, and the impact of Islam on relations among the new African states all noted that religion mattered in politics, but to what extent and in what ways could not be clearly formulated. In the concluding article, "Pan-Islamism in the Modern World," Princeton Orientalist Cuyler Young noted that Pakistan refrained from actively supporting Egypt during the Suez Crisis, leading Egypt to refuse a Pakistani military contingent among UN peacekeeping troops in the Gaza Strip.[22]

Indeed, symposium participants not only paid attention to policy differences among Muslim-majority countries but also rejected essentialist generalizations about Islam and the Muslim world. When the political scientist Dankwart Rustow quoted Bernard Lewis's 1953 claim of affinity between Islam and communism because both "profess a totalitarian doctrine, with complete and final answers to all questions on heaven and earth," and both harbor the "aggressive fanaticism of the believer"—the utterly different content of these beliefs being apparently insignificant—he did so in order to challenge and dismiss Lewis's argument.[23] The place of Muslim identity in world politics was, at this point, so multifaceted that it was no longer possible to maintain narratives of unitary pan-Islamism as both European and Muslim intellectuals had in the 1878–1924 period.

Another kind of intellectual debate cropped up in academic circles as decolonization proceeded into the early 1970s, as some scholars wondered if Muslim's faith in *ummah* was compatible with the reality of fifty nation-states.[24] In practice, this was an idle concern, as independent nation-states fulfilled the political and theological demands of many Muslims. Historically, it is even more irrelevant, as Muslims were never politically united during the previous millennium. And the nation-state framework did, in fact, accommodate the persistence of transnational identities, whether applied to politics, historical consciousness, charities, religious organizations, tourism, education, sports, or popular culture. The heroic profile of African American heavyweight champion and Muslim convert Muhammad Ali in many Muslim-majority societies was a case in point. Ali became a global figure of civil rights and antiracist activism all over the world, though his Muslim admirers seemed to cherish his defense of both African and Muslim causes. What made this issue of compatibility between Muslim faith and nation-state seem urgent, however, was new postcolonial governments' imposition of the idea of homogeneous and secular ethnic nationhood upon their societies. Each postcolonial nation-state had its own version of the role of Muslim identity in nationalist ideology, but there was a sense of primacy of national loyalties and patriotism. These debates and impositions fed later, and equally ahistorical, Cold War–era Islamist claims of contradiction between ethnic nationalism and the transnational community of Muslim believers.

Decolonization of Muslim societies, like so many historical processes, retrospectively appears rife with contradictions until one realizes that those involved sensed no discord. The period from the early 1950s until the mid-1970s witnessed little successful pan-Islamic mobilization, and yet Muslims won the dignity of self-rule, the increasing sympathy of non-Muslim political leaders and intellectuals, and the opportunity to participate in an at least formally equal global system under the aegis of the United Nations. It is only from a perspective of hindsight—or, more accurately, amnesia—promoted by modern Islamist ideologies that the Cold War–era politics of Muslim societies and supposedly timeless Muslim values could seem at odds.

The Postcolonial Politics of Islamic Civilization

By the mid-1960s, geopolitical discourses on the Muslim world inherited from the imperial era were almost entirely abandoned. The special ties of the British Empire to the Ottoman caliphate were long gone, rendering geopolitical pan-Islamism obsolete. Alternative universalistic ideologies such as socialism, Third-Worldism, pan-Arabism, pan-Africanism, humanism, and nationalism, along with economistic theories of development, overshadowed Muslim identities.

Similarly, there was no urgent need for racial apologetics advocating the equality and dignity of Muslims in the context of sovereign nation-states. But unlike geopolitical pan-Islam, notions of Islamic civilization and Islam as a world religion did not lie dormant. Instead they were detached from the imperial-era political context in which they served as antiracist rebukes to

European narratives of Muslim inferiority and were recycled for new purposes. In the postcolonial decades preceding the geopolitical pan-Islamic revival of the 1980s, Islamic principles and civilization were seen as solutions to the ills of global capitalist modernity. On their basis, more ethical and just communities might be crafted at both the national and the international level. Thus even as decolonization produced more territorial divisions among Muslims, visions of Islamic civilization as a source of moral politics knit them together.

We can observe the persistence of civilizational discourses on the Muslim world in the positive reception of the British historian Arnold Toynbee's ideas among humanist Muslim intellectuals. Toynbee, who died in 1975, considered the Islamic civilization one of the last in the world to survive Westernization. During the Cold War, Toynbee's writing was a repository of civilizational views in a world being redefined by nationalism. In part by embracing and reshaping Toynbee's ideas about world civilizations, Muslim writers kept pan-Islamic intellectual history alive amid decolonization.[25]

Throughout an academic and civil service career spanning from 1912 to 1955, Toynbee wrote extensively on the politics of Muslim societies, the Ottoman Empire, and modern Turkey. During World War I, he crafted anti-Ottoman propaganda for the British Empire. The geopolitics of Islam and the West were essential to his work. He questioned the loyalty of Indian Muslims with ties to Istanbul.[26] He wanted British colonial officers to argue that the Ottoman caliphate was illegitimate because the dynasty was not from the Prophet Muhammad's tribe, and thus dissuade Indian Muslims from asserting pro-Ottoman sympathies.[27] But during the interwar years, Toynbee's relationship with post-Ottoman Turkey improved, and he praised the republic's Westernization program.[28] In later discussions with the Japanese Buddhist leader and peace activist Daisaku Ikeda,

Toynbee recounted proudly the radical shift in his assessment of the Muslim Turks—once enemies, now friends.[29] He also lamented the future of the British Empire. One of the most influential aristocratic intellectuals of what Richard Overy has called Britain's "morbid age," Toynbee was convinced of the eventual decline of the West in relation to modernizing non-European societies.[30]

When Toynbee became a global celebrity for *A Study of History,* his monumental twelve-volume work of comparative world history published between 1934 and 1961 he was already well known in various Muslim-majority countries as a representative of British imperial internationalism and as a post–World War II critic of Western modernity.[31] To promote his books, Toynbee lectured in almost every major city in the world from the 1950s to the mid-1970s. Among these were Cairo, Beirut, Kabul, Tehran, Istanbul, and Islamabad, where he spoke to large audiences, taught courses as a visiting professor, and found the ear of government authorities and intellectual circles alike.[32]

Toynbee's influence peaked between 1950 and 1975, just when his major ideas were most at loggerheads with trends of the time. Embraced by both the United States and the Soviet Union, the era's ascendant modernization theory differed from the earlier, mission-oriented modernization project of imperialism, in which colonizers claimed to tutor backward people out of their inferiority.[33] And yet Muslim intellectuals embraced Toynbee's civilizational ideas precisely as nationalism was making colonial-era discourses of civilizational hierarchy appear archaic. Many of these intellectuals were from Turkey, Iran, Pakistan, Lebanon, and Egypt, where postcolonial elites were committed to modernizing and Westernizing rather than reviving civilizations. But revivalist, socialist, and liberal Muslim intellectuals and modernizing elites all frequently quoted Toynbee—especially his criticism of Western materialism and militarism and his celebration of alternatives offered by other civilizations.[34]

Given Toynbee's early commitment to the ideal of a British commonwealth, his admiration for the ostensible Hellenistic-Christian foundations of the modern world order, and his racist pre–World War I geopolitical views, his post–World War II internationalism and humanism demonstrate an impressive change of heart and mind. Toynbee had been heavily influenced by his Greek history professor Alfred Zimmern, a future founder of UNESCO, who saw the model of ancient Greece as a cure for the twentieth-century crisis of imperial legitimacy. Zimmern and the young Toynbee both believed the British Empire should eschew the Roman model by discarding late nineteenth-century notions of white racial superiority. Yet they also believed in a hierarchy of civilizations, with the West at its apex. What they sought was a "dialogue of civilizations" between the West and its surviving competitors.[35] By the 1920s, however, civilizational discourse had become a tool of anticolonial nationalism, empowering claims for racial equality and national liberation rather than justifying British imperial rule.[36] From Rabindranath Tagore and Okakura Tenshin to Sun Yat-sen and Nehru, Asian intellectuals used the idea of their civilizational heritage and greatness to refute the civilizing principles underlying Western colonialism.[37]

World War II was the decisive turning point in Toynbee's thinking. With the British Empire in retreat and Europe licking its wounds after another devastating war, Toynbee had lost confidence in Western civilization. By the 1950s, he no longer assumed or advocated its superiority. He hoped other civilizations would stop imitating the broken West and instead preserve their diverse traditions. Toynbee's changing intellectual commitments supported new politics. The one-time archimperialist was generally supportive of postwar nationalism. When news

of the 1956 Suez Crisis reached him in Japan, he vehemently condemned the British attack, bolstering his prestige among Arab
and Muslim intellectuals. On his return trip, he visited Indonesia, Pakistan, and Iran, where he often criticized Western
imperialism. In Pakistan, he was hosted by Prime Minister
Ayub Khan. Toynbee was also an opponent of Zionism and a
supporter of Palestinian demands.[38] After the historian Hugh
Trevor-Roper published a famously harsh critique of Toynbee
in June 1957, Zaki Saleh, an Iraqi intellectual, wrote a book defending the erstwhile antagonist of the Muslim world.[39] Most
of Toynbee's major writings were translated into Turkish, Arabic, Persian, and Urdu.[40]

Toynbee's historical framework, in which Islamic civilization
appears as one of the few durable civilizations able to resist the
materialism and destructiveness of the West, appealed to multiple ideological currents in postcolonial Muslim societies for
diverse reasons. But one thing Muslim intellectuals agreed on
regardless of their respective levels of piety and varied political
inclinations was that there was indeed a sharp distinction between the Islamic and Western worlds.

Among Toynbee's biggest fans were the kinds of thinkers
who later were known as Islamists, owing to their rejection of
Westernizing reforms initiated by nationalist regimes in Turkey,
Iran, and Egypt. For Islamists, Toynbee's world-historical model
was a bulwark against Eurocentrism and secular nationalism.
For example, Turkish Islamist Sezai Karakoç relied on Toynbee's ideas in formulating Islamic revival as an alternative to
both socialism and capitalism.[41] Toynbee's model of the modern
world suggested that modernity as promoted by the United
States and the Soviet Union was just an instance of Western
Christian civilization. As a critic of the West, Toynbee was
therefore a critic of modernity. Trevor-Roper understood this
as well the Islamists, writing, "At the foundation of Toynbee's

version of the present crisis of the West was a profound anti-modernism—a rejection of the contemporary secular decadence and a call for a neo-medieval flight from this world. [Philosopher] Karl Popper spoke for many critics when he disparaged this view as 'apocalyptic irrationalism.'"[42] Some non-Islamist Muslim readers of Toynbee argued that one could escape the secular decadence of the contemporary West by synthesizing Islamic civilization with positive aspects of modernity. Regardless of their particular prescriptions, Muslim intellectuals of varying political orientation were imagining solutions to the problems of the modern world by resurrecting Islamic civilization.

In one instance of that resurrection, Muslim scholars and popular writers returned to the discourse of the Islamic golden age by focusing once more on medieval Muslim scientific contributions. Again, one might have thought this early pan-Islamic trope would be politically insignificant after colonialism. Yet not only was the history of Muslim science still a source of pride and differentiation, but contemporary thinkers also updated their reading of that history in light of midcentury Western science. Now Muslim discourse stressed Islamic science's moral superiority, as compared to the materialism and destructiveness of Western science, responsible for environmental degradation and the atomic bomb. Meanwhile, the era's American and European historians of science had left behind the overt racism and mendacity of Ernest Renan and the like, but they joined him—and Islamic civilization revivalists—in insisting on a sharp distinction between Western science and the practices of Muslims and others, such as the Chinese.[43] Postcolonial social scientists and humanists of all stripes continued to labor under the assumption that there was a distinct Islamic civilization whose past glories and modern contributions needed to be emphasized.

Finally, Toynbee's civilizational view of world history appealed to Muslims and non-Muslims in Africa and Asia looking to displace Eurocentric methodologies in social science and historical scholarship. Civilizationism had long been a dominant theme in anticolonial discourse, whether pan-Islamic, pan-African, pan-Asian, or nationalistic. All challenged supposed Western supremacy by characterizing the West as decadent, violent, and declining.[44] Toynbee's writings were thus nothing new to Muslim and other Third World intellectuals, but they were still useful. In Toynbee, Muslim intellectuals found a celebrated British internationalist confirming a position they had held for a century.

The popularity of Toynbee's ideas, and those of agreeable Third World intellectuals, had discomfiting consequences in Muslim societies. Throughout decolonization, reformist Muslim elites trying to strengthen societies and establish new systems of governance looked to a paradigm of multiple modernities; they didn't equate modernity with the West. Many did not see selective and creative adoptions from Europe as an insult to their religious and cultural heritage. But if, as Toynbee argued, modernity was an extension of Western civilization, then Turkish, Iranian, Afghan, and Egyptian Westernization discarded the legacy of Muslim civilization in favor of a rival way of life tainted by violence, colonialism, and materialism. On this view, Atatürk, Nasser, and Reza Shah all appeared as culturally alienated traitors.[45] Some secular and socialist intellectuals, who should not have any use for civilizational ideas, bought in. Iranian intellectual Jalal Ali Ahmad's *Occidentosis: A Plague from the West* exemplifies this synthesis of Muslim tradition and socialism in criticizing the darker elements of top-down modernization amid an unjust Cold War international order.[46] Not only Indian Muslim revivalists but even secular,

French-educated North African Muslim intellectuals discussed similar issues.[47]

Civilizationism provided the epistemic basis for later Islamist ideas about a Muslim alternative to the failed internationalisms of the Cold War and to the perceived crisis of modernization. That Islamist figures such as Sayyid Qutb and Ali Shariati shared so much intellectual territory with Western critics of postcolonial modernity speaks to the historical novelty of Islamism—less an extension of traditional religious beliefs and education and more a participant in the global response to capitalism and the Enlightenment.[48] What enabled this similarity between Islamist and European intellectuals, who nonetheless posited an essential difference between destructive Western modernity and the traditional Muslim values, was the discourse of civilization that assumed the essential unities of Islamic and Western traditions. More important, a Toynbean view of sharp distinction between Islamic and Western civilization allowed Islamists to tar nationalism and socialism as programs of alienation that weakened the Muslim world by trying to imitate its enemies. In the 1970s, these discourses on alienation were used to explain both the humiliation of the Muslim world caused by suffering in Palestine and Kashmir, and postcolonial nation-states' failure to achieve economic progress, prosperity, and political participation.

The persistence of civilizational language during the Cold War did not immediately translate into geopolitical conflict, Islamophobia, or pan-Islamism. When Queen Elizabeth II opened the World of Islam Festival in London in the spring of 1976, the capital city of the former British Empire hosted an impressive series of cultural events, museum and library exhibits, and other activities showcasing the glories and contributions of Islamic civilization. About thirty-two independent Muslim countries contributed to this event, either financially or in terms of exhibit materials. Yet while the festival was going on in London in the aftermath of the 1973 Arab-Israeli war, the discourse of Islamic civilization was already entangled with geopolitics of Arab-Israeli wars and re-racialization of Muslims. Until the 1980s, a civilizational notion of the Muslim world could be adapted to any ideological and nationalist trend, including pro-Western ideologies. Comparison of Muslim, Chinese, and Japanese intellectuals is revealing in this regard. Toynbee's ideas were also popular in China, especially after the peak of Maoism, but the 1980s saw no great discourse of the Confucian and Buddhist worlds. In Japan, Toynbee's ideas merged with both liberal Buddhist internationalism and business-minded globalism. There was no association with pan-Asianism or the notion of a united Asian world. Japanese business leaders reveled in Toynbee's critique of Britain's sluggish economic performance and frequent labor unrest, which contrasted with Japan's rapid growth and more orderly management techniques. In superficial and patronizing terms, Toynbee praised both Islam and Shintoism, which he considered more peaceful than Christianity and better harmonized with the natural world. But there was never a Toynbee-inspired Shinto world or Pan-Buddhism. It is thanks to the particular synthesis of Toynbean civilizationism and geopolitical pan-Islamism—to which East Asian countries no longer had a serious analogue—that the idea of the Muslim world was reborn with renewed confidence.

The Caliph of the Cold War?
King Faisal's Pan-Islamism

The Cold War rivalry between the Soviet Union and the United States added a geopolitical cast to existing visions of Muslim solidarity. With Nasser close to the Soviet camp, the United States sought allies to lead the imagined Muslim world in an anticommunist direction. But American attempts to nurture a model of anticommunist modernity in the Muslim world would run into a problem that imperial forebears knew well: since the idea of Muslim unity was based on an illusion of racial and civilizational commonality, it was impossible to promote a single standard for diverse Muslim societies. Soviet efforts to propagandize the Muslim world relied on the same essentialist error. Indeed, while perpetuating the illusion of a unified Muslim world, the superpowers actually deepened divisions among the new Muslim-majority states.

Turkey, an aggressively modernizing and Western-looking country, seemed like just the model the United States was looking for. During the interwar period, Turkey had banned Sufi orders and *madrasas,* as well as the veiling of women in public spaces. The state abandoned the Arabic alphabet and the fez, both symbols of transnational Muslim identity. Iranian and Afghan leaders followed with similar secularizing reforms. Large numbers of influential Egyptians, Indonesians, and Indians also embraced Turkey's path.

Eager to expand the capitalist modernization theory's influence among Muslim-majority countries, against the appeal of the Soviet socialist model, American social scientists as well as government officials promoted Turkish secular nationalism to Muslim intellectuals across the globe. American modernization theory praised the achievements of Turkish Westernization but also wanted Turkey squarely in the imagined Muslim world, where it could influence fellow Muslim societies. Thus, just three decades after the British tried to demolish Ottoman leadership of the imagined Muslim world and Americans whipped themselves into a frenzy over "terrible Turks," the United States saw in Turkey a kind of ideal. This was not just an official position. For instance, *The Incredible Turk,* a 1958 documentary on Turkey narrated by Walter Cronkite, praised

Atatürk's secularizing reforms. Kemalism was, however, controversial in Muslim societies. By the 1950s, Muslim revivalist organizations had come to see Kemalism as a betrayal, as alienation from Muslim identity. Although that decade's multiparty democracy softened Turkey's position on religious expression in public life, the Turkish model remained divisive for other Muslim-majority nations.

Americans continued to favor the Turkish example into the 1960s, but along the way, the U.S. government hedged its bets. Although American policymakers generally feared Pakistan's pan-Islamism, there were U.S. State Department officials who did see it as a blessing for their anticommunist strategy. This view strengthened over time as Pakistan allied with the United States in the mid-1950s. During Prime Minister Ayub Khan's 1961 visit to the United States, American media wrote about Pakistan as another anticommunist model for the Muslim world. Cultivating Muslim partners seemed especially urgent at this time because the Soviet Union had begun to experiment with its own friendly policy toward the imagined Muslim world by emphasizing the religious freedom its Muslim citizens enjoyed. Muslim citizens of the Soviet Union could practice some of their religious rituals, under the guidance of the officially sanctioned Muslim clerical establishment, contrary to anti-Soviet propaganda that there was no place for religious expression under communist rule.[49]

Despite American hopes, neither Turkey's nor Pakistan's reputation among Muslim populations was sufficient to overcome the influence of the Soviet-aligned Nasser in postcolonial Arab countries. Nasser inspired regime change in Syria and facilitated an Egyptian-Syrian merger in the United Arab Republic (1958–1961). In 1966, when Egypt executed leading Muslim Brotherhood intellectual Sayyid Qutb against the expressed wishes of King Faisal, there was little by way of transnational

Muslim public reaction, illustrating the prestige and power of the Egyptian regime.

U.S. policy also seemed highly contradictory. On the one hand, the United States praised Saudi monarchs and the Iranian shah for their modernizing reforms. On the other, it criticized Nasser and Iran's Mosaddegh, themselves dyed-in-the-wool modernizers.[50] Soviet modernization theory seemed more consistent. Muslim-majority Soviet states such as Uzbekistan and Azerbaijan were making economic progress, with modern urban infrastructure and employment for its citizens, which suggested to Muslim-majority countries that Soviet-style modernization was compatible with Muslim faith and identity. Post-Stalin reforms reinforced this sense of compatibility by allowing Central Asian Muslims, including Communist Party members, to practice previously banned rituals such as circumcision, eid celebrations, and pilgrimage to a select number of Muslim sites. The Soviets also backed the Palestinian cause, earning much goodwill in Muslim societies.

In response to Soviet initiatives, the United States emphasized oppression of Muslims under communist rule. Mirroring World War II German propaganda directed toward Soviet Muslims, American anti-Soviet campaigns fostered the notion of essential conflict between Islam and communism.[51] Academic scholarship on Islam in the Soviet Union emphasized the harsh oppression of Muslim religious life under communist rule and how Islam tried to survive with underground and secret practices. Despite early failures to win over the imagined Muslim world, the United States was undaunted in its pursuit of a global Muslim leader to advance its interests. The Western bloc was in a sense searching for a new caliph, and, as the protector of the Muslim holy cities, King Faisal was an obvious candidate.[52] The Saudi Dynasty was also an ideological opponent of Nasser's radical Arab nationalism and confronted Egypt during the 1962–1970 North Yemen Civil War.[53]

Between 1964 and 1975, King Faisal embraced the opportunity to assert himself as a global Muslim leader. In travels that took him even to Africa's smallest independent Muslim countries, he reinvigorated and updated earlier pan-Islamic networks. His status as the protector of Mecca and Medina created opportunities to fashion and project his image as the wise king for all Muslims.

Faisal was seemingly born for global leadership. In 1919, at merely fourteen years old, he had visited London as his father's representative and as a guest of the British Foreign Service. From 1926 to 1930, he served as emir of Hejaz, which put him in contact with an immense number of pilgrims en route to Mecca, honing his diplomatic skills. From 1930 to 1962, Faisal served as foreign minister, a portfolio he maintained after ascending the throne. The vast scope of his travels, as well as his personal attention to Muslim-majority states and foreign leaders of Muslim minorities, made him the foremost symbol of transnational Muslim solidarity during the Cold War. Pakistani pan-Islamist writer Chaudri Nazir Ahmad Khan made that plain in his 1977 book *Thoughts on Pakistan and Pan-Islamism,* dedicated to "King Faisal bin Abdul Aziz of Saudi Arabia: the greatest Pan-Islamist of modern times who fell a martyr to an assassin's bullet in Riyadh on 25th March, 1975, as a result of a deep rooted and sinister conspiracy to remove the Helmsman of the World of Islam."[54]

King Faisal's popularity in Pakistan is significant because he needed the approval of Pakistani intellectuals and politicians to legitimate his claim to leadership of the imagined Muslim world. Prior to Bangladeshi independence, Pakistan was the most populous Muslim country, earning it considerable clout—though, as we have seen, not enough to successfully assert its own Muslim-world leadership. More important, South Asian Muslims represented the mainstream Sunni reaction to Saudi rule in the holy cities. Many had strong reservations about Wahhabism, which contradicted any number of practices hallowed by both Sunni and Shia Muslims. For instance, in 1926, the Saudis destroyed the sacred tombs of Muhammad's companions in Mecca and Medina on the grounds that the practice of tomb visitation deviated from authentic doctrine.

Shia Muslims continue to object to Wahhabi rule in the holy lands, but Sunnis gradually forgave (and forgot) such shocks. The Saudis did their best to encourage such forgiveness by, for instance, commissioning a national mosque in Islamabad in 1969. Completed after Faisal's assassination in 1975, the mosque was at the time the world's largest. It still carries the name of King Faisal and remains a symbol of Saudi-Pakistani alliance.[55] In 1961, Faisal established the Islamic University of Medina partly on the recommendation of Maududi and other Muslim thinkers from the Indian subcontinent, symbolizing the transfer of leadership from South Asia to Saudi Arabia.[56] Writers from T. E. Lawrence to Muhammad Asad, in his anti-Lawrence autobiography *The Road to Mecca,* romanticized Hejaz as the birthplace of authentic Arabness and Islam.[57] As oil soaked Saudi Arabia in riches, the idealization of Arabia become important for Saudi-based charities and educational institutions, as well as in Arab versions of Cold War Islamism.[58]

Egypt's Islamist opposition also supported Faisal, helping to establish his global credentials. Escaping from Nasser's oppression, many Muslim Brotherhood intellectuals and activists found positions and protection in King Faisal's service. They also spread to Syria, Palestine, and Jordan, helping to organize a pan-Islamic network opposed to Nasser's secular pan-Arabism and supportive of the Saudi king. Faisal sought to empower this base of support financially. For instance, his Muslim World Youth League sponsored Turkish and Urdu translations of books by the likes of Qutb.[59]

Faisal's relationship with Malcolm X further demonstrates Saudi leadership in the reactivation of the Muslim world. Through Rabitat Al Alam al-Islami (the Muslim World League), a nongovernmental organization he founded in 1962, Faisal was instrumental in coordinating pilgrimages and other trips to Mecca by Muslim leaders, especially those from minority communities.[60] African American civil rights leader Malcolm X was among these. When he undertook his pilgrimage, he was treated as a state guest and granted an audience with then-Prince Faisal.

The pilgrimage was a moment of great spiritual nourishment for Malcolm and therefore also a symbol of Faisal's deft political hand. For the two men were ideologically very much at odds. Malcolm was a devotee of pan-Africanism. He and Nasser openly admired each other, and the Egyptian president arranged scholarships for African American Muslims studying in Cairo. And yet, in a letter from Mecca to his assistant in Harlem, Malcolm glowed. "During the past eleven days here in the Muslim world, I have eaten from the same plate, drunk from the same glass, and slept on the same rug—while praying to the same God—with fellow Muslims, whose eyes were the bluest of blue, whose hair was the blondest of blond, and whose skin was the whitest of white," he wrote. "And in the words and in the deeds of the white Muslims, I felt the same sincerity that I felt among the black African Muslims of Nigeria, Sudan, and Ghana." There could hardly be a better illustration of Faisal's diplomatic aptitude, as he managed simultaneously to depoliticize Mecca— asserting its spiritual centrality for all Muslims, regardless of their worldly beliefs—and to politicize it by making it a symbol of pan-Islamic internationalism via Saudi networks of education, charity, and diplomacy.

King Faisal also boosted his Muslim-world leadership credentials through historical links to imperial-era pan-Islamism,
symbolized by his relationship with Abdurrahman Azzam, the
person who introduced Malcolm X to Saudi authorities. By the
time Azzam met Malcolm X in Jeddah in 1964, he had been a
pan-Islamic activist for fifty years. In 1912, young Azzam left his
medical studies in England to volunteer for the Ottoman army
in the Balkan Wars. While in the Balkans and Istanbul, he met
several prominent Young Turk leaders, including Enver Pasha,
who, as minister of war, was one of the most powerful figures of
the late empire. During World War I, Azzam left British-
controlled Egypt to join the Ottoman *jihad* in Libya and supported the Libyan resistance against Italy. Afterward he helped
to create a new Libyan republic and secure its international recognition. In 1922 Azzam returned to Egypt, where he became
the khedive's ambassador to the Saudi kingdom. In 1931 he
joined the Muslim World Congress in Jerusalem over official objections from Britain and Egypt. Then, as the war was winding
down in 1945, he became the first secretary-general of the Arab
League, a position from which he campaigned at the UN against
the partition of Palestine.[61] After the 1952 Revolution brought
the Egyptian dynasty to a close, Azzam left Egypt and the Arab
League for Saudi Arabia, where he was embraced by King Faisal.
The presence of Azzam Pasha and many other figures like him
in Saudi Arabia from the mid-1950s to the mid-1960s symbolized the presence of a group of people with the historical
memory of pan-Islamic ideas and arguments next to Prince
Faisal, when he was reactivating a new Muslim-world network
in the postcolonial context.

The post–World War II biography of Japanese pan-Asianist
Umar Mita Ryoichi offers another portrait of Faisal's attempts
to revive pan-Islamic networks built across space and generations. During the interwar period, Mita lived in Manchuria

and researched Islam in China. He learned about Islam from Haji Omer Yamaoka, who, in 1909, became the first Japanese Muslim to perform the hajj, which eventually led to Mita's conversion to Islam in 1941. The Japanese government sponsored Mita's pan-Asianist writings throughout the war, and he actively worked for Japan's Muslim-world policy. Upon Japan's defeat and abandonment of Pan-Asianism, Mita did not stop his Muslim practices. As president of the Japan Muslim Association in the 1960s, he wrote or translated multiple books on Muslim religious thought. In 1972, he became the first Japanese Muslim to translate the Quran into his native tongue. Mita's efforts in this period were financed by the Muslim World League in Mecca, as well as by King Faisal himself, who instructed Saudi Arabia's ambassador to Japan to finance Mita's translation.[62]

If these historic and geographic linkages helped to establish Faisal as a kind of Abdulhamid for the Cold War, it was not purely thanks to the king's outreach. As Azzam's story shows, pan-Islamists sought out Faisal, just as he did them. Indeed, many Islamist thinkers marginalized by postcolonial nationalism were desperate for pan-Islamic solidarity led by a Muslim great power. As the Pakistani economist and Islamic scholar Khurshid Ahmad, who was a spokesperson for Maududi's Islamist organization, wrote in the introduction to a 1967 collection of Maududi's speeches on Muslim-world unity:

> Muslims today constitute one-fifth of the Human race. . . . And despite all this, Muslims have no effective voice in the world affairs. They have become passive camp-followers of others. Imperialist powers of the East and the West are active in their lands. Their basic problems remain unattended, what to say of their solution. Palestine bleeds. Kashmiris groan. Turkish Cypriots cry. Eritrean Muslims are being crushed. Nigerians are being subjected to sabotage from within. Somalians grumble

and protest. But all these voices of agony and anguish fall on deaf ears. Problems are becoming more and more aggravated. Situation is worsening and we, the six hundred and fifty million Muslims stand bewildered and aghast, helpless spectators of our own ruin. This is a paradox and we must wriggle ourselves out of this unhappy state of affairs. The answer to this situation is that the Muslims must sincerely remodel their individual and collective life in accord with the principles of Islam and pool their resources to play their rightful role in the world. It is through Islamic Revival and Islamic Unity that we can change the course of events and fulfill our tryst with destiny.[63]

That South Asian Islamists such as Maududi found a new sponsor in the person of King Faisal, even before the oil boom turned Saudi Arabia into a wealthy power, shows just how desperate lingering geopolitical pan-Islamists were for leadership. Maududi helped Faisal to create and attract students and faculty to the Islamic University in Medina. Islamist figures like Maududi could look up to Faisal as a wise king who could sponsor various other pan-Islamic projects. Faisal enjoyed this international support for him and for Saudi Arabia, just when he was being threatened by the appeal of Arab nationalism of Egypt's Nasser.

Faisal had been elevating his standing in different Muslim countries both via bilateral relations and by links to nongovernmental intellectuals and movements, while his regional Cold War rival Nasser lost his political credibility with the humiliating defeat in the 1967 war against Israel. Faisal and Saudi public opinion supported Egypt and the Arab cause in this war, and they did not want Nasser defeated. Yet defeat and territorial loss damaged Nasser's transnational reputation. Although pan-Arabism continued—Libya's 1969 coup, which brought the pro-Nasser revolutionary Muammar Gaddafi to power, speaks to the Egyptian leader's ongoing influence—after 1967, Nasser was no longer seen as a credible challenge to the U.S.-led Cold War camp in the Middle East. Thus Faisal's elevated image as a wise pan-Islamic leader gained new political significance after the demise of Nasser. King Faisal had little military involvement internationally, but he was a staunch supporter of the Palestinian cause, which was that much more imperative now that Israel controlled Muslim holy sites in Jerusalem. Even though Faisal was a U.S. ally, his opposition to Israel's colonization of Palestine made him a potential leader of global Muslim solidarity that could help oppressed Palestinians.[64]

Faisal used his unique combination of pan-Islamic prestige, good relations with the United States, and credibility as a ruler sincerely concerned about the fate of Palestinians to establish himself as a negotiating partner on the Palestine question. He hoped to persuade the United States to rein in its client, Israel. In this process, Faisal again proved a shrewd operator. Although the Eastern bloc was widely seen as a friend of postcolonial Muslim societies, Faisal maintained American trust by positioning himself as anti-Soviet. This might have alienated Soviet-aligned Muslim rulers, but by establishing himself as the leading Muslim voice on Palestine, Faisal was able to head off strong Muslim opposition born of Cold War rivalry. This is in part why it was so important for him to organize his 1969 pan-Islamic congress about Jerusalem.[65]

Competition from Egypt was also reduced by an alliance with the Saudis lasting from 1971 until 1977. Saudi-Egyptian relations improved when the countries made their peace over the Yemeni Civil War. The Saudis backed Egypt in 1967 and felt more comfortable with Nasser after defeat lessened the challenge of pan-Arabism and secular Arab nationalism. Thus the Saudis strongly supported the 1973 Arab war against Israel, in part by leading the oil embargo, which proved to be the peak expression of Saudi soft power.

In the aftermath of the 1973 war, the Saudis also improved relations with Pakistan by cohosting the Second Islamic Summit in Lahore, to which all Muslim-majority countries sent official representatives. In many ways, the summit of 1974 was the most successful pan-Islamic event of the Cold War, demonstrating unprecedented levels of Muslim unity under the leadership of Anwar Sadat of Egypt, King Faisal of Saudi Arabia, and Zulfikar Ali Bhutto of Pakistan.[66] Even though Sadat delighted in the summit, where he was praised as a hero of the 1973 war and redeemer of Arab and Muslim dignity, it was Bhutto's and Faisal's leadership that mattered most. The Lahore summit, according to its supporters, represented the collective power of the Muslim world, bringing together the military, economic, and political resources of the leading Muslim-majority countries.[67]

The results of King Faisal's shrewd pan-Islamic diplomacy also appeared at the United Nations General Assembly. Gradually a voting bloc of Muslim countries emerged in alliance with countries belonging to socialist and Third World blocs on the issues of Palestine. On November 10, 1975, the solidarity of these three groups helped to pass Resolution 3379, condemning Zionism as a form of racism. Supporters included the Soviet Union, China, India, and many nonaligned countries.[68] Emergence of this voting bloc at the UN owed partly to Faisal's diplomatic achievement in creating the Organization of the Islamic Conference and co-organizing Islamic summits from 1969 to 1974.

Yet the passage of Resolution 3379 also revealed a key weakness of Muslim solidarity within the UN system. In spite of unity on the question of Palestine, nothing changed in the lives of Palestinians living under U.S.-backed Israeli occupation. King Faisal's activities and the oil wealth of the Arab monarchies raised expectations of the Muslim world's influence on the world stage, but rising expectations led to greater frustrations as no Great Power came to the Palestinians' aid. Muslims had money, strong militaries, and large populations, so why wasn't international cooperation achieving results? This question led to new rounds of pan-Islamic discourse critical of Saudi Arabia's international diplomacy on the eve of the Iranian Revolution in 1979.[69]

One of the sources of King Faisal's influence had been the failure of socialism and Third World internationalism to secure Muslim political objectives. But those objectives lingered, unmet, beyond his death. It was time for new tactics. Between 1975 and 1977, pan-Islamists allied with socialists and Third World internationalists to pressure the United States and to isolate Israel. There were opportunities at this point to resolve the Palestine question, one of the strongest pillars of pan-Islamic identity. But a series of unexpected events from 1978 to 1980—namely the Camp David Accords, the Iranian Revolution, and the Soviet invasion of Afghanistan—channeled the rising expectations of pan-Islamic popular opinion into new political projects and alliances with a distinctly anti-American perspective. Ayatollah Ruhollah Khomeini of Iran would exploit this new brand of pan-Islamism throughout the 1980s, redefining the meaning of the Muslim World as a postcolonial region still humiliated primarily by the United States, its European allies such as the British, and the postcolonial Muslim elites allied with the West, such as the Saudi and Egyptian leaders.[70]

Reemergence of the Muslim World, 1979–1988

In his 1978 book *Orientalism*, Edward Said isolated and criticized many of the epistemological foundations of Muslim essentialism.[71] His critique urged the scholarly community and general public to overcome the racist legacy of Islamophobia and Muslim-world geopolitics, and many responded. But the events of 1979 onward reversed this course. The Muslim world would soon play an ever-larger part in the imaginations of journalists, academics, and global publics. The discourse of the Muslim world in the 1980s looked much like that in the 1910s, despite all the intervening decades of war and decolonization. How could this be? The refashioning of pan-Islamism as an ally of assorted Third World internationalisms in the 1970s is a significant part of the answer. But to reach the heart of the matter, we have to consider contingent events, beginning with the Camp David Accords of September 1978.

Sadat's presidency, following Nasser's death in 1970, saw a strong uptick in pan-Islamic sentiment within Egypt and raised Egypt's profile among pan-Islamists elsewhere. Sadat dismantled Egypt's radical secular nationalism, creating space for Islamist activists to flourish. He also allied with Saudi Arabia, which under Faisal was promoting itself as the center of pan-Islamic thought. In 1973, when the Egyptian Army showed a new level of strength against Israel, Sadat gained an international reputation as both a pan-Arab and pan-Islamic hero. The Saudi-led oil boycott backed Egypt, furthering pan-Islamic geopolitical aspirations and helping to reestablish Egypt's centrality in the imagined Muslim world.

But Sadat would squander this goodwill and confidence at the Camp David Accords. A bilateral peace agreement between Egypt and Israel, the accords did nothing to solve the major problems of Palestinians and frustrated the rising pan-Islamic expectations. Indeed, the treaty recognized the dispossession of Palestinian lands and the denial of their statehood. As such, the agreement betrayed the pan-Arab and pan-Islamic solidarity surrounding Palestine. It was also condemned by the United Nations General Assembly for not including the Palestinians and denying Palestinians the right of return. With its separate peace, Egypt effectively abandoned its key role in the Palestinian liberation struggle.

Prioritizing national interests over pan-Islamic causes was, of course, nothing new. The Ottoman Empire, and later the Republic of Turkey, instrumentalized the notions of caliphate and Muslim world to serve their interests and eventually abandoned both. The Camp David Accords can be likened to the Turkish republic's desertion of the Muslim world in 1924, when the national parliament abolished the caliphate shortly after the Khilafat movement had been so helpful in pressuring Britain into the Lausanne Treaty. At times, Pakistan and Saudi Arabia too chose a limited sense of national interest of over global moral claims on behalf of the Muslim world. There was also nothing unique or anomalous about Sadat's choice within the context of pan-Arabism. Even in the heyday of Arab nationalism under Nasser, nation-state-based realpolitik was the norm among Arab states, despite the rhetoric of Arab unity. Egypt's union with Syria failed partly because it was impossible to reconcile the national interests of two component units of this federation. Thus the demise of pan-Arab nationalism was structural, not a contingent result of the 1967 defeat or self-serving moves, such as Sadat's at Camp David.[72]

The problem with Camp David was not that Egypt pursued its own goals but that Sadat first benefited from the global pressure of pan-Islamic and Third World public opinion to get the best deal for Egypt, and then could not deliver much in terms of tangible achievements for non-Egyptian Muslims and Arabs. He misjudged the sources of his own leverage. He thought his heroic standing after the 1973 war would allow him to get away with a separate peace at the expense of Palestinian goals. But whatever leverage he had within pan-Islamic discourse derived mainly from the perception that he championed the broader international cause beyond Egypt's national interests. By refusing to tackle the Palestinian issue at Camp David, he was seen as betraying the most important pan-Islamic concern of his time.

The unfairness of the accords as perceived by transnational Arab and Muslim populations led to pressure to isolate Egypt, symbolized by its decade-long expulsion from the Arab League. Anti-Sadat emotions ran high among Islamists and pan-Islamists.[73] As Egypt faltered, the Saudis appeared as the next big Arab and Muslim great power, despite their alliance with the United States. When it came to Israel and the Palestinians, the Saudis retained bona fides that Egypt now lacked.

King Faisal's successor, King Khalid, ruled a Saudi kingdom much richer and more prestigious than the one Faisal inherited. Given Saudi oil wealth and elevated global status, expectations for leadership of the imagined Muslim world were high. Yet it was also unrealistic to anticipate a Saudi-led pan-Islamic response to the disillusionment caused by Camp David. Saudi Arabia could achieve international pressure only in alliance with other Arab and Cold War allies. Given the Palestinian struggle's strong global links—to socialist Vietnam and China, Latin American countries, European leftists, and others—the Cold War alliance between the Soviet Union and the Arab bloc could have been strengthened to help create a solution. After all, the Camp David Accords were a kind of Monroe Doctrine in the Middle East, reshaping the regional map with America's blessing.[74] Surely the Soviets were not enamored of this development.

But the Soviet Union also had no effective response to Camp David, and after its invasion of Afghanistan it lost much of its credibility among Muslim publics. Communist China was seen as another power capable of supporting Third World solidarity projects, but it too stayed on the sidelines, uninterested in risking its economic reforms and improving relationship with the United States. Sadat was eventually assassinated by radical Islamists in October 1980. Feeling abandoned by non-Muslim allies, pan-Islamists decided that their own internationalism was the most credible tool for redressing Muslim and Arab grievances.[75]

The unexpected and unthinkable 1979 Islamic Revolution was born of this resurgent geopolitical pan-Islamism and also complicated it. Asserting his own claim to leadership of the Muslim world, Imam Khomeini articulated many pan-Islamic grievances concerning humiliating Western imperialism and U.S. hegemony in the Middle East. He and his followers dissolved the shah's alliance with Israel and the United States and turned over the Israeli embassy to the Palestine Liberation Organization. Iran financed projects committed to pan-Islamic geopolitical solidarity, effectively competing with the sponsorship role the Saudis had embraced under Faisal. And the Islamic Revolution inspired a renewed sense of Muslim internationalism throughout diverse Muslim societies, giving hope to Shia and Sunni Islamists alike. But its competition with Saudi Arabia devolved into sectarianism and led to a battle of divergent visions of the Muslim world.[76]

When the revolution occurred, there was no Shia-Sunni division of political consequence. Iran had always cultivated links with other Muslim societies, and Iranian pan-Islamists perceived themselves as part of a Muslim world incorporating all Islamic sects. For example, when Iraq's Shia clergy endorsed the Ottoman *jihad* in 1914 and joined Iraqi Kurds, Turkmen, and Sunni Arabs in rebellion against post–World War I British rule, Iranian clerics and publics expressed sympathy for the Ottoman side in the war. Such connections remained robust throughout the interwar period, as Turkey, Iran, and Afghanistan cooperated closely without sectarian strife. Shia-Sunni division was not even an issue to consider in the 1939 marriage between Prince Mohammad Reza Shah of Iran and Princess Fawzia of Egypt. Shia clerics and intellectuals were key participants at pan-Islamic congresses before and after World War II. Ayatollah Talagani, among Khomeini's inspirations, attended the nonsectarian Jerusalem Congress in the early 1950s. Iranians joined various Muslim organizations during the 1970s without regard to sectarian divides. Foreign policy under the shah was comparable to Turkey's and Indonesia's in that it maintained alliances with the Western powers, including the United States, while recognizing the significance of Muslim identity and global links to other Muslim societies regardless of sect.

The intellectual background of the revolution was also more diverse than the rigid doctrine instituted by the revolutionary government might suggest. Iranian Muslim internationalism had many roots that could not be traced to a primordial religious identity under pressure from a secular monarchy. The intellectual biography of Ali Shariati provides a case in point. Shariati was an internationalist, new-left writer who refashioned and mobilized a progressive image of Islam and in the process became an intellectual touchstone for leftist and youth movements that allied with Khomeini to overthrow the shah. Shariati claimed to merge the ideas of Ernesto "Che" Guevara and Patrice Lumumba with the religious symbolism of Imam Hussein, a grandson of the Prophet Muhammad and one of the early martyrs of Shiism. In that sense, he was little different from late nineteenth-century Muslim modernists such as Muhammad Abduh, who blended scientific progress and universal civilization with a reinterpretation of Islamic texts.

Shariati developed most of his key ideas while a graduate student in Paris. He was familiar with the writings of the Orientalist Henry Corbin, the sociologist Georges Gurvitch, Jean-Paul Sartre, Frantz Fanon, and their contemporaries, finding his way to a critique of both capitalism and socialism in line with Sartre's. Shariati did not quote any of the well-known Cold War Islamists such as Maududi and Qutb, but he was aware of Muhammad Iqbal and the Algerian scholar Malik Bennabi, as well as many other postcolonial Muslim thinkers. By the early 1970s, Shariati had synthesized these hybrid sources into a new-left ideology proud of the Muslim intellectual and religious legacy. He was concerned about the future of the Global South and, in particular, what he saw as one of its subcategories: the Muslim world.

Shariati's ideas held sway over Iranian youth and student activists in the early 1970s. Young Iranians appreciated his alternative to internationalist visions that had already proved to be dead ends. They were also attracted to the revival of geopolitical pan-Islam in light of the shah's simultaneous alliance with the United States and Israel.[77] It was already known that the shah had been brought to power with a CIA-backed coup in 1953; now his close relationship with Israel led to his image as an alienated leader who had sold out the Muslim world.

It should be clear, though, that the alliance between Shariati-influenced revolutionaries and those closer to Khomeini was, in important respects, one of convenience. Khomeini was a cleric with a different intellectual genealogy compared to Shariati, though both shared similar ideas about the Muslim world and the West. When he was a young scholar in 1944, Khomeini wrote in a visitors' book at a mosque in Yazd, "It is our selfishness and abandonment of an uprising for God that [has] led to our present dark days and subjected us to world domination. It is selfishness that has undermined the Muslim world."[78] During the 1950s, he remained connected to weak attempts at pan-Islamic gatherings to discuss the suffering of Palestinians, Algerians, or other colonized Muslims. In 1963, he was exiled from Iran due to his harsh critique of the shah's perceived subservient relationship to the United States. During his exile in the late Cold War period, in an Iraqi city that attracts Shia pilgrims from all over the world, Khomeini was aware of the demands for a new Muslim internationalism. Thus when his followers overthrew the shah and established an Islamic republic, support for the oppressed people of the Muslim world was one of the revolutionary Iranian government's stated goals.

Given the interconnectedness of Shia and Sunni pan-Islamic discourses and their shared vision of the Muslim world, the conflict between Iran and Saudi Arabia from the early 1980s onward should not be seen as an inevitable result of sectarian divisions. Revolutionary Iran and the kingdom of Saudi Arabia initially had more in common with each other than with Sadat's Egypt, as they both criticized the Camp David Accords and might have formed an alliance on behalf of the Palestinians. Revolutionary Iran also maintained good relations with secular, majority-Sunni Turkey. And both Saudi Arabia and revolutionary Iran supported the anti-Soviet *jihad* in Afghanistan.

Because Iran's revolutionary government singled out the United States as the Great Satan and condemned U.S.-allied Gulf monarchies and secular Arab nationalist regimes for perpetuating U.S. hegemony in the Middle East, the Saudi regime felt it had to respond. The two-week seizure of a Mecca mosque, beginning on November 20, 1979, by a group of messianic Sunni Saudis deepened the kingdom's insecurity about its own legitimacy in the eyes of Islamists. The fear of Iranian-inspired Islamist revolutions or Shia insurrections in the Arab Middle East, coupled with the challenge from Sunni Islamists at home, triggered another round of Saudi internationalism, but this time with a focus on a specifically Sunni message and supporting Sunni opponents of the newly assertive Shia leadership in Iran.[79] Just as the Iranian Revolution was coming to a head, the Soviets invaded Afghanistan in order to prop up the oppressive pro-Soviet government of Nur Mohammad Taraki, which had taken power in a coup and promptly executed thousands of political prisoners.

Thus Saudi Arabia spread its Sunni gospel by pouring money into the Afghan resistance to Soviet occupation. Iran too was sympathetic to the Afghan *jihad,* but its opposition to the United States prevented such full-throated support for the U.S.-backed *mujahideen,* leaving the Saudis with a relatively clear field in which to peddle influence. When Iraqi president Saddam Hussein, fearing perceived Iranian influence over Iraq's Shia populations, declared war on Iran in 1980, Saudi Arabia, other pro-U.S. Arab countries, and the United States itself supported the Iraqis.[80] Sectarian divisions were further amplified in 1982, when Iran backed the Syrian Baathist regime of Hafiz al-Asad against Sunni Islamist groups demanding democratization. As an Alawi, Asad came from a family that is considered an offshoot of Shia Islam. For various political reasons, Asad led the Syrian Baath Party regime, domestically supported by an Alawi base, allied with Iran against Saddam Hussein's Baath Party–led Iraq.

The various parties in these disagreements all justified their conflicts by reference to geopolitical illusions of Muslim salvation. Hence it is easy to look at the politics of Muslim-majority societies in the final decade of the Cold War and find Islamist defiance of the superpowers. But this was also the birth of a new era of Muslim disunity. The Saudis pushed Islamic unity with Mecca and Medina at the center of a global Wahhabi network aligned against the Soviets. Iran rejected the superpowers entirely and argued that its brand of Islam was the true path to the liberation of all Muslims. Just as Islamism was emerging as a global force, driven by passionate appeals for the moral and civic superiority of pan-Islamic ideologies, Muslims themselves were finding new sources of geopolitical divisions and intra-Muslim conflicts.[81]

Competing and conflicting pan-Islamisms helped to revive dormant Islamophobia in Europe and the United States. Some of the very Muslims fighting each other also challenged U.S. and European interests by urging pan-Islamic solidarity against the Christian West. After Iranian student groups took U.S. embassy personnel hostage in November 1979, and as Westerners were taken hostage in Lebanon throughout the 1980s, Western journalism took on a strongly Islamophobic cast, reinforcing the clash-of-civilizations arguments among pan-Islamic groups in Islamic societies. Both U.S. embassy personnel kept hostage in Tehran for more than a year and European and American hostages in Lebanon were seen as innocent Western victims of a militant and assertive Islamic world. Ayatollah Khomeini's 1988 *fatwa* encouraging the murder of Salman Rushdie in response to his novel *The Satanic Verses,* along with book burnings organized by English Muslims, further inspired Western intellectuals and journalists to create a narrative of untrustworthy Muslims rejecting Western modernity and liberal values in the name of an unchanging Islamic tradition. Western observers were already concerned about Muslim solidarity in the Middle East, which had left scars in the form of rising anti-Arab discourses in the media since 1973. Now that fear and hatred of seemingly anti-Western Muslims in the Middle East began to be linked with the presence, demands, and agency of Muslims living in Europe and the United States.[82] Pictures of British Muslims burning a copy of Rushdie's book in protest, and then some of them agreeing with Khomeini's *fatwa* endorsing his assassination, added a new theme to European Islamophobia: that their racialized Muslim neighbors and citizens did not agree with liberal Western values such as freedom of speech.

A comparison between the attempts to ban *The Satanic Verses* in 1988 with the cancellation of Sir Thomas Henry Hall Caine's play *Mohamet* in London in 1890 illustrates continuities as well as dramatic changes in the geopolitical consequences of the racial imagination of the Muslim world. As we saw in Chapter 3, even though the play depicted the Prophet Muhammad and Islam respectfully, Indian Muslim leaders successfully petitioned the British Empire to cancel it so as not to offend the religious sensibilities of its Muslim subjects. In that context, the empire behaved according to the demands of imperial strategy, thinking not only about its legitimacy in the eyes of Indian Muslims but also of its relationship with the Ottoman Empire. Imperial civility reigned, and there were no calls for *jihad*.

In the case of Rushdie's perceived insults to Islam and Muslims a century later, the leadership of the imagined Muslim world was claimed not by a caliph-sultan eager to maintain his place in the international system but by a cleric who claimed to reject the global order of nation-states. The perceived insults against Islam were penned by a brown-skinned Indian of Muslim background, not a white British writer. But Rushdie, like British Muslims of the late nineteenth century, lived amid racialization of European Muslims—in his case, immigrants rather than imperial subjects—and widespread media-driven Islamophobia not unlike that of the imperial age. Rushdie himself criticized the racialized treatments of Indians in England; he wrote harsh words about Islam as a faith tradition but not about Muslims as a brown race. Khomeini's call for Muslims in Europe to protest and punish Rushdie carried the pan-Islamism of Abdulhamid and King Faisal in a new direction. While Abdulhamid searched for cooperation with the British Empire and King Faisal was hoping to empower the Muslim bloc in the UN system of world order in alliance with the United States, Khomeini tried to reach subaltern Muslims and Muslim public opinion directly, thanks to a network of Western satellite television channels that seemed terrified of an anti-Western Muslim religious cleric issuing a death order for a writer.

Saudi Arabia attempted to stake out a less radical position, condemning *The Satanic Verses* at a meeting of the Organization of the Islamic Conference but refraining from threatening Rushdie's life or suggesting that anyone else do so.[83] But Khomeini had successfully stoked the anger of subaltern Muslims the world over, demonstrating his emergence as spokesman for the illusory Muslim world. The fearful response in America and England and the rest of Europe, as much as any actions taken by Muslims themselves, demonstrated that postcolonial Muslim populations living in England were now seen as extensions of a threatening Muslim world into the heart of Western civilization.

In short, the Iranian Revolution exemplified the possibility of a new form of politics that challenged both camps of the Cold War in the name of a pan-Islamic solidarity centered in Tehran, prompting, on the one hand, admiration and emulation among other Islamists and, on the other, competition and opposition in the name of Sunni pan-Islamism.[84] It was something of an ironic turn, given that, at this very moment, Edward Said was making critical headway against civilizational thinking and Eurocentrism in academic scholarship. Thus an updated idea of the Muslim world appeared in the late Cold War period, not only in European and American writings on geopolitics but also in the political visions of Islamist groups challenging the failures of secular nationalism. For example, the era's pan-Islamists and Western Islamophobes agreed that Islam was incompatible with nationalism and the nation-state-based world order, no matter how strongly academic scholarship debunked this thesis.[85] While there emerged radical Islamists who considered democracy a Western ideology alien to their faith, there were also open expressions of doubts whether Muslim citizens in Europe and America would ever accept the standard norms of liberal democracy, a generalization about Muslims that became part of

Islamophobia. It was against this background that the American media's propagation of an Orientalist view of the Muslim world became worse, inspiring Said to write *Covering Islam* in 1981 to critique a new form of mass media racism against Muslims as a sequel to *Orientalism.*[86]

Amid the renewed discourse of civilizational competition, even anti-Orientalist scholarship seemed, to some, simply anti-Western. Many pan-Islamists in the 1980s read Said's book as a defense of real and essential Islam from the West's Islamophobic misrepresentations. In a review of *Orientalism,* the Syrian academic Sadiq Jalal al-Azm noted this "Orientalism in reverse" whereby Muslim intellectuals began to identify primarily with Muslim universalism and Muslim-world identity in the process of articulating essentialist condemnations of the West.[87] What Al-Azm observed in Said's readers in the Arab world were contemporary manifestations of a century-long legacy of Muslim self-Orientalizing in pursuit of assorted political goals. Muslim leftists also read Said in these terms, fearing that he buttressed rising Islamist tendencies that weakened leftist aims.[88]

◆ ◆ ◆

The genocide of Bosnian Muslims from 1992 to 1995 offered another opportunity for lazy generalizations about an unending clash of civilizations. Atrocities against Muslims in Southeast Europe, former borderlands of the Ottoman and Habsburg empires, recalled the tropes and sentiments of Islamophobia's Western birthplace, linking nineteenth-century racism to the new Islamophobia inspired by the Arab-Israeli conflict and the Iranian Revolution. Serbian nationalists subjecting Bosnian Muslims to genocide used tropes of anti-Muslim racism traced back not only to the late Ottoman era but also to the 1980s, such as the fear of Muslim fundamentalism, to justify why they needed to ethnically cleanse Europe of Muslims. During the pan-Islamic

mobilization of the 1990s, different Muslim-majority countries, from Turkey and Pakistan to Iran and Saudi Arabia, tried
to help Bosnians who were subjected to genocide because of
their Muslim identity. Observing initial sympathies toward
Serbian nationalists from Greece to Russia, as well as Western
governments' reluctance to accept a Muslim-majority independent Bosnia in Europe, coupled with transnational Muslim
mobilization to support Bosnian Muslims, inspired Samuel
Huntington to write his influential article "The Clash of Civilizations?," in which he predicted that the Muslim world would
be the Western world's next enemy after the collapse of the
Soviet Union.[89] Thus there emerged important continuities in
the ways the Muslim world was imagined as a geopolitical,
religious, and civilizational unity from the late nineteenth to
the late twentieth century.[90]

   Throughout this period, from the Iranian Revolution to the
conclusion of the Bosnian War, attention was focused on the
rise of Islamist parties and movements. These transnational
Muslim ideologies and movements seemed a unique aspect of
the Muslim world, compared to the seemingly secular and nationalist politics in the West, Asia, and Africa. But this view
misdiagnosed the situation in revealing ways. Muslim societies were no different from the rest of the world in terms of
their primary political experiences within sovereign nation-
states. Even the charter of the Organization of the Islamic
Conference affirmed and universalized the global norms underlying the UN charters, such as respect for sovereignty and the
right of self-determination.[91] Muslim organizations, people,
and ideas, ranging from socialists to feminists, crossed national
boundaries, but this is hardly unusual. Christian and Buddhist
missionaries, charities, and nongovernmental organizations—
some operating in the name of African, Asian, or Western
values—also traversed the globe. Even the presence of Islamist

parties and organizations, and shared themes and slogans among some of them, were not exceptional. Secularist, socialist, liberal, and environmentalist ideas also cross national borders. At the same time, postcolonial Muslims from Indonesia to Sub-Saharan Africa and the Soviet Union to the United States experienced immense diversity in their personal and political lives. Religious revivalism, even fundamentalism, did not warrant belief in a unique Muslim-world unity among either Islamists or Islamophobes—no more than it did Christian, Buddhist, or African unity. Yet post-1980s Islamist ideologies that call for international solidarity of the imagined Muslim world with reference to their own interpretation of Muslim faith tradition give the false illusion to Western observers that Islamists are authentic representatives of pious Muslims, an illusion used to justify Western Islamophobia.

The obsession about the geopolitical and civilizational unity of the Muslim world further inflated expectations of Muslim solidarity as a tool to solve Muslim societies' problems, ranging from economic development and establishing good governance to tackling international conflicts in Palestine, Kashmir, or Afghanistan. As these expectations went unmet, frustration at the weakness of the *ummah* prompted further calls for solidarity as well as anger that the majority of Muslims are not up to their faith's requirements. The pan-Islamic hopes were often unreasonable. Just as there was little chance that an African Union army or a black race *ummah* could liberate South African blacks from apartheid, it was equally improbable that Muslim cooperation alone would help Palestinian, Bosnian, and Kashmiri Muslims in their political struggles. As a problem created by the imperial world order and the United Nations, the subjugation of Palestinian Arabs, for example, has always lent itself to a solution truly international in scope. But such reasoning did nothing to eliminate the feedback loop of rising expectations and humiliation, leading to deepening fundamentalism and Islamophobia, all of which bolstered obsolete geopolitical imaginations of the Muslim world.

As ever, flawed assumptions of a separate and unified Muslim world superficially benefited pan-Islamic activists, who took advantage of perceived solidarity in order to gain support from faraway Muslims. But recourse to racial and religious identity also has been a source of weakness for pan-Islamism, undermining its universalist appeals. Pan-Islamism has long contained a strong measure of globalism, visible in alliances with theosophists, pan-Africanists, pan-Asianists, socialists, Third World movements, and nationalists committed to self-determination for all. Yet the persistent illusion of an insular Muslim world restricts such internationalism and relegates Muslims to reactionary and parochial positions, often against Western claims to universality. The multilayered discourse on the Muslim world—geopolitical, religious, and civilizational—also privileged the internationalism of Islamist parties over the existing diversity of Muslim political experiences. In scholarly and journalistic analysis, the wide range of governance styles within Muslim-majority countries became largely irrelevant, with preference and attention given to the supposedly univocal message of Islamisms asserting themselves as the ideologies of all Muslims. By the mid-1990s, these mutually reinforcing cycles of Islamist and Islamophobic outburst had entrenched the illusion of the Muslim world, suffocating the diverse voices and political demands of actual Muslims in different parts of the world.

Conclusion

Recovering History and
Revitalizing the Pursuit
of Justice

The 1980s witnessed a puzzling repetition. Imperial-era racial notions of pan-Islamism and the Muslim world that originally emerged in the 1880s were refashioned and revived in the late Cold War period. This intellectual context coincided with political and military conflicts producing millions of shattered lives.

Conflicts in Palestine, Lebanon, Syria, Iran, Iraq, and Afghanistan collectively buttressed claims of a clash between Islam and the West. Just when these seemed to be ending, Iraq's invasion of Kuwait and the subsequent first Gulf War, a civil war in Algeria, and the genocide of Muslims in Bosnia further reinforced the sense of a clash. A wide range of global actors, from Middle Eastern clerics and secular journalists to American academics and European novelists and ordinary news consumers of every stripe, thought this state of affairs ordinary. True, Cold War exigencies sometimes resulted in an alliance across the imagined borders of these illusionary worlds, but the idea that Islam and the West constituted separate, internally coherent entities with defined contours became immutable common sense.

This era spawned a new generation of radical Islamist groups and movements justifying violence in the name of a Muslim world besieged and victimized by the West, a narrative that continued to gain adherents through the turn of the twenty-first century.[1] Although today Muslims in Iraq, Syria, Yemen, and Afghanistan wage protracted wars against each other, and Muslim societies are more divided than ever, the resort to Muslim unity persists. In spite of the obvious differences obliterated in this narrative, the narrative goes on doing its work of racializing Muslims, especially in Europe and the United States.

In response, some liberals in Muslim-majority societies and beyond have pointed out that there are in fact multiple Islams and that to be Muslim involves diverse life experiences. But this is an insufficient debunking of epistemological and political assumptions of Muslim-world unity. Countering essentialism demands engagement with history—specifically how the discriminatory and racialized governing practices of European empires collectivized the political struggles and destinies of societies where Muslims lived in large numbers.

At the turn of the twentieth century, being Muslim in India, West Africa, Central Asia, or Southeast Asia had racial connotations. The Muslim world partly constituted by these regions was therefore seen as a rival of and sometimes a threat to white supremacy. Under such conditions, Muslim humiliation at the hands of the West emerged as the shared history of Muslim societies, whether under Christian imperial rule or observing the effects of that rule from within Ottoman domains. The narrative of eternal conflict between the Muslim world and the West originated in the late nineteenth century, yet non-Muslims and Muslims alike assumed that this narrative reflected a historical reality prevailing since the seventh century.

The challenges Muslim-majority societies faced in the twentieth century reflected legacies of imperial racism, so it is understandable that the proposed solution to that racism—Muslim unity—survived decolonization and its profusion of new political ideals. Postcolonial nationalist and internationalist ideologies popular in Muslim societies often sought salvation of the victimized Muslim world from the humiliation of Western hegemony. The adherents of these ideologies were sometimes rivals, and their perceptions of problems and solutions varied greatly. Yet their object was always the same: redemption for the integrated, amalgamated Muslim body.

Thus today's counternarratives against the essentialization of Islam and the Muslim world must account for the historical context that produced the conditions and content of that essentialization. It is not enough to demonstrate that presumptions of unity are just that. Islamists and Islamophobes alike can respond by recourse to endless conflict and the textual core of Muslim thought and identity. Contemporary diversity can be shunted aside as alienation or aberration from enduring faith and history. It is these stories, repeated or just assumed by billions, that must be shown to be false; recent and contingent, they were the inventions of, on the one hand, imperial racism and, on the other, the pan-Islamic claims of Muslim reformers who conjured history and beliefs as befit their political projects.

Amnesia about the late nineteenth-century origins of Muslimness helps to explain the thorniest question of contemporary Islamophobia and pan-Islamism: why the essentialist narrative of Islam versus the West has peaked in global public opinion in the past three decades, amid an unprecedented wave of books, scholars, and organizations debunking the racial and civilizational theories making essentialism possible. Countless efforts emphasize all that is shared by Islam and its fellow Abrahamic traditions, Christianity and Judaism. Others highlight the humanism and pluralism of Islam in theory and practice. Still others continue to shatter myths about so-called Islamic civilization, showing its civility and contribution to global modernity. Historians of science and technology avoid using terms such as "Islamic science" in order to avoid contributing to new essentialisms of dividing human history into Islamic and its Western other. Other historians commit themselves to the connected history of all peoples and no longer build theories atop frameworks of civilization.

But while contemporary scholars and activists do well to avoid essentialism as well as tropes of immutable faith and civilization, avoidance leaves the wounds of essentialism to fester. We must not just shun others' errors but must also reflect on the modern political struggles that bred notions of Muslim unity in the first place. Today, as in the imperial era, apologia celebrating good Muslim faith, real Muslim faith, and the Islamic golden age are supposed to combat the geopolitical fears inherent in Islamophobia, yet they only fortify the essentialism without which Islamophobia is impossible.

If instead we trace the evolution of Muslim-world narratives across 150 years, we can appreciate that geopolitical projects responsive to momentary exigencies are the basis of both Islamism and Islamophobia, warring twins crudely and falsely proclaiming enduring religious and civilizational identity. Historicizing the formation of major pan-Islamic narratives also shows the many possibilities that could have been realized but were not, further distancing us from any sense that today's fears of the Muslim world and dreams of Muslim internationalism have any deep basis resistant to contingent politics.

Once we recognize that Renan, Gladstone, and Hurgronje were not merely prejudiced but were talking about the rights of fellow imperial subjects, and once we recognize that Muslim modernism and pan-Islamism were aimed at a Western audience in an attempt to counter the racism that justified mistreatment, we not only leave deep history behind but also can take more sober stock of antiracist strategies that sadly and unwittingly are repeated to this day. Muslims themselves strategically essentialized a notion of the Muslim world that contradicted the lived imperial, national, global, and local experiences of Muslim societies. Pan-Islamists from Jamal ad-Din al-Afghani and Abdulhamid II to Syed Ameer Ali, Shakib Arslan, and Abul Ala Maududi were not acting as pious interpreters of God's divine will as revealed in sacred texts, though they may at times have claimed as much. Rather, what drove them was political will: the ideology they brought to their particular historical context.

Today's ahistorical narratives of the Muslim world and the West ignore the political contexts in which these categories were born. That political context was empire: the desire to preserve imperial borders, maintain strategic alliances, and achieve the cosmopolitan ideal of equal rights and dignity within and across empires. More than Wahhabi and other fundamentalist interpretations of Islam, it was the Muslim-ness constructed in the conversation between European Orientalists and Muslim modernists that created current obsessions with Islamic texts, cut off from a millennium of diverse Muslim religious and political experience.

The real nineteenth- and twentieth-century history of Islamophobia also demonstrates clearly that it is a form of racism, skin color aside. Consider how hard Muslim modernists worked to stave off imputations of inferiority and difference. Turkish leaders under Mustafa Kemal Atatürk tried, of their own will, to become Western by erasing their visible Muslim identity. But the project failed in the long term because no amount of Westernization or secularism could eliminate the markers of Muslim difference. Bosnians and Kosovar Albanians suffered similar fates; their cosmopolitan secularism and integration into Yugoslav culture could not prevent the genocide against them in the 1990s. Clearly, the Muslim identity constructed through both pan-Islamism and Islamophobia supports discrimination and hatred even in the absence of biological notions of race.

Nor need Islamophobia be explained with recourse to timeless religious difference. Though Christian missionary polemics, sometimes drawing on medieval Christian prejudices, contributed to European bias against Muslims, the notion of the Muslim world—the idea that Muslims constitute a global community with shared habits, concerns, and politics differing from those of non-Muslims—is itself secular. There is no better evidence of this than the coproduction of the Muslim world in the past 150 years of by Islamophobic and pan-Islamic discourses. If we are to have a new conversation on Muslim political agency and Islamophobia today, this coproduction of essential difference, without biological or doctrinal theories, must be front and center.

Islamophobia is neither transhistorical nor ahistorical; it would be wrong to describe just any critique of the practices of Muslims as Islamophobia. Persians fighting the early Muslim armies were not Islamophobes. Nor could Habsburg propagandists writing against the Ottoman-French alliance in the mid-sixteenth century fairly be called Islamophobic. To do so is to construct a false narrative of millennium-long, continuous European Christian enmity toward all Muslims, from the Crusades onward. The roots of modern Islamophobia lie in the particular moment in the late nineteenth century when Muslim societies shared the same imperial political system with European Christians and could claim their rights within these empires.

But while there is continuity between late nineteenth-century and current conceptions of the Muslim world, it would also be wrong to portray even this recent evolution as linear or inevitable. The Muslim world is in an ongoing process of creation. Ruptures, mutations, and reinventions surround the caliphate, *ummah,* and pan-Islamism. Even though the All-India Muslim League's Muhammad Ali Jinnah and Muslim Brotherhood founder Hasan al-Banna are seen as progenitors of late Cold War political Islam, neither Jinnah nor al-Banna would recognize or willingly take responsibility for Islamist *jihads* of the 1980s. The increasingly violent political Islam of the 1980s was enriched and shaped by Cold War ideologies.

There may be no more vivid example of the nostalgia at work in today's Islamist politics than zeal for the establishment of a caliphate. Present-day caliphate movements pursue lifestyles and political sensibilities utterly alien to those of the Ottoman caliphs whom they see as predecessors. Whereas Ottoman caliphs embraced cosmopolitan empire, today's caliphate builders impose their variety of original and true Islam as nation-state policy. The Indian Khilafat movement of the early 1920s, with its explicit pursuit of Muslim solidarity, may seem a more direct predecessor of today's Islamists, as it was focused on preserving the existing caliphate; but it too embodied a set of values radically different from those of any Islamist group of the 1980s and since. Khilafat activists agitated on behalf of Muslim rights and dignity within the imperial world. They neither rejected the global order nor sought the imposition of Islamic law over any population, whether Muslim or non-Muslim. When the Ottoman Empire collapsed, and the caliphate soon after, Khilafat supporters did not dig in their heels to reject nationalism but, as their own lives reflect, adjusted to changing sensibilities and circumstances.

Indeed, even the Islamists of the 1980s, who mostly tried to control a nation-state and run it according to their own visions in harmony with the international community, cannot easily comprehend the brutal messianism of ISIS in Iraq and Syria after 2014. Even though ISIS's roots lie in the policies of the U.S. occupation of Iraq after 2003, its ideology relies on an ahistorical caricature of the caliphate, one that seems derived more from Islamophobic stereotypes than from Abbasid or Ottoman practices.

American and European political elites are similarly afflicted by amnesia. They deny their own complicity in creating the conditions that fostered imperial-era racialization of Muslims, geopolitical othering of an imaginary Muslim world, Cold War Islamism, al-Qaida, and ISIS, instead blaming Muslims and the Muslim world. The goal is to perpetuate a self-righteous narrative of Western innocence. The result is increasing European and American Islamophobia, with considerable legal and political implications. This robust Islamophobia benefits militant Islamist groups, who argue that the Muslim world is still being humiliated and thus needs pan-Islamic solidarity.

As evidence for this humiliation, Islamists point to, among other things, the very chaos and division they sow and exploit. The imposition of particular pan-Islamic visions of forced unity itself reveals and aggravates the natural diversity of ethnicity, language, class, gender, and ideological orientations among Muslims. The post-1979 bloom of pan-Islamic discourses has created a new and varied set of conflicts within Muslim societies. It is safe to say that the "Muslim world," as a catchall description of people recognizing themselves as Muslims, has never been more delusional.

If both Islamists and Islamophobes are ever to be rid of this delusion, they must come to appreciate the contingent politics of the ideas they hold dear. Useful in that process will also be revision of Eurocentric notions of world history, the humanities, and the social sciences, which too often continue to rely on binary distinctions between Islamic and Western civilizations. The appeal of this binary model is probably clearest in its embrace and preservation by generations of Muslim reformers and nationalists crafting a narrative of the morally superior Muslim world and its victimization. But simplistic and ahistorical frameworks of European empires versus non-European subaltern colonized masses must be scrapped and replaced with the history of the world as it actually existed. In reality, Muslim and Asian empires, kingdoms, and princely states played important roles in intellectual and political history. For instance, Napoleon's invasion of Egypt in 1798 was not a turning point in Western imperial hegemony over Muslim societies, because Muslim dynasties—Ottoman, Persian, Omani, Afghan, and Egyptian—adjusted in response. Seeking empowerment within the world order of their own time, they modernized and clawed their way toward imperial legitimacy. Even when unfairness and subjugation eventually prompted debates on Islamic decline and renewal, producing the new, late nineteenth-century discourses of Islamic civilization and the Muslim world, Muslim dynasties pragmatically instrumentalized the new pan-Islamism. Hence for the Ottomans, the Muslim world was a strategic tool of foreign policy. Much later, leaders of postcolonial Muslim-majority nation-states such as Pakistan, Egypt, Saudi Arabia, and Iran strategically refashioned older ideas of the Muslim world as befit their global and regional rivalries. Today's attempt to overcome racialized narratives of civilizational conflict must involve self-reflection and critique on the part of Muslims, to recover and acknowledge their agency in reproducing these narratives.

This sort of self-criticism is of greater importance when one realizes that it was not just elites, European and Muslim, who embraced pan-Islamic solidarity and the illusion of the Muslim world. Disempowered Muslim populations joined them in pursuit of bargaining power over colonial rulers and global governance institutions. Subaltern Muslims spoke out and wrote against racism. They talked back, contesting the Euro-American discourse on the inferiority of their religion, race, and community. The image of the "argumentative Indian," articulating his demands on the basis of British law and notions of imperial legitimacy, is apt.[2] Subaltern Muslims also appealed to both imperial and international mechanism and notions of justice. Critically, they talked to each other, all over the world, and to non-Muslim Asians and Africans, about solidarity against imperial domination. They traveled; read newspapers, books, and magazines; protested and organized; published books and pamphlets; and attended international gatherings.

It is time to reflect on whether their solidarity movements actually worked to the advantage of those comprising them. Pan-Islamists figures often saw themselves as weak actors in need of Great Power sponsorship, whether provided by the Ottomans, the British, the Axis or Allied powers, the United Nations, or postcolonial internationalisms. Yet Great Power sponsors and the ideologues of universalistic doctrines constantly disappoint, prioritizing their own interests over the struggle for rights of disempowered groups. The struggle on behalf of the Muslim world has been especially prone to co-optation because there is no clear limit to who might speak on behalf of an imagined entity. Just about anyone can claim its custodianship and then betray the people who believed themselves at last represented. Whether the claimant was the Ottoman Empire, the Saudi kingdom, postcolonial Egypt, or revolutionary Iran, the interests of states were impossible to align with those of subaltern Muslim internationalism.

The dispiriting trajectory of the idea of the Muslim world does not entail that contemporary Muslims are beyond their rights in imagining their own humanitarian or political solidarity. On the contrary, Muslims of all kinds have every right to be concerned about the conditions and future of their coreligionists, and they have a right to act on their internationalist and humanitarian visions. But in doing so, Muslims and their non-Muslim allies must stop relying on imaginary geographical unities and theoretical ideals and ask themselves what the experiences of Muslim societies actually has been. All would be well advised to reconsider their essentializing assumptions about the experience of being Muslim in the modern world.

Historicizing the Muslim world and reflecting on the role of both Muslims and Euro-Americans in fostering racialization can vitalize the struggle for rights and justice. Muslim publics and intellectuals have never been wrong in seeking fairness and justice. The problem has always been the essentializing moves they made along the way, which repeatedly backfired by fostering Islamophobic fears from without and, later, in concert with those fears, Islamist rage from within. The failure lay in an inability to recognize that their demands and criticisms were not limited to the good of the imaginary Muslim world but in fact extended to all humanity. After all, how can you achieve justice for a geopolitical illusion that does not exist?

Notes

Introduction

1. The *New York Times* online edition introduced this speech thus: "The following is a text of President Obama's prepared remarks to the Muslim world, delivered on June 4, 2009, as released by the White House." "Text: Obama's Speech in Cairo," *New York Times*, June 4, 2009, http://www.nytimes.com/2009/06/04/us/politics/04obama .text.html?pagewanted=all&_r=0.

2. *A Call to Divine Unity: Letter of Imām Khomeinī, The Great Leader of the Islamic Revolution and Founder of the Islamic Republic of Iran, to President Mikhail Gorbachev, Leader of the Soviet Union* (Tehran, 2008) For the online text, see http://www.fouman.com/Y/Get_Iranian _History_Today.php?artid=1387.

3. Samuel P. Huntington, *The Clash of Civilizations and the Remaking of World Order* (New York: Simon & Schuster, 1996); Erik Zurcher, *Jihad and Islam in World War I: Studies on the Ottoman Jihad on the Centenary of Snouck Hurgronje's "Holy War Made in Germany"* (Leiden: Leiden University Press, 2016).

4. Ansev Demirhan, "Female Muslim Intellectuals: Understanding the History of Turkey's Woman Question through the Construction of Islamic Tradition" (MA thesis, University of North Carolina–Chapel Hill, 2014); Nile Green, "Spacetime and the Muslim Journey West:

Industrial Communications in the Making of the 'Muslim World,'"
American Historical Review 118, no. 2 (April 2013): 401–429.

5. For polyvocality argument, see Jonathan Berkey, *The Formation of Islam: Religion and Society in the Near East, 600–1800* (New York: Cambridge University Press, 2003). This does not mean that Muslim scholars before the nineteenth century were immune from any form of essentialism. A book by al-Suyuti, titled *The Perfect Guide to the Sciences of the Qur'an (Al-Itqān fi 'Ulum Al-Qur'an)* (Reading, UK: Garnet, 2010) would obviously have its author's firm conviction about how to read and understand the Quran. But al-Suyuti and many others in his generation would not feel the need to think of writing a book just on Islam or "Islam and Christianity" as abstract, global, and systematic religious traditions. Questions such as "Which interpretation of Islam, when and where, and understood by whom?" would seem to qualify the scholarship on Muslim faith tradition before the late nineteenth century, when Muslim scholars responded to essentialist writings of Orientalism and missionaries about Islam with equally apologetic or polemical essentialist abstractions.

6. Katharina A. Ivanyi, "God's Custom Concerning the Rise and Fall of Nations: The Tafsir al-Manar on Q 8: 53 and Q 13: 11," *Maghreb Review: Majallat al-Maghrib* 32, no. 1 (2007): 91–103.

1. An Imperial *Ummah* before the Nineteenth Century

1. Kate Brittlebank, *Tipu Sultan's Search for Legitimacy: Islam and Kingship in a Hindu Domain* (Delhi: Oxford University Press, 1997); Mohibbul Hasan, *Waqai-i manazil-i Rum: Tipu Sultan's Mission to Constantinople* (Delhi: Aakar Books, 2005). For a discussion of the significance of this Indian-Ottoman correspondence, see Azmi Özcan, "Attempts to Use the Ottoman Caliphate as the Legitimator of British Rule in India," in *Islamic Legitimacy in a Plural Asia,* ed. Anthony Reid and Michael Gilsenan (London: Routledge, 2007), 71–80. See also Virginia Aksan, "Ottoman Political Writing, 1768–1808," *International Journal of Middle East Studies* 25, no. 1 (1993): 53–69; Azmi Özcan, *Pan-Islamism: Osmanlı Devleti, Hindistan Müslümanları ve İngiltere (1877–1924)* (Ottoman state, Indian Muslims and England, 1877–1924) (Istanbul: Isam, 1991), 20; Yusuf Bayur, "Maysor Sultan Tipu ile Osmanlı

Padişahlarından Abdulhamid, III. Selim Arasındaki Mektuplaşma"
(Correspondence between the Sultan of Mysore and Ottoman rulers
Abdulhamid and Selim IIIrd), *Belleten* 12, no. 47 (1948): 617-654.
   2. Ian Almond, *Two Faiths, One Banner: When Muslims Marched
with Christians across Europe's Battlegrounds* (Cambridge, MA: Harvard University Press, 2009).
   3. Sayyid Abu al-'Ala Mawdudi, *A Short History of the Revivalist
Movement in Islam* (Lahore: Islamic Publications, 1963); Ali Shariati,
Ali Shariati's Red Shi'ism (Tehran: Shariati Foundation, 1979).
   4. Hamid Dabashi, *Being a Muslim in the World* (Basingstoke, UK:
Palgrave Macmillan, 2013).
   5. Mohammad Hassan Khalil, *Between Heaven and Hell: Islam, Salvation, and the Fate of Others* (Oxford: Oxford University Press, 2013).
   6. For a broader perspective on Muslim societies in world history,
see Marshall G. S. Hodgson, "The Role of Islam in World History," *International Journal of Middle East Studies* 1, no. 2 (1970): 99-123. See
also Edmund Burke III, "Islamic History as World History: Marshall
Hodgson, 'The Venture of Islam,'" *International Journal of Middle East
Studies* 10, no. 2 (1979): 241-264.
   7. Talal Asad, *The Idea of an Anthropology of Islam* (Washington,
DC: Center for Contemporary Arab Studies, Georgetown University,
1986).
   8. Ahmet Karamustafa, "Kaygusuz Abdal: A Medieval Turkish
Saint and the Formation of Vernacular Islam in Anatolia," in *Unity in
Diversity: Mysticism, Messianism and Construction of Religious Authority
in Islam,* ed. Orkhan Mir Kasimov (Leiden: Brill, 2013), 329-342.
   9. Guy Burak, "The Second Formation of Islamic Law: The Post-
Mongol Context of the Ottoman Adoption of a School of Law," *Comparative Studies in Society and History* 55, no. 3 (2013): 579-602; Zvi
Ben-Dor Benite, *The Dao of Muhammad: A Cultural History of Muslims
in Late Imperial China* (Cambridge, MA: Harvard University Asia
Center, 2005).
   10. For Christian alliances with Muslims, see Richard Tuck, "Alliances with Infidels in the European Imperial Expansion," in *Empire
and Modern Political Thought,* ed. Sandar Muthu (New York: Cambridge University Press, 2012), 61-83.
   11. Muzaffar Alam and Sanjay Subrahmanyam, "The Making of a
Munshi," *Comparative Studies of South Asia, Africa and the Middle East*

24, no. 2 (2004): 61–72; Ebba Koch, "How the Mughal Padshahs Referenced Iran in Their Visual Construction of Universal Rule," in *Universal Empire: A Comparative Approach to Imperial Culture and Representation in Euroasian History*, ed. Peter Fibiger Bang and Dariusz Kolodziejczyk (Cambridge: Cambridge University Press, 2012), 194–209.

12. Cemal Kafadar, "A Rome of One's Own: Reflections on Cultural Geography and Identity in the Lands of Rum," in *Muqarnas: An Annual on the Visual Culture of the Islamic World*, vol. 24, ed. Gulru Necipoglu and Sibel Bozdogan (Leiden: Brill, 2007), 7–25; Giancarlo Casale, "The Ethnic Composition of Ottoman Ship Crews and the 'Rumi Challenge' to Portuguese Identity," *Medieval Encounters* 13, no. 1 (2007): 122–144; Anna Contadini and Claire Norton, *The Renaissance and the Ottoman World* (Surrey, UK: Ashgate, 2013); Gerald M. MacLean, *Re-orienting the Renaissance: Cultural Exchanges with the East* (New York: Palgrave Macmillan, 2005).

13. Hanifi Şahin, "Câmiu't-Tevârîh'e Göre Gâzân Hân'in Müslümanligi ve Bunun Ilhanli Toplumuna Yansimalari" (Gazan Khan's Muslim-ness according to Camiu't Trevarih and its reflection on Ilkhanid Society), *Bilig* 73 (Spring 2015): 207–230.

14. Denise Aigle, "The Mongol Invasions of Bilâd al-Shâm by Ghâzân Khân and Ibn Taymîyah's Three 'Anti-Mongols' Fatwas," *Mamluk Studies Review* 11, no. 2 (2007): 89–120. See also R. Amitai-Preiss, "Ghazan, Islam and the Mongol Tradition: A View from the Mamluk Sultanate," in *Muslims, Mongols and Crusaders*, comp. G. R. Hawting (London: RoutledgeCurzon, 2005), 253–262.

15. A. N. Poliak, "The Influence of Chingiz-Khan's Yasa upon the General Organization of the Mamluk State," in *Muslims, Mongols and Crusaders*, comp. G. R. Hawting (London: RoutledgeCurzon, 2005), 27–41.

16. Ovamir Anjum, *Politics, Law and Community in Islamic Thought: The Taymiyyan Moment* (Cambridge: Cambridge University Press, 2012).

17. Azfar Moin, *The Millennial Sovereign: Sacred Kingship and Sainthood in Islam* (New York: Columbia University Press, 2012); Lisa Balabanlýlar, *Imperial Identity in the Mughal Empire: Memory and Dynastic Politics in Early Modern South and Central Asia* (London: I. B. Tauris, 2012); Said Amir Arjomand, "Perso-Islamicate Political Ethic in Re-

lation to the Sources of Islamic Law," in *Mirror for the Muslim Prince: Islam and the Theory of Statecraft*, ed. Mehrzad Boroujerdi (Syracuse, NY: Syracuse University Press, 2013), 82–106.

18. Cihan Yüksel Muslu, *The Ottomans and the Mamluks: Imperial Diplomacy and Warfare in the Islamic World*. (London: I. B. Taurus, 2014).

19. See Namık Sinan Turan, *Hilafetin Tarihsel Gelişimi ve Kaldırılması* (Historical evolution and abolishment of the caliphate) (Istanbul: Altın Kitaplar, 2004).

20. Hüseyin Yılmaz, *Caliphate Redefined: The Mystical Turn in Ottoman Political Thought* (Princeton, NJ: Princeton University Press, 2017).

21. Gulru Necipoglu, "Süleyman the Magnificent and the Representation of Power in the Context of Ottoman-Hapsburg-Papal Rivalry," *Art Bulletin* 71, no. 3 (1989): 401–427; Dariusz Kolodjiejczyk, "Khan, Caliph, Tzar and Imperator: The Multiple Identities of the Ottoman Sultan," in *Universal Empire: A Comparative Approach to Imperial Culture and Representation in Euroasian History*, ed. Peter Fibiger Bang and Dariusz Kolodziejczyk (Cambridge: Cambridge University Press, 2012), 175–193; Koch, "How the Mughal Padshahs Referenced Iran."

22. Cornell Fleischer, *Bureaucrat and Intellectual in the Ottoman Empire: The Historian Mustafa Ali, 1541–1600* (Princeton, NJ: Princeton University Press, 1986); Kaya Şahin, *Empire and Power in the Reign of Süleyman: Narrating the Sixteenth-Century Ottoman World* (Cambridge: Cambridge University Press, 2013); Muzaffar Alam, "A Muslim State in a Non-Muslim Context," in *Mirror for the Muslim Prince: Islam and the Theory of Statecraft*, ed. Mehrzad Boroujerdi (Syracuse, NY: Syracuse University Press, 2013), 160–189.

23. For the claims of the Moroccan sultan's caliphate in the western Mediterranean at the same time the Ottomans promoted their caliphate in the Indian Ocean, compare Stephen Cory, *Reviving the Islamic Caliphate in Early Modern Morocco* (Surrey, UK: Ashgate, 2013) with Giancarlo Casale, *The Ottoman Age of Exploration* (Oxford: Oxford University Press, 2010).

24. Cihan Yüksel Muslu, "Ottoman-Mamluk Relations and the Complex Image of Bayezid II," in *Conquête Ottomane De l'Égypte (1517): Arrière-plan, Impact, Échos*, ed. Benjamin Lellouch (Leiden: Brill, 2013).

25. John Obert Voll, "Islam as a Special World-System," *Journal of World History* 5, no. 2 (1994): 213-226.

26. Abdullah al-Ahsan, *Ummah or Nation? Identity Crisis in Contemporary Muslim Society* (Leicester, UK: Islamic Foundation, 1992), 26-27. See also Sayyid Abul A'la Mawdudi, *Unity of the Muslim the Muslim World* (Lahore: Islamic Publications, 1967), 14-15.

27. Ibn Batuta, *Ibn Battuta in Black Africa,* ed. Said Hamdun, trans. Noel Quinton King (Princeton, NJ: Markus Wiener, 1994). See also Ibn Batuta, *The Travels of Ibn Battuta in the Near East, Asia and Africa 1325-1354,* trans. Samuel Lee (Mineola, NY: Dover, 2004).

28. Robert Dankoff, "Ayp değil! (No Disgrace!)," *Journal of Turkish Literature* 5 (2008): 77-90.

29. Evliya Celebi, *An Ottoman Traveller: Selections from the Book of Travels by Evliya Celebi,* ed. and trans. Robert Dankoff and Sooyong Kim (New York: Eland, 2011); Evliya Celebi, *Evliya Chelebi Travels in Iran and the Caucasus, 1647-1654,* trans. Hasan Javadi and Willem Floor (Washington, DC: Mage, 2010).

30. Mehmet İpşirli, "Hasan Kafi Akhisari ve Devlet Düzenine Ait Eseri: Usûlü'l-hikem fi Nizami'l Alem," in *Tarih Enstitütüsü Dergisi* (Journal of the Historical Institute) (Istanbul: Edebiyat Fakültesi Matbaasi, 1981), 239-278.

31. Şener Aktürk, "September 11, 1683: The Myth of a Christian Europe and Massacre of Norway," *Insight Turkey,* Winter 2012, 1-11.

32. Christos S. Bartsocas, "Alexander Mavrocordatos (1641-1709): Physician and Statesman," *Journal of the History of Medicine and Allied Sciences* 28, no. 4 (1973): 392-395.

33. Casale, *The Ottoman Age of Exploration.*

34. For Ottoman indifference to the defeat of Persia against the Russian expansion, see Virginia Aksan, *Ottoman Wars 1700-1870: An Empire Besieged* (Harlow, UK: Longman / Pearson, 2007).

35. See Kate Brittlebank, "Islamic Responses to the Fall of Srirangapattana and the Death of Tipu Sultan (1799)," *South Asia: Journal of South Asian Studies* 22, no. 1 (1999): 79-86.

36. Kemal Karpat, *The Politicization of Islam* (Oxford: Oxford University Press, 2001), 48-67.

37. For more on Russia's attempt at integrating Muslim populations after 1774 with new policies, see Alan W. Fisher, "Enlightened Despotism and Islam under Catherine II," *Slavic Review* 27, no. 4 (1968):

542-553. See also Alan W. Fisher, "Şahin Girey, the Reformer Khan, and the Russian Annexation of the Crimea," *Jahrbücher für Geschichte Osteuropas, Neue Folge* 15, no. 3 (1967): 341-364.

38. Ahmad S. Dallal, "The Origins and Early Development of Islamic Reform," in *The New Cambridge History of Islam,* vol. 6: *Muslims and Modernity: Culture and Society since 1800,* ed. Robert W. Hefner (Cambridge: Cambridge University Press, 2010), 107-147.

39. Juan Cole, *Napoleon's Egypt: Invading the Middle East* (New York: Palgrave, 2007).

40. Thomas Naff, "Reform and the Conduct of Ottoman Diplomacy in the Reign of Selim III, 1789-1807," *Journal of the American Oriental Society* 83, no. 3 (1963): 295-315. See also Nihat Karaer, "Fransa'da İlk İkamet Elçiliğinin Kurulması Çalısmaları Ve İlk İkamet Elçimiz Seyyid Ali Efendi'nin Paris Büyükelçiliği (1797-1802) Sürecinde Osmanlı-Fransız Diplomasi İliskileri" (Attempts to establish the first Ottoman resident embassy in France, and the Paris embassy experience of Seyyid Ali Efendi, the first resident ambassador [1797-1802]), *Ankara Üniversitesi Dil ve Tarih-Coğrafya Fakültesi Tarih Bölümü Tarih Araştırmaları Dergisi* (History journal of the History Department of Ankara University's School of Languages, History and Geography) 31, no. 51 (1963): 63-92.

41. Maya Jasanoff, *The Edge of Empire: Lives, Culture and Conquest in the East, 1750-1850* (New York: Vintage, 2006), 138-147.

42. 'Abd al-Raḥmān Jabartī, *Napoleon in Egypt: Al-Jabartī's Chronicle of the French Occupation, 1798* (Princeton, NJ: Markus Wiener, 2004).

43. Ian Coller, *Arab France: Islam and the Making of Modern Europe, 1798-1831* (Berkeley: University of California Press, 2011).

44. Kahraman Sakul, "Ottoman Attempts to Control the Adriatic Frontier in the Napoleonic Wars," in *The Frontiers of the Ottoman World,* Proceedings of the British Academy, ed. Andrew Peacock (Oxford: Oxford University Press, 2009), 253-271.

45. Brittlebank, *Tipu Sultan's Search for Legitimacy.*

46. A provincial notable of Ottoman Palestine, Cezzar Ahmad Pasha, is a good example to show the ultimate loyalty of these decentralizing figures to the Ottoman center in the face of outside invasions. Thomas Philipp, *Acre: The Rise and Fall of a Palestinian City, 1730-1831* (New York: Columbia University Press, 2001).

47. It was these Ottoman decentralized area dynasties in Libya, Tunisia (Husainid Dynasty), and Algiers (plus independent Morocco) that had a war with the United States in the first Barbary Wars between 1801 and 1805. Morocco also claims to be the first country that recognized the young American republic.

48. For the long-term impact of Nader Shah's invasion and a counterfactual history based on the possibility of his stay in India, see Sanjay Subrahmanyam, "Un Grand Dérangement: Dreaming an Indo-Persian Empire in South Asia, 1740-1800," *Journal of Early Modern History* 4, nos. 3-4 (2000): 337-378.

2. Reinforcing the Imperial World Order (1814-1878)

1. H. K. Sherwani, "The Political Thought of Sir Syed Ahmad Khan," *Indian Journal of Political Science* 5 (1944): 306-328.

2. Edward W. Blyden, "Mohammedanism and the Negro Race," *Fraser's Magazine*, November 1875.

3. Nihat Karaer, *Paris, Londra, Viyana: Abdülaziz'in Avrupa Seyahati* (Paris, London and Vienna: Abdulaziz's trip to Europe) (Ankara: Phoenix Yayınları, 2007).

4. Cemal Kutay, *Avrupa'da Sultan Aziz* (Sultan Aziz in Europe) (Istanbul: Posta Kutusu Yayýnlarý, 1977).

5. For Musurus Pasha and other Greeks serving the Ottoman Empire, see Nicholas Doumanis, *Before the Nation: Muslim-Christian Coexistence and Its Destruction in Late-Ottoman Anatolia* (Oxford: Oxford University Press, 2012) and Christine Philliou, "Communities on the Verge: Unraveling the Phanariot Ascendancy in Ottoman Governance," *Comparative Studies in Society and History* 51, no. 1 (2009): 151-181.

6. For Ismail's speech on the opening of the Suez Canal in 1869 see Pierre Crabiteìs, *Ismail: The Maligned Khedive* (London: G. Routledge and Sons, 1933).

7. Aziz Ahmad, "Sayyid Aḥmad Khān, Jamāl al-dīn al-Afghānī and Muslim India," *Studia Islamica* 13 (1960): 55-78.

8. Bağdatlý Abdurrahman Efendi, *Brezilya'da Ilk Müslümanlar: Brezilya Seyahatnamesi* (First Muslims in Brazil: Travel accounts in

NOTES TO PAGES 43-47

Brazil), trans. from Arabic to Ottoman and then Turkish by Mehmet Şerif and N. Ahmet Özalp (Istanbul: Kitabevi, 2006).

9. For a broader discussion of Muslims in various European empires, see David Motadel, "Islam and the European Empires," *Historical Journal* 55, no. 3 (2012): 831–856.

10. For the process of the nineteenth-century Egyptian reforms, see Kenneth Cuno, "Egypt to c. 1919," in *The New Cambridge History of Islam*, vol. 5: *The Islamic World in the Age of Western Dominance*, ed. Francis Robinson (Cambridge: Cambridge University Press, 2010), 79–106.

11. Ilham Khuri-Makdisi, "Ottoman Arabs in Istanbul, 1860–1914: Perceptions of Empire, Experience of the Metropole through the Writings of Ahmad Faris al-Shidyaq, Muhammad Rashid Rida and Jirji Zaydan," in *Imperial Geographies in Byzantine and Ottoman Space*, ed. Sahar Bazzaz, Yota Batsaki, and Dimiter Angelov (Cambridge, MA: Harvard University Press, 2013), 159–182.

12. Kevin Reinhart, "Civilization and Its Discussants: *Medeniyet* and Turkish Conversion to Modernism," in *Converting Cultures: Religion, Ideology, and Transformations of Modernity*, ed. Denise Washburn and Kevin Reinhart (Leiden: Brill, 2007), 267–290, 281–282. See also Cemil Aydin, "Mecmua-i Fünûn ve Mecmua-i Ulûm Dergilerinin Medeniyet ve Bilim Anlayýþý" (Discourses on civilization and science in the Ottoman journals of Mecmua-i Fünûn ve Mecmua-i Ulûm) (MA thesis, Istanbul University, 1995).

13. P. J. Vatikiotis, *The History of Egypt: From Muhammad Ali to Sadat* (Baltimore: Johns Hopkins University Press, 1980); Khaled Fahmy, *Mehmed Ali: From Ottoman Governor to Ruler of Egypt* (Oxford: Oneworld, 2009).

14. For racial and colonial aspects of Egyptian rule over Sudan, see Eve M. Troutt Powell, *A Different Shade of Colonialism: Egypt, Great Britain, and the Mastery of the Sudan* (Berkeley: University of California Press, 2003).

15. Beatrice Nicolini, *The First Sultan of Zanzibar: Scrambling for Power and Trade in the Nineteenth-Century Indian Ocean* (Princeton, NJ: Markus Wiener, 2012).

16. Jeremy Prestholdt, "From Zanzibar to Beirut: Sayyida Salme bint Said and the Tensions of Cosmopolitanism," in *Global Muslims in*

the Age of Steam and Print, ed. James Gelvin and Nile Green (Berkeley: University of California Press, 2014), 204-226.

17. Khayr al-Dîn Tunisi, *The Surest Path: The Political Treatise of a Nineteenth-Century Muslim Statesman* (Cambridge, MA: Harvard University Press, 1967). See also Carl Brown, *The Tunisia of Ahmad Bey, 1837-1855* (Princeton, NJ: Princeton University Press, 1974).

18. For a recent reassessment of Khayr al-Din Tunisi, see Syed Tanvir Wasti, "A Note on Tunuslu Hayreddin Paşa," *Middle Eastern Studies* 36, no. 1 (January 2000): 1-20.

19. Ismael M. Montana, *Abolition of Slavery in Ottoman Tunisia* (Gainesville: University Press of Florida, 2013).

20. Hakan Erdem, *Slavery in the Ottoman Empire and Its Demise, 1800-1909* (Hampshire, UK: Macmillan, 1996).

21. For reforms during the nineteenth-century Qajar rule in Iran, see Nikki Keddie, "Iran under the Later Qajars, 1848-1922," in *Cambridge History of Iran*, vol. 7: *From Nader Shah to the Islamic Republic*, ed. Peter Avery, Gavin R. G. Hambly, and Charles Melville (Cambridge: Cambridge University Press, 1991), 174-212; Abbas Amanat, *Pivot of the Universe: Nasir al-Din Shah Qajar and the Iranian Monarchy, 1831-1896* (Berkeley: University of California Press, 1997). For reforms in Morocco during the nineteenth century, see Amira K. Bennison, "The 'New Order' and Islamic Order: The Introduction of the *Nizami* Army in the Western Maghrib and Its Legitimation, 1830-73," *International Journal of Middle East Studies* 36 (2004): 591-612.

22. Mehmet Yıldız, "1856 Islahat Fermanına Giden Yolda Meşruiyet Arayışlar: Uluslararası Baskılar ve Cizye Sorununa Bulunan Çözümün Islami Temeller" (Search for legitimacy in the process leading up to 1856 Reform Edict: International pressures and solving the *jizya* problem with Islamic foundations), *Türk Kültürü İncelemeleri Dergisi* (Journal for the Study of Turkish Culture) 7 (Fall 2002): 75-114.

23. On the Tunisian legal system in the nineteenth century, see Julia Clancy-Smith, *Mediterranean North Africa and Europe in an Age of Migration, c. 1800-1900* (Berkeley: University of California Press, 2010).

24. H. L. Bulwer, *Life of Palmerston*, 3 vols. (London, 1870-1874), 2:298, quoted in M. E. Yapp, "Europe in the Turkish Mirror," *Past and Present* no. 137 (November 1992): 155. For the connection and comparisons between Metternich and Ottoman reformists, see Ilber Ortaylı,

NOTES TO PAGES 49-52

"Tanzimat Bürokratları ve Metternich" (Ottoman bureaucrats and Metternich), in *Osmanlı İmparatorluğu'nda İktisadi ve Sosyal Değişim: Makaleler* (Articles on economic and social change in the Ottoman Empire), vol. 1 (Ankara: Turhan Kitabevi, 2000). Ortaylı rightly emphasizes that Tanzimat reformists were less reactionary and conservative than Metternich.

25. Thomas Sanders, Ernest Tucker, and Gary Hamburg, ed. and trans., *Russian-Muslim Confrontation in the Caucasus: Alternative Visions of the Conflict between Imam Shamil and the Russians, 1830-1859* (New York: RoutledgeCurzon, 2004).

26. Robert D. Crews, *For Prophet and Tsar: Islam and Empire in Russia and Central Asia* (Cambridge, MA: Harvard University Press, 2006).

27. For Christians in Ottoman-ruled Balkan territories, see Barbara Jelavich, *History of the Balkans: Eighteenth and Nineteenth Centuries* (Cambridge: Cambridge University Press, 1983).

28. Christine May Philliou, *Biography of an Empire: Governing Ottomans in an Age of Revolution* (Berkeley: University of California Press, 2011).

29. Stathis Gourgouris, *Dream Nation: Enlightenment, Colonization, and the Institution of Modern Greece* (Stanford, CA: Stanford University Press, 1996).

30. For an analysis about the broader vision of Greek nationalism that included all Orthodox Christians of the empire, see Victor Roudometfor, "From Rum Millet to Greek Nation: Enlightenment, Secularization, and National Identity in Ottoman Balkan Society, 1453-1821," *Journal of Modern Greek Studies* 16, no. 1 (1998): 11-48.

31. On philhellenism, see Suzanne L. Marchand, *Down from Olympus: Archaeology and Philhellenism in Germany, 1750-1970* (Princeton, NJ: Princeton University Press, 2003).

32. Thomas Hope, *Anastasius; or, Memoirs of a Greek* (London: Harper, 1831).

33. David Urquhart, *England, France, Russia, and Turkey* (London: J. Ridgway and Sons, 1835); Nazan Çiçek, *The Young Ottomans: Turkish Critics of the Eastern Question in the Late Nineteenth Century* (New York: Tauris Academic Studies, 2010).

34. See Eric Weitz, "From the Vienna to the Paris System: International Politics and the Entangled Histories of Human Rights, Forced

Deportations, and Civilizing Missions," *American Historical Review* 113, no. 5 (2008): 1313–1343, 1317.

35. Nurdan Şafak, "Bir Tanzimat Diplomatý Kostaki Musurus Paşa" (Portrait of Kostaki Musurus Pasha as a Tanzimat diplomat) (PhD dissertation, Marmara Üniversitesi Sosyal Bilimler Enstitüsü Tarih Anabilim Dalý, Istanbul, 2006).

36. Bruce Vandervort, *Wars of Imperial Conquest in Africa, 1830–1914* (Bloomington: Indiana University Press, 1998).

37. Jennifer Pitts, "Liberalism and Empire in a Nineteenth-Century Algerian Mirror," *Modern Intellectual History* 6, no. 2 (2009): 287–313.

38. Candan Badem, *The Ottoman Crimean War, 1853–1856* (Boston: Brill, 2010).

39. William Dalrymple, *The Last Mughal: The Emperor Bahadur Shah Zafar and the Fall of Delhi, 1857* (London: Bloomsbury, 2006).

40. Azmi Özcan, "Attempts to Use the Ottoman Caliphate as the Legitimator of British Rule in India," in *Islamic Legitimacy in a Plural Asia*, ed. Anthony Reid and Michael Gilsenan (London: Routledge, 2007), 71–80.

41. William Wilson Hunter, *The Indian Musalmans: Are They Bound in Conscience to Rebel against the Queen?* (London: Trübner, 1871).

42. Aziz Ahmad, "Sayyid Ahmad Khan, Jamal al-Din al-Afghani and Muslim India," in *Studia Islamica* no. 13 (1960): 55–78. Ahmad quotes from Sayyid Ahmad Khan's article "Truth about the Khilafat" on 71–72.

43. Ali Altaf Mian and Nancy Nyquist Potter, "Invoking Islamic Rights In British India: Mawlana Ashraf 'Ali Thanawi's Huquq al-Islam," *Muslim World* 99 (April 2009): 312–334.

44. A. A. Powell, "Maulânâ Rahmat Allâh Kairânawî and Muslim-Christian Controversy in India in the Mid-19th Century," *Journal of the Royal Asiatic Society* 20 (1976): 42–63; Avril A. Powell, *Scottish Orientalists and India: The Muir Brothers, Religion, Education and Empire* (Woodbridge, UK: Boydell Press, 2010). See also Christine Schirrmacher, "The Influence of German Biblical Criticism on Muslim Apologetics in the 19th Century," in *Festschrift for Rousas John Rushdoony*, http://www.contra-mundum.org/schirrmacher/rationalism .html.

45. Edward W. Blyden, *Christianity, Islam and the Negro Race* (Edinburgh: Edinburgh University Press, 1967), 3.

46. Ismail Hakký Göksoy, "Ottoman Aceh Relations as Documented in Turkish Sources," in *Mapping the Acehnese Past*, ed. Michael Feener, Patrick Daily, and Anthony Reid (Leiden: KITLV Press, 2011), 65-96.

47. On the Aceh ruler's demand for aid from the Ottoman Empire, see Anthony Reid, "Nineteenth Century Pan-Islam in Indonesia and Malaysia," *Journal of Asian Studies* 26, no. 2 (February 1967): 275-276. Reid's article demonstrates the role played by pilgrims, students, scholars, and merchants who connected Indonesia with Mecca, Cairo, and Istanbul and revived the notion of Islamic solidarity during the 1860s and 1870s. For the broader context of Indonesian-Ottoman links during the colonial era, see Engseng Ho, *Graves of Tarim: Genealogy and Mobility in the Indian Ocean* (Berkeley: University of California Press, 2006).

48. Hodong Kim, *Holy War in China: The Muslim Rebellion and State in Chinese Central Asia, 1864-1877* (Stanford, CA: Stanford University Press, 2004), 146-150.

49. Mümtazer Türköne, *Siyasi Ýdeoloji Olarak Ýslamcýlýðýn Doðuþu* (Origins of Islamism as a political ideology) (Ankara: Lotus Yayýnlarý, 2003), 143.

50. Azmi Özcan, "İngiltere'de Hilafet Tartışmaları, 1873-1909" (Debates on the caliphate in England, 1873-1909), in *Hilafet Risaleleri* (Books and pamphlets on the caliphate), vol. 1, ed. Ismail Kara (Istanbul: Klasik Yayınları, 2002), 65-67.

51. For Gladstone's influential speech on Ottoman atrocities in Bulgaria, see W. E. Gladstone, *Bulgarian Horrors and the Question of the East* (London: John Murray, 1876).

52. For Disraeli and the Ottoman Empire, see Milos Kovic, *Disraeli and the Eastern Question* (Oxford: Oxford University Press, 2011).

53. Robert H. Patton, *Hell before Breakfast: America's First War Correspondents Making History and Headlines, from the Battlefields of the Civil War to the Far Reaches of the Ottoman Empire* (New York: Pantheon Books, 2014).

54. Azmi Özcan, *Pan-Islamism, the Ottoman Empire and Indian Muslims* (Leiden: Brill, 1997).

55. Weitz, "From the Vienna to the Paris System."

56. Nikkie Keddie, *An Islamic Response to Imperialism* (Berkeley: University of California Press, Berkeley, 1968).

57. Wilfred Scawen Blunt, *The Future of Islam* (London: Kegan Paul, 1882).

3. Searching for Harmony between Queen and Caliph
(1878-1908)

1. Hakan Kırımlı and İsmail Türkoğlu, *İsmail Bey Gaspıralı ve Dünya Müslümanları Kongresi* (İsmail Bey Gaspıralı and the Muslim World Congress), Islamic Area Studies Project, Central Asian Research Series, no. 4 (Tokyo: Tokyo University, 2002).

2. Ibid., 17.

3. The concept of spiritual sovereignty of the caliphate is best formulated in Lale Can's study on the relationship between Central Asian Muslims and the Ottoman Caliphate. See Lale Can, "Trans-Imperial Trajectories: Pilgrimage, Pan-Islam, and Ottoman–Central Asian Relations, 1865-1914" (PhD diss., New York University, 2011).

4. For the diversity of political and intellectual loyalties of European Orientalism, see Katherine Watt, "Thomas Walker Arnold and the Re-evaluation of Islam, 1864-1930," *Modern Asian Studies* 36, no. 1 (2002): 1-98.

5. M. E. Yapp, "'That Great Mass of Unmixed Mahomedanism': Reflections on the Historical Links between the Middle East and Asia," *British Journal of Middle Eastern Studies* 19, no. 1 (1992): 3-15.

6. Amira K. Bennison, "Muslim Internationalism between Empire and Nation-State," in *Religious Internationals in the Modern World: Globalization and Faith Communities since 1750,* ed. Abigail Green and Vincent Viaene (Basingstoke, UK: Palgrave, 2012), 163-185, 172-174.

7. Umar Ryad, "Anti-Imperialism and Pan-Islamic Movement," in *Islam and the European Empires,* ed. David Motadel (Oxford: Oxford University Press, 2014), 131-149.

8. We still have English, German, and French journals with the same title. The Japanese journal *Kaikyo Sekai* is very important in this regard. Syed Amir Ali, *The Life and Teachings of Mohammed: The Spirit of Islam* (London: W. H. Allen, 1891); Hindli Abdulmecid, *Ingiltere ve Alem-i Islam* (England and the world of Islam) (Istanbul: Matbaai Amire, 1910); Abdurreşid Ibrahim, *Alem-i Islam ve Japonya'da Intişarı Islamiyet* (The world of Islam and spread of Islam in Japan) (Istanbul: Ahmet Saik Bey Matbaasi, 1911).

9. For the English translation of Renan's 1883 lecture "Islam and Science," see Ernest Renan, *The Poetry of the Celtic Races and Other Studies* (London: Walter Scott, 1896), 84-108.

10. On multiple Muslim modernist responses to Renan, see Dücane
Cündioğlu, "Ernest Renan ve 'Reddiyeler' Bağlamında İslam-Bilim
Tartişmalarina Bibliyografik bir Katkı" (A bibliographic contribution
to the Islam and science debate in the context of refutations against Er-
nest Renan's arguments), *Divan* no. 2 (Istanbul 1996): 1–94. For a
British contemporary response to Gladstone, see H. A. Munro Butler-
Johnstone, *Bulgarian Horrors, and the Question of the East: A Letter
Addressed to the Right Honorable W. E. Gladstone, M.P.* (London: Wil-
liam Ridgway, 1876).

11. For Kemal's response to Renan's speech, see Namik Kemal,
Renan Müdafaanamesi: Islamiyet ve Maarif (Refutation against Renan:
Islam and education) (Ankara: Milli Kültür Yayınları, 1962). For
Afghani's response, see Jamal al-Afghani, "Answer of Jamal ad-Din to
Renan," in *An Islamic Response to Imperialism*, ed. Nikkie Keddie
(Berkeley: University of California Press, 1968), 181–187. For the re-
sponse of Ataullah Bayezidof, see his *Islam ve Medeniyet* (Ankara:
TDV Yayınları, Ankara, 1993). For an account of Afghani's relationship
with Renan in Paris, see Elie Kedourie, *Afghani and Abduh* (London:
Cass, 1966), 41–46.

12. Ahmed Riza, *La faillite morale de la politique occidentale en Orient*
(The moral bankruptcy of Western policy toward the East) (Tunis: Édi-
tions Bouslama, 1979); Ahmed Riza and Ismayl Urbain, *Tolérance de
l'islam* (Tolerance in Islam) (Saint-Ouen, France: Centre Abaad, 1992).

13. Marwa Elshakry, *Reading Darwin in Arabic, 1860–1950* (Chicago:
University of Chicago Press, 2013).

14. Carter Vaughn Findley, "An Ottoman Occidentalist in Europe:
Ahmed Midhat Meets Madame Gulnar, 1889," *American Historical Review* 103, no. 1 (1998): 15–49.

15. For the modernism of the salafi thought during the late nineteenth century, see David Dean Commins, *Islamic Reform: Politics
and Social Change in Late Ottoman Syria* (New York: Oxford University Press, 1990).

16. Samira Haj, *Reconfiguring Islamic Tradition: Reform, Rationality
and Modernity* (Stanford, CA: Stanford University Press, 2009), 91.

17. All of the major themes in Muslim modernist and anti-imperial
responses to Christian missionaries can be seen in a comprehensive
book prepared in response to a letter sent to Istanbul's Chief Muslim
Office (Seyhülislamlik) by the Anglican Church in England. A response

by Abdulaziz Jawish, a pan-Islamist Ottoman Arab of Moroccan Egyptian origin, was published in the context of the British occupation of Istanbul in 1923. Abdulaziz Jawish, *Anglikan kilisesine cevap* (Response to the Anglican Church), trans. Mehmet Akif (Istanbul: Evkaf-i İslamiye Matbaası, 1923).

18. Jason Ānanda Josephson, *The Invention of Religion in Japan* (Chicago: University of Chicago Press, 2012).

19. Umar Ryad, *Islamic Reformism and Christianity: A Critical Reading of the Works of Muhammad Rashid Rida and His Associates (1898-1935)* (Leiden: Brill, 2009); Kazuo Morimoto, *Sayyids and Sharifs in Muslim Societies: The Living Links to the Prophet* (London: Routledge, 2012).

20. Syed Ameer Ali, *The Spirit of Islam: A History of the Evolution and Ideals of Islam with a Life of the Prophet* (London: Methuen, 1967).

21. Muḥammad 'Abduh, *The Theology of Unity* (London: George Allen and Unwin, 1966).

22. Tomoko Masuzawa, *The Invention of World Religions, or, How European Universalism Was Preserved in the Language of Pluralism* (Chicago: University of Chicago Press, 2005); Dietrich Jung, *Orientalists, Islamists and the Global Public Sphere: A Genealogy of the Modern Essentialist Image of Islam* (Sheffield, UK: Equinox, 2011).

23. Christopher Shackle and Javed Majeed, trans., *Hali's Musaddas: The Flow and Ebb of Islam* (Delhi: Oxford University Press, 1997).

24. On the empowerment of Hadrami Arab diaspora merchants within the British Empire, see Engseng Ho, *The Graves of Tarim Genealogy and Mobility across the Indian Ocean* (Berkeley: University of California Press, 2006).

25. Halil Halid, *The Crescent versus the Cross* (London: Luzac, 1907).

26. A pan-Islamist Ottoman who published extensively in England about issues of the Muslim world, Halil Halid studied and taught at Cambridge University. See Syed Tanvir Wasti, "Halil Halid: Anti-Imperialist Muslim Intellectual," *Middle Eastern Studies* 29, no. 3 (July 1993): 559-579. For Halid's own autobiography, see Halil Halid, *The Diary of a Turk* (London: A. C. Black, 1903). Similarly, the first comprehensive book on pan-Asianism was written by a Japanese graduate of Columbian College of Law in Washington, DC, around the turn of the century: Kodera Kenkichi, *Dai Ajiashugi Ron* (Tokyo: Hôbunkan, 1916).

27. Lothrop Stoddard, *The New World of Islam* (New York: Scribner's, 1921).

28. For its Arabic translation, see Lûthrub Stûdard, *Hadir al-Alam al-Islami,* trans. 'Ajjâj Nuwayhid, ed. al-Amîr Shakîb Arslân (Cairo: Matbaa-i Salafiyah, 1924). For the Ottoman translation of the same work: *Yeni Alem-i Islam,* trans. Ali Riza Seyfi (Istanbul: Ali Şükrü Matbaasi, 1922).

29. Samuel Zwemer, *Islam, a Challenge to Faith: Studies on the Mohammedan Religion and the Needs and Opportunities of the Mohammedan World from the Standpoint of Christian Missions* (New York: Laymen's Missionary Movement, 1909).

30. Thomas Kidd, *American Christians and Islam: Evangelical Culture and Muslims from the Colonial Period to the Age of Terrorism* (Princeton, NJ: Princeton University Press, 2009); Samuel Marinus Zwemer, ed., *The Moslem World* (London: Published for the Nile Mission Press by the Christian Literature Society for India, 1911). This journal was later moved to Hartford Seminary in 1938 and is still being published. The main German magazine also carried the title: Deutsche Gesellschaft für Islamkunde, *Die Welt des Islams = The World of Islam = Le Monde de l'Islam* (Leiden: E. J. Brill, 1913). A French journal on the Muslim world started earlier, in 1906: Mission scientifique du Maroc, *Revue du monde musulman* (Paris: Mission scientifique du Maroc, 1906). Around the same time, pan-Islamist figures published their own journals with similar titles. See *Alemi-i Islam* (The Muslim world), Istanbul, 1911–1912, edited by Abdurreşid Ibrahim.

31. Wilfrid Blunt, *The Future of Islam* (London: Kegan Paul, 1882).

32. Ryad, "Anti-Imperialism and the Pan-Islamic Movement."

33. Renee Worringer, " 'Sick Man of Europe' or 'Japan of the Near East'? Constructing Ottoman Modernity in the Hamidian and Young Turk Eras," *International Journal of Middle Eastern Studies* 36, no. 2 (2004): 207–223. Also see Cemil Aydin, "A Global Anti-Western Moment? The Russo-Japanese War, Decolonization and Asian Modernity," in *Conceptions of World Order, ca. 1880–1935: Global Moments and Movements,* ed. Sebastian Conrad and Dominic Sachsenmaier (New York: Palgrave, 2007), 213–236.

34. Mustafa Abdelwahid, *Duse Mohamed Ali (1866–1945): The Autobiography of a Pioneer Pan-African and Afro-Asian Activist* (Trenton, NJ: Read Sea Press, 2011). At the Chicago World Parliament

of Religions in 1893, Muslim representation was relatively small, mainly the Ottoman envoy Ismail Hakkı Bey and Alexander Russell Webb. However, there were many non-Muslim delegates who gave speeches about the civilized life of Muslims and the Ottomans, among them Esmeralda Cervantes, Herant Kiretchijian, Teresa Viele, and Christopher Jibara. See Richard Hughes Seager, ed., *The Dawn of Religious Pluralism: Voices from the World's Parliament of Religions, 1893* (La Salle, IL: Open Court, 1993).

35. Umar F. Abd-Allah, *A Muslim in Victorian America: The Life of Alexander Russell Webb* (Oxford: Oxford University Press, 2006).

36. Mushir Hosain Kidwai's book *Pan-Islamism* mentions that the magazine *Theosophist* published a positive account of the establishment of London's pan-Islamic Society in its November 1907 issue. Mushir Hosain Kidwai, *Pan-Islamism* (London: Lusac, 1908).

37. For Theosophists and the nationalist connection, see Mark Frost, " 'Wider Opportunities': Religious Revival, Nationalist Awakening and the Global Dimension in Colombo, 1870-1920," *Modern Asian Studies* 36, no. 4 (2002): 937-967. For the impact of positivism, see Axel Gasquet, "Ernesto Quesada, a Positivist Traveler: Between Cosmopolitanism and Scientific Patriarchy," *Culture & History Digital Journal* 1, no. 2 (2012): 1-17.

38. Michael Goebel, *Anti-Imperial Metropolis: Interwar Paris and the Seeds of Third World Nationalism* (New York: Cambridge University Press, 2015).

39. On Muslim loyalty in the army, see Nile Green, *Islam and the Army in Colonial India: Sepoy Religion in the Service of Empire* (Cambridge: Cambridge University Press, 2009). On Muslim critiques of British Islamophobia, see Ron Geaves, *Islam in Victorian Britain: The Life and Times of Abdullah Quilliam* (Leicester, UK: Islamic Foundation, 2009).

40. Shrabani Basu, *Victoria and Abdul: The True Story of the Queen's Closest Confidant* (New Delhi: Rupa, 2010).

41. W. E. Gladstone, *Bulgarian Horrors and the Question of the East* (London: John Murray, 1876).

42. Various Indian Muslim defenses of the Ottoman Empire compare the empire's inclusion of Greek and Armenian bureaucrats in high-level positions to limitations on Muslims and Hindus for social mobility in the British Empire. Cheragh Ali lists almost a hundred

Christian officers working for the Ottoman Empire at that time to make this point. See Moulavi Cheragh Ali, *The Proposed Political, Legal and Social Reforms in the Ottoman Empire and Other Mohammadan States* (Bombay: Education Society's Press, 1883), 40-43.

43. Seema Alavi, *Muslim Cosmopolitans in the Age of Empire* (Cambridge, MA: Harvard University Press, 2014).

44. William Henry Abdullah Quilliam, *The Faith of Islam: An Explanatory Sketch of the Principal Fundamental Tenets of the Moslem Religion* (Liverpool, UK: Wilmer Bross, 1892).

45. William Henry Quilliam, *The Troubles in the Balkans: The Turkish Side of the Question. Verbatim Report of the Speech Delivered by the Sheikh-Ul-Islam of the British Isles (W. H. Quilliam) on the 22nd October, 1903, at the Town Hall, Liverpool* (Liverpool, UK: Crescent, 1904), 62.

46. Geaves, *Islam in Victorian Britain*, 66.

47. Quilliam's journals, both *Crescent* and *Islamic World*, have discussions of Armenian massacres, often defending the Ottoman position. For an example of Quilliam's defense of the Ottoman Empire, see Quilliam, *The Troubles in the Balkans*.

48. Blunt, *The Future of Islam*.

49. For many texts on the validity of the caliphate and the trajectory of this debate, see İsmail Kara, ed., *Hilafet Risaleleri* (Istanbul: Klasik Yayınları, 2002), 1:65-67.

50. Double loyalty to the Ottoman caliph and the British king became very difficult to advocate for British Muslims during World War I, especially given Lloyd George's anti-Ottoman Christian rhetoric and ideas of a British Crusade in Palestine. Lloyd George called the Greek invasion of Anatolia an "emancipation of vast territory . . . from the blighting influence of the Turks as one of the finest tasks for civilization upon which Britain had ever embarked" (Humayun Ansara, *The Infidel Within: Muslims in Britain since 1800* [London: Hurst and Company, 2004], 80).

51. Amal N. Ghazal, *Islamic Reform and Arab Nationalism: Expanding the Crescent from the Mediterranean to the Indian Ocean (1880s-1930s)* (New York: Routledge, 2010), 51-57.

52. Edmund Burke, "Pan-Islam and Moroccan Resistance to French Colonial Penetration, 1900-1912," *Journal of African History* 13, no. 1 (1972): 97-118.

53. See Faiz Ahmed, *Constituting Afghanistan* (Cambridge, MA: Harvard University Press, 2017).

54. Abu Bakar of Johor visited Istanbul on the way back from England in 1870, at the time of Sultan Abdulaziz, and then after his pilgrimage to Mecca in 1893, at the time of Sultan Abdulhamid II. The first concubine from the Ottoman palace married Abu Bakar's brother (and, after divorces, two other Malay dignitaries). One of her grandsons, Hussein Onn, became prime minister of the modern Malaysian state. The second concubine, Hadija, was married to Abu Bakar himself.

55. Lale Can, "Connecting People: A Central Asian Sufi Network in Turn-of-the-Century Istanbul," *Modern Asian Studies* 46, no. 2 (2012): 373–401.

56. For pan-Islamism in the Iranian-Ottoman context, see Mehrdad Kia, "Pan-Islamism in Late Nineteenth-Century Iran," *Middle Eastern Studies* 32, no. 1 (1996): 30–52.

57. Nejat Göyünç, "Muzafferüddin Şah ve II. Abdülhamid Devrinde Türk İran Dostluk Tezahürleri" (Turkish-Iranian friendship during the era of Muzaffarudding Shah and Sultan Abdulhamid II), in *İran Şehinşahliğinin 2500.uncu Kuruluş Yıldönümüne Armağan* (Memorial book celebrating the 2,500th anniversary of the foundation of the Persian Empire) (Istanbul: Milli Eğitim Bakanlığı Yayınları, 1971), 140–145.

58. For the importance of the hajj in the era of imperial globalization, see Michael Christopher Low, "Empire and the Hajj: Pilgrims, Plagues, and Pan-Islam under British Surveillance, 1865–1908," *International Journal of Middle East Studies* 40, no. 2 (2008): 269–290; Benjamin Claude Brower, "The Colonial Haj: France and Algeria, 1830–1962," in *The Hajj: Collected Essays,* ed. Venetia Porter and Liana Saif (London: British Museum Press, 2013), 108–114; John Slight, "The Haj and the Raj: From Thomas Cook to Bombay's Protector of Pilgrims," in *The Hajj: Collected Essays,* ed. Venetia Porter and Liana Saif (London: British Museum Press, 2013), 115–121; Eileen Kane, *Russian Hajj: Empire and the Pilgrimage to Mecca* (Ithaca, NY: Cornell University Press, 2015).

59. C. Van Dijk, "Colonial Fears, 1890–1918: Pan-Islamism and the Germano-Indian Plot," in *Transcending Borders: Arabs, Politics, Trade and Islam in Southeast Asia,* ed. Huub De Jonge and Nico Kaptein (Leiden: KITLV Press, 2002), 53–89.

60. Mustafa Akyol, "A Sultan with Swat," *Weekly Standard*, December 26, 2005, 16-18.

61. For the memoirs of the Ottoman scholars who went to South Africa, see Ebubekir Efendi Ebubekir, *Ümitburnu Seyahatnâmesi* (Accounts of travel to Capetown), ed. Hüseyin Yorulmaz (İstanbul: Ses Yayınları, 1994).

62. Almost all the major international law books of the late nineteenth century were translated and taught in the Ottoman Empire. There were also original works written by Ottoman Muslim intellectuals. For an example, see Celal Nuri, *Kendi Noktai Nazarimizdan Hukuk-i Düvel* (International law from our point of view) (Istanbul: Osmanlı Şirketi Matbaasi, 1911). See also Aimee Genell, "The Well-Defended Domains: Eurocentric International Law and the Making of the Ottoman Office of Legal Counsel," *Journal of the Ottoman and Turkish Studies Association* 3, no. 2 (November 2016): 255-275.

63. Arnulf Becker Lorca, "Universal International Law: Nineteenth-Century Histories of Imposition and Appropriation," *Harvard International Law Journal* 51, no. 2 (2010): 475-552.

4. The Battle of Geopolitical Illusions (1908-1924)

1. Hüseyin Âtıf, *Bey Sultan II. Abdülhamid'in sürgün günleri 1909-1918: Hususi doktoru Âtıf Hüseyin Bey'in hatıratı* (Exile years of Sultan Abdülhamid, 1909-1918: Memoirs of his private doctor Atif Hüseyin Bey) (Prepared by Metin Hülagu) (Istanbul: Pan, 2003).

2. This issue was noted by Toynbee as a major reason for Ottoman-British estrangement. For the broader context of Ottoman-British confrontation in Africa and Arabia, see Mostafa Minawi, *The Ottoman Scramble for Africa: Empire and Diplomacy in the Sahara and the Hijaz* (Stanford, CA: Stanford University Press, 2016).

3. See Azmi Özcan, "İngiltere'de Hilafet Tartışmaları, 1873-1909" (Debates on caliphate in England), in *Hilafet Risaleleri*, vol. 1, ed. Ismail Kara (<AU: Istanbul: Klasik Yayınları, 2002), 63-94.

4. See Şükrü Hanioğlu, "1906 Yılında Sabahaddin Bey, MacColl, Vambery, ve Kidvai Arasında Geçen Osmanlı Hilafeti Tartışması" (Debate on the Ottoman caliphate among Prince Sebahattin Bey, MacColl, Vambery and Kidwai in 1906) in *Hilafet Risaleleri*, (Books

and pamphlets on the caliphate), vol. 2, ed. Ismail Kara (Istanbul: Klasik Yayınları, 2002), 419-437.

5. Muhammad Barakatullah, "A Mohammedan View of the Macedonian Problem," The North American Review 177, no. 564 (November 1903): 739-750.

6. Yusuf Akçura, *Üç Tarzı Siyaset* (Three methods of grand politics) (Ankara: Türk Tarih Kurumu Basımevi, 1987), 39-40.

7. Ali Fehmi Muhammad, "Islam Hilafeti ve Osmanlı Ittihadi" (The Islamic caliphate and Ottoman unity), in *Hilafet Risaleleri* (Books and pamphlets on the caliphate), vol. 3, ed. Ismail Kara (Istanbul: Klasik Yayınları, 2003), 77-100.

8. Renee Worringer, *Ottomans Imagining Japan: East, Middle East, and Non-Western Modernity at the Turn of the Twentieth Century* (New York: Palgrave Macmillan, 2014).

9. *Punjabee* was a triweekly published in English by Muh Chand in Lahore. See Ikram Ali Malik, *Punjab Muslim Press and the Muslim World, 1888-1911* (Lahore: South Asian Institute, University of the Punjab1974), 59-60.

10. For the ethnic cleansing of the Muslims in the Balkans, see the sections on the Balkan Wars in Justin McCarthy, *Death and Exile: The Ethnic Cleansing of Ottoman Muslims, 1821-1922* (Princeton, NJ: Darwin Press, 1995), 135-164.

11. After about six months of negotiation, during which a second Balkan War occurred, the Treaty of London, signed on May 30, 1913, ended the Balkan Wars. With that treaty, Turkey ceded most of its territory in Europe.

12. For the most comprehensive biography of Ahmed Hilmi, see M. Zeki Yazıcı, "Şehbenderzade Ahmet Hilmi: Hayatı ve Eserleri" (Life and works of Şehberderzade Ahmet Hilmi) (PhD diss., Istanbul University, 1997).

13. For the English translation of Hilmi's novel on universal mystical thought, see Ahmed Hilmi Şehbenderzade, *Awakened Dreams: Raji's Journeys with the Mirror Dede*, trans. Refik Algan and Camille Helminski (Putney, VT: Threshold Books, 1993).

14. Şeyh Mihridin Arusi (pseud. for Şehbenderzade Ahmed Hilmi), *Yirminci Asırda Alem-i İslam ve Avrupa-Müslümanlara Rehber-i Siyaset* (The Muslim world and Europe in the twentieth century: A political guide to Muslims) (Istanbul: Hikmet, 1911). Ismail Kara has

NOTES TO PAGES 109-113

published a good selection from this work (2-11, 66-73, 87-96) in his edited collection *Türkiye'de Islamcılık Düsüncesi* (Islamist thought in Turkey), vol. 1 (Istanbul: Risale Yayınları, 1986), 86-101.

15. See Kara, *Türkiye'de Islamcılık Düsüncesi*, 1:100-101.

16. Ibid., 1:86-87.

17. Özdemir (pseud. for Şehbenderzade Ahmed Hilmi), *Türk Ruhu Nasıl Yapılıyor? Her Vatanperverden, Bu Eserciği Türklere Okumasını ve Anlatmasını Niyaz Ederiz* (How is the Turkish spirit is formed? We ask that each patriot read and relate this pamphlet to the Turks) (Istanbul: Hikmet Matbaa-yı İslamiyesi, 1913).

18. Celal Nuri, *İttihad-i İslam: İslamin Mazisi, Hali, İstikbali* (Muslim unity: past, present and future of Islam) (Istanbul: Yeni Osmanli Matba'asi, 1913). The Arabic translation of this work was published in Cairo in 1920, the year of the Paris Peace Conference. See Jalal Nuri Bek (Celal Nuri Bey), *Ittihad al-Muslimin: al-Islam, madihi wahadiruhu wa mustaqbaluhu* (Muslim unity: past, present and future of Islam) trans. Hamzah Tahir and Abd al-Wahhab 'Azzam (Cairo, 1920). Celal Nuri published a similar work on pan-Islamism, just on the eve of World War I, but focused more on its potential relations with German grand policy. See Celal Nuri, *İttihat-i İslâm ve Almanya* (Muslim unity and Germany) (Istanbul: Yeni Osmanli Matbaasi, 1914).

19. Nuri, *İttihad-i İslam*, 3.

20. Ibid., 5.

21. Ibid., 10-11.

22. Ibid., 479.

23. Ibid., 480-482.

24. Ibid., 139.

25. Ibid., 139-140.

26. Ibid., 141-142.

27. Ibid., 292-320.

28. Ibid., 150.

29. *Siyasetü'l-Etrak ve'l-Hilafe* (Turkish policy and the caliphate) (Istanbul: Matbaatu'l-Adl, 1913/1331); Professor Vayt (pseud.), *Muharebeden Sonra: Hilafet Siyaseti ve Türklük Siyaseti* (After the Balkan Wars: Politics of caliphate and Turkism), trans. Habil Adem (Istanbul: Ikbal Kütüphanesi, 1915). Habil Adem also wrote on pan-Germanism and pan-Slavism, indicating his interest in the politics of pan-ideologies in world affairs. See Habil Adem (pseud.), *Pan Cermanizm, Pan*

Islavizm (Pan-Germanism and pan-Slavism) (Istanbul: Seda-yi Millet Matbaasi, 1916).

30. Vayt, "Muharebeden Sonra."

31. David Motadel, *Islam and Nazi Germany's War* (Cambridge, MA: Harvard University Press, 2014).

32. Maia Ramnath, *Haj to Utopia: How the Ghadar Movement Charted Global Radicalism and Attempted to Overthrow the British Empire* (Berkeley: University of California Press, 2011), 189–193.

33. Azmi Ozcan, *Pan-Islamism: Indian Muslims, the Ottomans and Britain, 1877–1924* (Leiden: Brill, 1997), 179.

34. Kees van Dijk, "Religion and the Undermining of British Rule in South and Southeast Asia during the Great War," in *Islamic Connections: Muslim Societies in South and Southeast Asia,* ed. Michael Feener and Terenjit Sevea (Singapore: ISEAS, 2009), 109–133.

35. Hamdi Paşa, *İslam Dünyası ve İngiliz Misyoneri: İngiliz Misyoneri Nasıl Yetiştiriliyor?* (The Muslim world and the British missionary: How do they train British missionaries?) (1916; reprint, Izmir: Tibran Yayıncılık, 2006); Hindli Abdülmecid, *İngiltere ve Alem-i Islam* (England and the Muslim world) (Istanbul: Matbaa-i Amire, 1910); Şehbenderzade Ahmed Hilmi, *Senusiler ve Sultan Abdulhamid* (Sanusi order of Africa and Sultan Abdulhamid II) (Istanbul: Ses Yayınları, 1992).

36. *Mir Islama* (Petersburg) 1, nos. 2–3 (1912).

37. See Carlo Alfonso Nallino, *Caliphate* (Cairo, 1918); Carlo Alfonso Nallino, *Notes sur la Nature du Califat en Generale et sur le Pretendu Califat Ottoman* (Rome: Printed at the Press of the Foreign Office, 1919).

38. George Samne, *Le Khalifet et le Panislamisme* (Paris: Imprimerie Dudois et Bauer, 1919).

39. Arnold J. Toynbee, "The Question of the Caliphate," *Contemporary Review,* February 1920, 192–196.

40. A. T. Olmstead, *The New Arab Kingdom and the Fate of the Muslim World* (Urbana: War Committee of the University of Illinois, 1919).

41. E. Dinet and Sliman Ben Ibrahim, *The Life of Mohammed: The Prophet of Allah* (Paris: Paris Book Club, 1918) is a book dedicated to Muslims who died while serving the French Empire. The authors criticize the French metropole's Islamophobia against Muslims in their introduction.

42. Michael A. Reynolds, *Shattering Empires: The Clash and Collapse of the Ottoman and Russian Empires, 1908-1918* (Cambridge: Cambridge University Press, 2011).

43. Michael J. Mortlock, *The Egyptian Expeditionary Force in World War I: A History of the British-Led Campaigns in Egypt, Palestine, and Syria* (Jefferson, NC: McFarland, 2011), 149. Mustafa Kemal Atatürk, who was in Berlin on the day of the loss of Jerusalem in the winter of 1917, repeatedly told Shakib Arslan Raja Adal, an Arab-Ottomanist intellectual, of his desire to take Jerusalem back. Shakib Arslan Raja Adal, "Constructing Transnational Islam: The East-West Network of Shakib Arslan," in *Intellectuals in the Modern Islamic World*, ed. Stephane A. Dudoignon, Komatsu Hisao, and Kosugi Yasushi (New York: Routledge, 2006), 176-210, 180.

44. Seema Alavi, *Muslim Cosmopolitans across Empires* (Cambridge, MA: Harvard University Press, 2015).

45. Mark Mazower, *No Enchanted Palace: The End of Empire and the Ideological Origins of the United Nations* (Princeton, NJ: Princeton University Press, 2009), 28-65. Article 22 of the League of Nations covenant includes the Mandate principle: "To those colonies and territories which as a consequence of the late war have ceased to be under the sovereignty of the States which formerly governed them and which are inhabited by peoples not yet able to stand by themselves under the strenuous conditions of the modern world, there should be applied the principle that the well-being and development of such peoples form a sacred trust of civilization." "Covenant of the League of Nations," part 1, article 22 of the Treaty of Versailles, quoted in Eric D. Weitz, "From the Vienna to the Paris System: International Politics and the Entangled Histories of Human Rights, Forced Deportations, and Civilizing Missions," *American Historical Review* 113, no. 5 (2008): 1313-1343, 1340.

46. Mushirul Hasan and Margrit Pernau, eds., *Regionalizing Pan-Islamism: Documents of the Khilafat Movement* (New Delhi: Manohar, 2005).

47. Abul Kalam Azad, "Khilafat and Jaziratul-Arab" (The caliphate and the Arabian Peninsula), address delivered at the Bengal Provincial Khilafat Conference (Bombay: Central Khilafat Committee, 1920). See also Syed Mahmud, *The Khilafat and England* (Patna, India: Imtiyaz, 1920).

48. Perin Gürel, *The Limits of Westernization: A Cultural History of America in Turkey* (New York: Columbia University Press, 2017).

49. John Willis, "Debating the Caliphate: Islam and Nation in the Work of Rashid Rida and Abul Kalam Azad," *International History Review* 32, no. 4 (2010): 711–732.

50. Syed Ameer Ali, "Address by the Right Hon. Syed Ameer Ali on Islam in the League of Nations," in *Transactions of the Grotius Society*, vol. 5: *Problems of Peace and War,* Papers Read before the Society in the Year 1919 (London: Grotius Society, 1919), 126–144.

51. Lothrop Stoddard, *The New World of Islam* (New York: Scribner's, 1921).

52. Surendra Gopal, *Indian Freedom-Fighters in Tashkent, 1917–1922: Contesting Ideologies, Nationalism, Pan-Islamism and Marxism* (Kolkata: Maulana Abul Kalam Azad Institute of Asian Studies, 2002); John Riddell, *To See the Dawn: Baku, 1920—First Congress of the Peoples of the East* (New York: Pathfinder, 1993).

53. Selçuk Esenbel's study of Japanese diplomatic correspondence from Occupied Istanbul shows this negotiation. See Selçuk Esenbel, "Friends in Opposite Camps or Enemies from Afar: Japanese and Ottoman Turkish Relations in the Great War," in *The Decade of the Great War: Japan and the Wider World in the 1910s*, ed. Tosh Minohara et al. (Leiden: Brill, 2014), 257–278.

54. Allied and Associated Powers (1914–1920), *Treaty of Peace with Turkey and Other Instruments Signed at Lausanne on July 24, 1923, Together with Agreements between Greece and Turkey Signed on January 30, 1923, and Subsidiary Documents Forming Part of the Turkish Peace Settlement* (London: Her Majesty's Stationery Office, 1923).

55. Esenbel, "Friends in Opposite Camps or Enemies from Afar."

56. Mim Kemal Öke, *Mustafa Kemal Paşa Ve İslam Dünyası: Hilafet Hareketi* (Mustafa Kemal Paşa and the Muslim world: The caliphate movement) (Istanbul: Aksoy Yayıncılık, 1999).

57. Lord Eversley, *The Turkish Empire from 1288 to 1914 (and from 1914 to 1924 by Sir Valentine Chirol)*, 3rd ed. (London: T. Fisher Unwin, 1924), 464.

58. Andre Servier, *Islam and the Psychology of the Musulman* (London: Chapman & Hall, 1924), 262–263.

59. Chiara Formichi, "Mustafa Kemal's Abrogation of the Ottoman Caliphate and Its Impact on the Indonesian National Movement," in

Demystifying the Caliphate: Historical Memory and Contemporary Contexts, ed. Madawi al-Rasheed et al. (New York: Columbia University Press, 2013), 95–115.

60. Sam Moyn uses the term "truncated discourses of rights." See Samuel Moyn, *The Last Utopia: Human Rights in History* (Cambridge, MA: Harvard University Press, 2010).

5. Muslim Politics of the Interwar Period (1924–1945)

1. Mona F. Hassan, *Longing for the Lost Caliphate: A Transregional History* (Princeton, NJ: Princeton University Press, 2009). See also Martin van Bruinessen, "Muslims of the Dutch East Indies and the Caliphate Question," *Studia Islamika* 2, no. 3 (1995): 115–140; Anthony Milner, "The Impact of the Turkish Revolution on Malaya," *Archipel* 31 (1986): 117–130.

2. Elie Kedouire, "Egypt and the Caliphate, 1915–1952," in *The Chatham House Version, and Other Middle-Eastern Studies* (New York: Praeger, 1970), 177–212.

3. Ali Abdul Raziq, *Al Islam wa usul al-hukm* (Islam and the principles of government), ed. Muhammad Amara (Beirut: al-Muasasa al-Arabiyaa lil Dirasat wa al-Nashr, 1972). For an English translation, see Ali Abdelraziq, *Islam and the Foundations of Political Power,* trans. Maryam Loutfi, ed. Abdou Filali-Ansary (Edinburgh: Edinburgh University Press, 2012).

4. Joshua Teitelbaum, *The Rise and Fall of the Hashemite Kingdom of Arabia* (London: C. Hurst, 2001).

5. John Willis, "Azad's Mecca: On the Limits of Indian Ocean Cosmopolitanism," *Comparative Studies of South Asia, Africa and the Middle East* 34, no. 3 (2014): 574–581.

6. Amrita Malhi, "Raise the Bendera Stambul: The Ottoman Caliphate and Anti-colonial Action on the Malay Peninsula, 1870s–1928," in *From Anatolia to Aceh: Ottomans, Turks and Southeast Asia,* Proceedings of the British Academy, ed. Andrew Peacock and Annabel Teh Gallop (Oxford: Oxford University Press, 2015).

7. Michael Francis Laffan, *Islamic Nationhood and Colonial Indonesia: The Umma below the Winds* (London: RoutledgeCurzon, 2003).

8. For the significance of the Rif wars for anticolonial intellectual networks in Paris, see Michael Goebel, *Anti-Imperial Metropolis: Interwar Paris and the Seeds of Third World Nationalism* (Cambridge: Cambridge University Press, 2015), 263–267.

9. Rashid Khalidi, Lisa Anderson, Muhammad Muslih, and Reeva S. Simon, eds., *The Origins of Arab Nationalism* (New York: Columbia University Press, 1991).

10. John Willis, "Debating the Caliphate: Islam and Nation in the Work of Rashid Rida and Abul Kalam Azad," *International History Review* 32, no. 4 (2010): 711–732.

11. William Cleveland, *Islam against the West: Shakib Arslan and the Campaign for Islamic Nationalism* (Austin: University of Texas Press, 1985).

12. Homa Katouzian, *State and Society in Iran: The Eclipse of the Qajars and the Emergence of the Pahlavis* (New York: I. B. Tauris, 2006).

13. Mian Abdul Aziz, *The Crescent in the Land of the Rising Sun* (London: Blades, East & Blades, 1941).

14. M. Naeem Qureshi, "Atatürk's Impact on Muslim India, 1919–1938," "The Image of Atatürk and Turkey in Urdu Literature," and "Atatürk's Reforms and the Muslim World Bordering South Asia," in *Ottoman Turkey, Atatürk and Muslim South Asia: Perspectives, Perceptions and Responses* (Karachi: Oxford University Press, 2014), 143–160, 161–188, and 216–235.

15. For the significance of the Kemalist model for later Muslim political and intellectual history, see Salman Sayyid, *A Fundamental Fear: Eurocentrism and the Emergence of Islamism* (London: Zed Books, 2003).

16. For a discussion of this episode in Habib Bourguiba's memoirs, see Julia Clancy Smith, *Mediterraneans: North Africa and Europe in an Age of Migration, c. 1800–1900* (Berkeley: University of California Press, 2010).

17. The British Empire had six separate memberships in the League, for the United Kingdom, Canada, Australia, South Africa, New Zealand, and India.

18. Basil Matthews, *Young Islam on Trek: A Study in the Clash of Civilizations* (New York: Friendship Press, 1926); Lothrop Stoddard, *The New World of Islam* (New York: Charles Scribner's Sons, 1921).

19. Matthews, *Young Islam on Trek,* 17.

20. Ibid., 22.

21. Ibid., 196.

22. Muhammad Asad, *Islam at the Crossroads* (Lahore: Wassanpura, Arafat Publications, 1934).

23. Safvet Halilovic, *Islam and the West in the Thought of Muhammad Asad (Leopold Weiss)* (Sarajevo: Dobra Knjiga, 2013).

24. Muhammad Asad, *The Road to Mecca: An Autobiography* (New York: Simon and Schuster, 1954); Muhammad Asad, *The Message of the Qur'an* (Mecca: Muslim World League, 1964).

25. Muhammad Asad, *Principles of State and Government in Islam* (Berkeley: University of Calfornia Press, 1961). Originally published in Arabic as *Minhaj al-Islam fi al-Hukm* (Beirut: Darul ilm vel Malayin, 1957), this book was then translated into every major language.

26. Beth Baron, *The Orphan Scandal: Christian Missionaries and the Rise of the Muslim Brotherhood* (Stanford, CA: Stanford University Press, 2014).

27. Hasan al-Banna, *Five Tracts of Hasan Al-Banna (1906–1949): A Selection from teh Majmu'at Rasail al-Imam al-Shahid Hasan al-Banna,* translated from the Arabic and annotated by Charles Wendell (Berkeley: University of California Press, 1978).

28. Gudrun Kramer, *Hasan al-Banna* (Oxford: Oneworld, 2010).

29. S. V. R. Nasr, *Mawdudi and the Making of Islamic Revivalism* (New York: Oxford University Press 1996).

30. Shakîb Arslan, *Our Decline: Its Causes and Remedies,* new edition (Kuala Lumpur: Islamic Book Trust, 2004). This text is based on a translation from the Arabic original. Shakib Arslan, *Li Madha ta'akhhar al-Muslimun wa li madha taqaddam ghayruhum?* (Why did Muslims decline and why did others progress?) (Cairo: Isa al-Babi al-Halabi, 1939).

31. William L. Cleveland, *Islam against the West: Shakib Arslan and the Campaign for Islamic Nationalism* (Austin: University of Texas Press, 1985).

32. Basheer Nafi, *Arabism, Islamism and the Palestine Question, 1908–1941: A Political History* (Reading, UK: Ithaca Press, 1998); Zvi Elpeleg, *Through the Eyes of the Mufti: The Essays of Haj Amin* (London: Vellentine Mitchell, 2009).

33. Basheer M. Nafi, "General Islamic Congress of Jerusalem Reconsidered," *Muslim World* 86, nos. 3–4 (October 1996): 243–272; Philip Mattar, *The Mufti of Jerusalem: Al-Hajj Amîn al-Ḥusaynî and the Palestinian National Movement* (New York: Columbia University Press, 1988).

34. Aiyaz Husain, *Mapping the End of Empire: American and British Strategic Visions in the Postwar World* (Cambridge, MA: Harvard University Press, 2014).

35. Chaudhry Khaliquzzaman, *Pathway to Pakistan* (Lahore: Longmans, Pakistan Branch, 1961).

36. For the image of Jinnah in Muslim societies, see Atique Zafar Sheikh and Mohammad Riaz Malik, eds., *Quaid-e-Azam and the Muslim World: Selected Documents, 1937–1948* (Karachi: Royal Book Co., 1978).

37. See Report by Abdur Rahman Siddique, countersigned by Chaudhri Khaliquzzaman, on the Activities of the All-India Muslim League Palestine Delegation, 28 June 1939, Quaid-e-Azam Papers, file 49, pp. 117–132, in ibid., 84–106.

38. A. Nielsen, "The International Islamic Conference at Jerusalem," *Moslem World* 22 (1932): 340–354.

39. Abdul-Rahman Azzam, *Imperialism: The Barrier to World Peace*, Arab League Pamphlets on International Relations, no. 1: Causes of World Unrest (Cairo: Government Press, 1947). For the book of Azzam Pasha that influenced Malcolm X's thinking about Islam, see Abd al-Rahman Azzam, *The Eternal Message of Muhammad*, trans. from Arabic by Caesar E. Farah (New York: Devin-Adair, 1964).

40. Michael Goebel, *Anti-Imperial Metropolis: Interwar Paris and the Seeds of Third World Nationalism* (Cambridge: Cambridge University Press, 2015).

41. David Motadel, *Islam and Nazi Germany's War* (Cambridge, MA: Harvard University Press, 2014).

42. For Italy's Muslim and Middle Eastern policy, see Nir Arielli, *Fascist Italy and the Middle East, 1933–1940* (New York: Palgrave Macmillan, 2010).

43. Cemil Aydin, "The Muslim World in Japanese Imperial Thought," in *Islam and Empire*, ed. David Motadel (Oxford: Oxford University Press, 2014), 287–302. See also Abu Talib Ahmad, *The Malay Muslims, Islam and the Rising Sun, 1941–1945* (Selangor: Malaysian Branch of the Royal Asiatic Society 2003).

44. See Dai Nippon Kaikyô Kyôkai, *Kunô Suru So-Ren Kaikyô Minzoku* (Suffering of the Muslim peoples in the Soviet Union), (Tokyo: Dai Nippon Kaikyô Kyôkai, 1939), 13.

45. Italy's Islam policy was also described and discussed as a potential model for Japan by Sakurai Masashi, *Dai Toa Kaikyô Hattenshi*

(History of the development of Muslims in greater East Asia) (Tokyo: Sanseido, 1943), 8.

46. Dai Nippon Kaikyô Kyôkai, *Sekai Kaikyôto Seisaku no Hitsuyôsei ni Tsuite* (On the necessity of developing a special policy toward world Muslims) (Tokyo: Dai Nippon Kaikyô Kyôkai, 1939). There were Muslim nationalists exiled from Russia who were supported by both Japan and Germany. See Matsunaga Akira, "Ayazu Ishaki to Kyokutô no Tatarujin Comuniti" (Azas Ishaki and the Tatar Muslim community), in *Kindai Nihon to Toruko Sekai* (Modern Japan and the Turkic world), ed. Ikei Masaru and Sakamoto Tsutomu (Tokyo: Keisô Shobo, 1999), 219-263.

47. *Isuramu Bunka* (Islamic Culture) 1, no. 1 (November 1932). This manifesto-like English-language text was on the back cover of the journal, illustrating the attempt to announce to the Euro-American scholarly community a particularly unique Japanese perspective on the Muslim World.

48. The journal lasted for six and a half years, from July 1938 to December 1944.

49. Nile Green, "Founding the First Mosque in Japan," in *Terrains of Exchange: Religious Economies of Global Islam* (Oxford: Oxford University Press, 2014), 235-279.

50. Abdul Rauf, "The British Empire and the Mujāhidīn Movement in the N.W.F.P. of India, 1914-1934," *Islamic Studies* 44, no. 3 (October 2005): 409-439.

51. Israel Gershoni, *Arab Responses to Fascism and Nazism: Attraction and Repulsion* (Austin: University of Texas Press, 2014).

6. Resurrecting Muslim Internationalism (1945-1988)

1. Gerald De Gaury, *Faisal: King of Saudi Arabia* (Louisville, KY: Fonts Vitae, 2007).

2. Matthew Jones, "Perils and Promise of Islam: The United States and the Muslim Middle East in the Early Cold War," *Diplomatic History* 30 (September 2006): 705-739, 730.

3. Ibid., 705.

4. Abd al-Rahman Azzam, *The Eternal Message of Muhammad*, translated from Arabic by Caesar E. Farah (New York: Devin-Adair, 1964). The Arabic original was first published in 1946 with the title

Al-Risalah al-Khalidah (Cairo: Matba'at Lajnat al-Ta'lif wa-al-Tarjamah wa al-Nashr, 1946).

5. Matthieu Rey, "Fighting Colonialism versus Non-Alignment: Two Arab Points of View on the Bandung Conference," in *The Non-Aligned Movement and the Cold War*, ed. Nataša Miškoviæ, Harald Fischer-Tiné, and Nada Boškovska (London: Routledge, 2014), 163-183.

6. Richard Wright, *The Color Curtain: A Report on the Bandung Conference*, foreword by Gunnar Myrdal (Cleveland, OH: World, 1956).

7. On the Palestine vote at the United Nations in 1947, see "United Nations Vote for Palestine Partition," November 29, 1947, WOR Collection, Library of Congress.

8. For Turkey's vote at the UN against Algerian claims, see Şinasi Sönmez, "Cezayir Baðýmsýzlýk Hareketinin Türk Basýnýna Yansýmalarý (1954-1962)" (Turkish press coverage of the Algerian War of Independence), *ZKÜ Sosyal Bilimler Dergisi* 6, no. 12 (2010): 289-318.

9. Faisal Devji, *Muslim Zion: Pakistan as a Political Idea* (Cambridge, MA: Harvard University Press, 2013).

10. "Letter from the President of Muslim Brotherhood, Cairo, to M. A. Jinnah, 29 May 1947," in *Quaid-e-Azam and the Muslim World: Selected Documents, 1937-1948,* ed. Atique Zafar Sheikh and Mohammad Riaz Malik (Karachi: Royal Book Co., 1990), 308; telegraph from Quaid-e-Azam Papers, file 138, 209-210.

11. Carolien Stolte, " 'The Asiatic Hour': New Perspectives on the Asian Relations Conference, New Delhi, 1947," in *The Non-Aligned Movement and the Cold War: Delhi-Bandung-Belgrade*, ed. Nataša Miškoviæ, Harald Fischer-Tiné, and Nada Boškovska (London: Routledge, 2014), 57-75.

12. Ayesha Jalal, *The Sole Spokesman: Jinnah, the Muslim League and the Demand for Pakistan* (Cambridge: Cambridge University Press, 1994).

13. Venkat Dhulipala, *Creating a New Medina State Power, Islam, and the Quest for Pakistan in Late Colonial North India* (Cambridge: Cambridge University Press, 2014).

14. *Studies on Commonwealth of Muslim Countries,* comp. Secretariat of the Motamar al-Alam al-Islami (Muslim World Congress) (Karachi: Umma Publishing House, 1964), 5.

15. On Hindu-Muslim unity in 1857 and the Khilafat movement, see Zakir Husain, *Communal Harmony and the Future of India: The Study*

of the Role and Thoughts of Nation Builders for India's Unity, 1857-1985 (Bareilly, India: Prakash Book Depot, 1985).

16. For the princely state of Hyderabad and pan-Islamic networks, see Eric Lewis Beverley, *Hyderabad, British India, and the World: Muslim Networks and Minor Sovereignty, c. 1850-1950* (Cambridge: Cambridge University Press, 2015). For the impact of the Partition of Pakistan, see Srinath Raghavan, *1971: A Global History of the Creation of Bangladesh* (Cambridge, MA: Harvard University Press 2013).

17. Edward Curtis, "'My Heart Is in Cairo': Malcolm X, the Arab Cold War, and the Making of Islamic Liberation Ethics," *Journal of American History* 102, no. 3 (2015): 775-798.

18. Matthew Connelly, *A Diplomatic Revolution: Algeria's Fight for Independence and the Origins of the Post-Cold War Era* (Oxford: Oxford University Press, 2002).

19. Christiane-Marie Abu Sarah, "Palestinian Guerrillas, Jewish Panthers: 1960s Protest and Global Revolution in Israel-Palestine" (MA thesis, George Mason University, 2011).

20. J. Harris Proctor, ed., *Islam and International Relations* (New York: Frederick A. Praeger, 1965), vii.

21. Fayez A. Sayegh, "Islam and Neutralism," in *Islam and International Relations,* ed. J. Harris Proctor (New York: Frederick A. Praeger, 1965), 61-93, 61-62.

22. T. Cuyler Young, "Pan-Islamism in the Modern World," in *Islam and International Relations,* ed. J. Harris Proctor (New York: Frederick A. Praeger, 1965), 194-221, 199.

23. Dankwar Rustow, "The Appeal of Communism to Islamic Peoples," in *Islam and International Relations,* ed. J. Harris Proctor (New York: Frederick A. Praeger, 1965), 40-60, 41-42. Rustow quotes from Bernard Lewis, "Communism and Islam," in *The Middle East in Transition,* ed. Walter Z. Laqueur (New York: Praeger, 1958), 302.

24. James P. Piscatori, *Islam in a World of Nation-States* (Cambridge: Cambridge University Press, 1986); Abdullah Ahsan, *Ummah or Nation? Identity Crisis in Contemporary Muslim Society* (Leicester, UK: Islamic Foundation, 1992).

25. For good biographies of Arnold Toynbee, see W. McNeill, *Arnold J. Toynbee: A Life* (New York: Oxford University Press, 1990) and M. Perry, *Arnold Toynbee and the Crisis of the West* (Washington, DC: University Press of America, 1982).

NOTES TO PAGES 192-193

26. For his wartime reflections on British-Ottoman relations, see A. J. Toynbee, *Turkey: A Past and a Future* (London: Hodder & Stoughton, 1917). For Toynbee's anti-Ottoman propaganda writings, see A. Toynbee, *Armenian Atrocities: The Murder of a Nation* (London: Hodder & Stoughton, 1915) and A. Toynbee, *The Murderous Tyranny of the Turks,* preface by Viscount Bryce (London: Hodder & Stoughton, 1917).

27. Arnold Toynbee, *Nationality and the War* (London: J. M. Dent & Sons, 1915), 399–404. Toynbee's introduction to the book was written in February 1915, at the beginning of the war, before the Gallipoli campaigns. It does reflect the mood of the early declaration of *jihad* by the Ottoman Empire and Indian Muslim public opinion.

28. The change in Toynbee's attitude toward Turkey can be seen in his later writings. A. J. Toynbee, *The Western Question in Greece and Turkey: A Study in the Contact of Civilisations* (London: Constable, 1923).

29. Daisaku Ikeda, *Words of Wisdom,* http://www.ikedaquotes.org /stories/arnold_toynbee.

30. Richard Overy, *The Morbid Age: Britain and the Crisis of Civilisation, 1919–1939* (London: Penguin, 2010).

31. A. J. Toynbee, *A Study of History,* 12 vols. (London: Oxford University Press, 1934–1961). It was the one-volume abridgement of the first ten volumes rather than the multivolume project that became an international best seller in multiple translations. A. J. Toynbee, *A Study of History,* abridgement of vols. 1–10 by D. C. Somervell (New York: Oxford University Press, 1957).

32. For the text of some of his speeches in the Middle East and Asia, see *The Toynbee Lectures on the Middle East and Problems of Underdeveloped Countries* (Cairo: National Publications House, 1962); A. J. Toynbee, *Four Lectures Given by Professor Arnold Toynbee in United Arab Republic* (Cairo: United Arab Republic, Public Relations Dept., 1965).

33. For modernization theory and the Cold War connection, see D. C. Engerman et al., eds., *Staging Growth: Modernization, Development, and the Global Cold War* (Amherst: University of Massachusetts Press, 2003); N. Gilman. *Mandarins of the Future: Modernization Theory in Cold War America* (Baltimore: Johns Hopkins University Press, 2003); M. Latham, *Modernization as Ideology: American Social Science and "Nation Building" in the Kennedy Era* (Chapel Hill: University of North Carolina Press, 2000).

34. For an early example of his relatively positive assessment of the survival of Islamic civilization despite the hegemony of the West, see the section "Islam, the West and the Future," in A. J. Toynbee, *Civilization on Trial* (New York: Oxford University Press, 1948). For a good example of how Toynbee's ideas can be in conversation with the Buddhist revival in Cold War-era Japan at the peak of its modernization, see A. J. Toynbee, *Choose Life: A Dialogue between Arnold Toynbee and Daisaku Ikeda*, ed. R. L. Gage (Oxford: Oxford University Press, 1976).

35. For Alfred Zimmern's imperial internationalism, see A. Zimmern, *The Prospect of Civilization* (New York: Farrar & Rinehart, 1939) and *Spiritual Values and World Affairs* (Oxford: Clarendon Press, 1939).

36. P. Duara, "The Discourse of Civilization and Pan-Asianism," *Journal of World History* 12, no. 1 (Spring 2001): 99-130.

37. For the broader politics of the discourse of civilization, see C. Aydin, *The Politics of Anti-Westernism in Asia: Visions of World Order in Pan-Islamic and Pan-Asian Thought, 1882-1945* (New York: Columbia University Press, 2007).

38. See chapter 10, "Toynbee as a World Figure," in McNeill, *Arnold J. Toynbee.*

39. H. Trevor-Roper, "Arnold Toynbee's Millennium," *Encounter* 8, no. 6 (June 1957): 14-18; Z. Saleh, *Trevor-Roper's Critique of Arnold Toynbee: A Symptom of Intellectual Chaos* (Baghdad: Al-Ma'eref Press, 1958).

40. For translations of Toynbee's works into Turkish, see A. J. Toynbee, *Dünya ve Garp* (The world and the West) (Istanbul: Türkiye İş Bankası Kültür Yayınları, 1952); *Tarih Üzerine: İki Konferans* (Civilization on trial) (Istanbul: Fakülteler Matbaası, 1962); *Tarih Bilinci* (A study of history) (Istanbul: Bateş Yayınları 1978); *Medeniyet Yargılanıyor* (Civilization on trial), trans. Ufuk Uyan (Istanbul: Yeryüzü Yay, 1980).

41. Cemil Aydin and Burhanettin Duran, "Arnold Toynbee in Cold War Era Islamism: Sezai Karakoç's Civilizational Cosmopolitanism," *Comparative Studies of South Asia, Africa and the Middle East* 3 (Summer 2015): 310-323.

42. Trevor-Roper, "Arnold Toynbee's Millennium," 18.

43. On the history of Islamic science literature during the Cold War decolonization period, see Aydin Mehmed Sayılı, "The Institutions of

Science and Learning in the Moslem World" (PhD diss., Harvard University, 1941) and Seyyed Hossein Nasr, *Science and Civilization in Islam* (Cambridge, MA: Harvard University Press, 1968).

44. For the usage of civilizationism in anticolonial discourses, see S. N. Hay, *Asian Ideas of East and West: Tagore and His Critics in Japan, China, and India* (Cambridge, MA: Harvard University Press, 1970); C. Aydin, "Beyond Civilization: Pan-Islamism, Pan-Asianism and the Revolt against the West," *Journal of Modern European History* 4, no. 2 (Fall 2006): 204-223.

45. For an influential book that depicts all Westernization and modernization movements in the late Ottoman and republican periods in Turkey as alienation from one's native civilization, see Mehmet Doğan, *Batılılaşma İhaneti* (A betrayal called Westernization) (Istanbul: Dergah Yayınları, 1975).

46. Jalal Ali Ahmad, *Occidentosis: A Plague from the West*, trans. R. Campbell and Hamid Algar (Berkeley, CA: Mizan Press, 1983).

47. Abulhasan Ali Nadvi, *Mādhā khasira al-ʿālam bi-inḥiṭāṭ al-Muslimīn* (What did the world lose with the decline of Muslims) (Cairo: Lajnat al-Taʾlīf wa-al-Tarjamah wa-al-Nashr, 1950); English translation: Abulhasan Ali Nadvi, *Islam and the World* (Lahore: Academy of Islamic Research & Publications, 1961); Turkish translation: Ebüʾl Hasan Ali el-Haseni Nadvi, *Müslümanların gerilemesiyle dünya neler kaybetti* (What did the world lose with the decline of Muslims) (Istanbul: Tevhid Yayınları, 1966); Hichem Djait, *Europe and Islam: Cultures of Modernity* (Berkeley: University of California Press, 1985). This book by Djait was first published in French as *L'Europe et L'Islam* (Paris: Editions du Seuil, 1978).

48. Roxanne Euben, *Enemy in the Mirror: Islamic Fundamentalism and the Limits of Modern Rationalism* (Princeton, NJ: Princeton University Press, 1999).

49. Eren Murat Tasar, "Soviet and Muslim: The Institutionalization of Islam in Central Asia, 1943-1991" (PhD diss., Harvard University, 2010).

50. Hemant Shah, *The Production of Modernization: Daniel Lerner, Mass Media, and the Passing of Traditional Society* (Philadelphia: Temple University Press, 2011); Daniel Lerner, *The Passing of Traditional Society: Modernizing the Middle East* (Glencoe, IL: Free Press, 1958).

51. Alexandre Benningsen and Chantal Lemercier-Quelquejay, *Islam in the Soviet Union* (New York: Praeger, 1967).

52. Salim Yaqub, *Containing Arab Nationalism: The Eisenhower Doctrine and the Middle East* (Chapel Hill: University of North Carolina Press, 2004).

53. On Egypt in Yemen, see Jesse Ferris. *Nasser's Gamble: How Intervention in Yemen Caused the Six-Day War and the Decline of Egyptian Power* (Princeton, NJ: Princeton University Press, 2013).

54. Chaudri Nazir Ahmad Khan, *Thoughts on Pakistan and Pan-Islamism,* intro. by David Iqbal (Lahore: Al-Ahibba, 1977).

55. Nehemia Levtzion, *International Islamic Solidarity and Its Limitations* (Jerusalem: Manges Press of the Hebrew University, 1979).

56. Michael Farquhar, "Saudi Petrodollar, Spiritual Capital, and the Islamic University of Medina: A Wahhabi Missionary Project in Transnational Perspective," *International Journal of Middle East Studies* 47 (2015): 701–721.

57. T. E. Lawrence, *Seven Pillars of Wisdom: The Complete 1922 Text,* new edition (Fordingbridge, UK: J. and N. Wilson, 2004); Muhammad Asad, *The Road to Mecca* (New York: Simon and Schuster, 1955).

58. There were non-Arab essentializations of Islam that did not reduce Islam to Arabs. Tom Reiss, *The Orientalist: Solving the Mystery of a Strange and Dangerous Life* (New York: Random House, 2005).

59. William Ochsenwald, "Saudi Arabia and the Islamic Revival," *International Journal of Middle East Studies,* 13, no. 3 (1981): 271–286.

60. For Muslim internationalism after World War II, see Reinhard Schulze, *A Modern History of the Islamic World* (New York: NYU Press, 2002), 200–201.

61. Ralph Coury, *The Making of an Egyptian Arab Nationalist: The Early Years of Azzam Pasha, 1893–1936* (Reading, UK: Ithaca Press, 1998).

62. Mita Ryōichi, *Sei kuruān: Nichia taiyaku chūkai* (Tōkyō: Nihon Musurimu Kyōkai, 1982); Hans Martin Kramer, "Pan-Asianism's Religious Undercurrents: The Reception of Islam and Translation of the Qur'ān in Twentieth-Century Japan," *Journal of Asian Studies* 73, no. 3 (2014): 619–640.

63. S. Abul A'la Maududi, *Unity of the Muslim World* (Lahore: Islamic Publications, 1967). The introduction by Khurshid Ahmad was signed February 17, 1967.

64. For King Faisal's reign and impact, see A. M. Vasil'ev, *King Faisal of Saudi Arabia: Personality, Faith and Times* (London: Saqi, 2012).

65. Saad Khan, *Reasserting International Islam: A Focus on the Organization of the Islamic Conference and Other Islamic Institutions* (Karachi: Oxford University Press, 2001); Stephane Lacroix, *Awakening Islam: The Politics of Religious Dissent in Contemporary Saudi Arabia* (Cambridge, MA: Harvard University Press, 2011).

66. Robert Tignor, *Anwar Al-Sadat: Transforming the Middle East* (New York: Oxford University Press, 2016).

67. *Report on Islamic Summit, 1974 Pakistan, Lahore, February 22-24, 1974* (Islamabad: Department of Films and Publications, Ministry of Information and Broadcasting, Government of Pakistan, 1974). See also Zahid Malik, *Re-Emerging Muslim World* (Lahore: Pakistan National Centre, 1974).

68. Walid Khalidi, *From Haven to Conquest: Readings in Zionism and the Palestine Problem until 1948* (Washington, DC: Institute for Palestine Studies, 1987).

69. Shaukat Ali, a professor of political science at Southeastern Massachusetts University, published a book on this topic in 1976, before the 1980s revival of pan-Islamism, based on Western literature on pan-movements: *Pan-Movements in the Third World: Pan-Arabism, Pan-Africanism and Pan-Islamism* (Lahore: Publishers United, 1976).

70. For the irony of pan-Islamic Saudi Arabia's close ties to America via ARAMCO, see Robert Vitalis, *America's Kingdom: Mythmaking on the Saudi Oil Frontier* (Stanford, CA: Stanford University Press 2007).

71. Edward W. Said, *Orientalism* (New York: Vintage Books, 1978).

72. Rashid Khalidi, "The 1967 War and the Demise of Arab Nationalism: Chronicle of a Death Foretold," in *The 1967 Arab-Israeli War: Origins and Consequences,* ed. Wm. Roger Louis and Avi Shlaim (Cambridge: Cambridge University Press, 2012), 264-284.

73. Fawaz A. Gerges, "The Transformation of Arab Politics: Disentangling Myth from Reality," in *The 1967 Arab-Israeli War: Origins and Consequences,* ed. Wm. Roger Louis and Avi Shlaim (Cambridge: Cambridge University Press, 2012), 285-313.

74. Rashid Khalid, *Soviet Middle East Policy in the Wake of Camp David* (Beirut: Institute for Palestine Studies, 1979).

75. Paul Thomas Chamberlin, *The Global Offensive: The United States, the Palestine Liberation Organization, and the Making of the Post-Cold War Order* (Oxford: Oxford University Press, 2012).

76. Simon Mabon, *Saudi Arabia and Iran Soft Power Rivalry in the Middle East* (London: I. B. Tauris, 2013).

77. Ali Rahnama, *An Islamic Utopian: A Political Biography of Ali Shari'ati* (London: I. B. Tauris, 1996).

78. For Khomeini's political views in 1944, see Baqer Moin, *Khomeini: Life of the Ayatollah* (New York: Thomas Dunne Books, 2000), 60.

79. Thomas Hegghammer, *Jihad in Saudi Arabia: Violence and Pan-Islamism since 1979* (Cambridge: Cambridge University Press, 2010).

80. Lawrence Potter and and Gary Sick, eds., *Iran, Iraq, and the Legacies of War* (New York: Palgrave Macmillan, 2004).

81. Odd Arne Westad, *The Global Cold War* (Cambridge: Cambridge University Press, 2007), 288-330.

82. David Farber, *Taken Hostage: The Iran Hostage Crisis and America's First Encounter with Radical Islam* (Princeton, NJ: Princeton University Press, 2005). For the Rushdie affair, see Talal Asad, "Multiculturalism and British Identity in the Wake of the Rushdie Affair," *Politics and Society* 18, no. 4 (December 1990): 455-480.

83. Naveed S. Sheikh, *The New Politics of Islam: Pan-Islamic Foreign Policy in a World of States* (London: Routledge Curzon, 2003), 67.

84. John L. Esposito, ed., *The Iranian Revolution: Its Global Impact* (Miami: Florida International University Press, 1990); Maryam Panah, *The Islamic Republic and the World: Global Dimensions of the Iranian Revolution* (London: Pluto Press, 2007).

85. James P. Piscatori, *Islam in a World of Nation States* (Cambridge: Cambridge University Press, 1986).

86. Edward W. Said, *Covering Islam: How the Media and the Experts Determine How We See the Rest of the World* (New York: Pantheon Books, 1981).

87. Sadiq Jalal al-Azm, "Orientalism and Orientalism in Reverse," *Khamsin* no. 8 (1988): 5-26, reprinted in Alexander Lyon Macfie, ed., *Orientalism: A Reader* (New York: New York University Press, 2000), 217-238.

88. Fadi Bardawil, "Sidelining Ideology: Arab Theory in the Metropole and Periphery, c. 1977" (unpublished conference paper, Princeton University, October 2011).

89. Samuel Huntington, "The Clash of Civilizations?," *Foreign Affairs* 72, no. 3 (Summer 1993): 22-49.

90. Michael Anthony Sells, *The Bridge Betrayed: Religion and Genocide in Bosnia* (Berkeley: University of California Press, 1998).

91. Saad S. Khan, *Reasserting International Islam: A Focus on the Organization of the Islamic Conference and Other Islamic Institutions* (Karachi: Oxford University Press, 2001).

Conclusion

1. For the transformation of modern Islamist thought from the 1920s to the 2000s, see Roxanne L. Euben and Muhammad Qasim Zaman, *Princeton Readings in Islamist Thought: Texts and Contexts from al-Banna to Bin Laden* (Princeton, NJ: Princeton University Press, 2009). See also Peter Mandaville, *Global Political Islam* (New York: Routledge, 2007).

2. Barbara Metcalf, "An Argumentative Indian: Maulana Husain, Ahmad Madani, Islam, and Nationalism in India," in *Islamic Legitimacy in a Plural Asia,* ed. Anthony Reid and Michael Gilsenan (London: Routledge, 2008), 81-97; Barbara D. Metcalf, *Husain Ahmad Madani: The Jihad for Islam and India's Freedom* (Oxford: Oneworld, 2009).

Acknowledgments

After the publication of my previous book, *The Politics of Anti-Westernism in Asia,* I was initially planning to write a sequel, a comparative study on the trajectory of pan-Asian and pan-Islamic thought in the post–World War II period. I ended up writing a different book, the current one, with a focus solely on the history of pan-Islamism and the invention of the Muslim world. This decision derived from a concern to understand the process of the reracialization of Muslims in world politics. Out of all the pan-nationalist projects of the age of empire across Asia and Africa, pan-Islamism and Islamist internationalism seemed to be making more of the headlines and news in the past thirty years. At the same time, a wave of strong anti-Muslim discourse in Europe and America relying on manufactured fear of the Muslim world has become a political force affecting the lives of millions of Muslims living in those societies. It is the puzzling similarity between the debates on the Muslim world in the early twenty-first century and the early twentieth century that prompted my decision to write a book on the history of the idea of the Muslim world rather than a comparative book on pan-nationalism in the postcolonial period.

This book is greatly inspired by conversations with my partner, Juliane Hammer, about scholarship and theory on Islam as a religious tradition, and the historical and systemic origins of the concept of religion itself. It is my great fortune to be married to someone who is

ACKNOWLEDGMENTS280

also my best friend and intellectual interlocutor. During the writing of this book, I also benefited from the amazingly beautiful garden and home she created for all of us. Our daughters, Leyla and Mehtap, contributed to this book not only by making my life more joyful but also in terms of content. I am amazed how, as American Muslims at elementary-school age, they have articulated some of the best critiques of racism and Islamophobia I have ever heard. They respond to their own teachers' and friends' ideas about "the Muslim world" with wonderful humor and serious analysis, even in the seemingly innocent staging of a play about Aladdin.

I want to acknowledge my debt to colleagues, librarians, friends, students, and family members who helped me to think about the main questions of this book. I started research for this book during a postdoctoral fellowship at Princeton University's Near Eastern Studies Department, when I benefited greatly from the conversations with Michael Cook, Şükrü Hanioğlu, Bernard Haykel, Michael Laffan, Mike Reynolds, and Qasim Zaman. Further research was enabled by the University of North Carolina-Chapel Hill's history department research leave and the Epsy Family Faculty Fellowship from UNC's Institute for Arts and Humanities. Scholars of Muslim societies and Asia at UNC and Duke campuses helped me with engaging conversations and feedback. Special thanks to Hasan Aksakal, Fadi Bardawil, Carl Ernst, Emma Flatt, Kathleen Foody, Erdağ Göknar, Engseng Ho, Vasant Kaiwar, Lloyd Kramer, Charlie Kurzman, Sucheta Mazumdar, Ebrahim Moosa, Susan Pennybacker, Omid Safi, Iqbal Sevea, Sarah Shields, and Eren Taşar. The librarians at UNC made sure that I had all the library resources I needed for my research.

A group of friends and colleagues were generous with their suggestions and comments about the main ideas of this book. Ali Vural Ak, Harun Anay, Ertan Aydin, Erol Çatalbaş, Ismail Coşkun, Ahmet Demirhan, Mehmet Süreyya Er, Cemal Kafadar, Michael Muhammed Knight, Sadaf Knight, Alison Kysia, Kareem Kysia, Fırat Oruç, Cengiz Şişman, Himmet Taşkömür, Hüseyin Yılmaz, and Hayrettin Yücesoy would recognize ideas discussed over meals and coffee in the pages of this book. Mustafa Aksakal, Seema Alavi, Lale Can, Houchang Chehabi, Sebastian Conrad, Marwa Elshakry, Nile Green, Madeleine Herren-Oesch, Ismail Kara, Michael Christopher Low, David Motadel, Dominic Sachsenmaier, Glenda Sluga, Carolien Stolte, and

Halil Ibrahim Yenigün answered questions over email and in person. Masashi Haneda at the University of Tokyo encouraged me to pursue this line of inquiry in personal conversations and with his own publications. Over the past six years, I have had the chance to discuss some of the ideas in this book in various conference and lecture venues. I would like to thank colleagues at Cambridge University, the University of Helsinki, Duke University, Heidelberg University, Harvard University, Sarajevo International University, Portland State University, Columbia University, NYU New York, NYU Abu Dhabi, the University of California, Berkeley, Georgetown University, Ewha Women's University, Sogang University, Tokyo University, and Hokkaido University for hosting these meetings and facilitating the exchange of ideas.

I would like to thank Joyce Seltzer at Harvard University Press, who supported this project from the beginning and pushed it over the finish line. The book benefited greatly from Simon Waxman's careful suggestions and copy editing.

Last but not least, I want to express my thanks to members of the Aydin family in Istanbul and Ankara, and the Hammer and Steckel family in Berlin and Gardelegen who have offered their homes and hospitality during summer vacations and continue to cheer me on.